Quantum
Technologies

Julian Jang-Jaccard • Philippe Caroff •
Evan Blezinger • Valentin Mulder •
Alain Mermoud • Vincent Lenders
Editors

Quantum Technologies

Trends and Implications
for Cyber Defense

Editors
Julian Jang-Jaccard
Cyber-Defence Campus
armasuissse
Lausanne, Switzerland

Evan Blezinger
Cyber-Defence Campus
armasuisse
Lausanne, Switzerland

Alain Mermoud
Cyber-Defence Campus
armasuisse
Lausanne, Switzerland

Philippe Caroff
Quantum Science and Engineering
EPFL
Lausanne, Switzerland

Valentin Mulder
Cyber-Defence Campus
armasuisse
Lausanne, Switzerland

Vincent Lenders
Cyber-Defence Campus
armasuisse
Lausanne, Switzerland

ISBN 978-3-031-90726-5   ISBN 978-3-031-90727-2   (eBook)
https://doi.org/10.1007/978-3-031-90727-2

This work was supported by armasuisse. This book is an open access publication.

© The Editor(s) (if applicable) and The Author(s) 2026. This book is an open access publication.

Open Access This book is licensed under the terms of the Creative Commons Attribution 4.0 International License (http://creativecommons.org/licenses/by/4.0/), which permits use, sharing, adaptation, distribution and reproduction in any medium or format, as long as you give appropriate credit to the original author(s) and the source, provide a link to the Creative Commons license and indicate if changes were made.
The images or other third party material in this book are included in the book's Creative Commons license, unless indicated otherwise in a credit line to the material. If material is not included in the book's Creative Commons license and your intended use is not permitted by statutory regulation or exceeds the permitted use, you will need to obtain permission directly from the copyright holder.
The use of general descriptive names, registered names, trademarks, service marks, etc. in this publication does not imply, even in the absence of a specific statement, that such names are exempt from the relevant protective laws and regulations and therefore free for general use.
The publisher, the authors and the editors are safe to assume that the advice and information in this book are believed to be true and accurate at the date of publication. Neither the publisher nor the authors or the editors give a warranty, expressed or implied, with respect to the material contained herein or for any errors or omissions that may have been made. The publisher remains neutral with regard to jurisdictional claims in published maps and institutional affiliations.

This Springer imprint is published by the registered company Springer Nature Switzerland AG
The registered company address is: Gewerbestrasse 11, 6330 Cham, Switzerland

If disposing of this product, please recycle the paper.

Foreword I

Throughout history, military operations have gone hand in hand with technological innovation. From cryptography to radar, breakthroughs have reshaped the battlefield and changed the way nations defend themselves. Today, quantum technologies are at the forefront of scientific discovery, and while much is still unknown, it is clear that they will have a profound impact on national security—particularly in the realm of cyber defense. For those of us in defense and security, the question is not only how quantum technologies will evolve, but how we must prepare for a future shaped by them.

Quantum computing challenges long-standing assumptions about secure communications and critical infrastructure, as current encryption methods may become vulnerable once quantum computers reach advanced capabilities. However, quantum technologies also present opportunities to enhance military operations, from optimizing logistics and battlefield planning to improving threat detection with quantum sensing. Realizing this potential requires deeper exploration and collaboration across military, academic, and industrial domains.

This book invites readers to explore the emerging opportunities and strategic significance of quantum technologies in the context of cybersecurity. It brings together the latest trends and insights into the evolution of quantum computing and quantum communication, offering valuable guidance. While the path forward remains uncertain, this moment is pivotal. By expanding our understanding of quantum technologies, we can position ourselves to lead with foresight rather than react in this transformative era of digital defense.

As military leaders, it is our duty to remain curious and engaged with the unknown. Quantum technologies present both challenges and opportunities, and understanding their implications will be essential to ensuring national security in the decades to come. I encourage readers to use this book as a resource to deepen their knowledge and ask the critical questions that will help us stay ahead of the curve in this rapidly evolving field.

Chief of the Swiss
Armed Forces Cyber Command, Bern,
Switzerland
February 2025

Major General Simon Müller

Foreword II

Quantum technologies have the potential to reshape the future of cybersecurity. The ongoing progress in quantum computing and communication presents a dual-edged reality: offering promising new capabilities while simultaneously raising complex challenges, especially in relation to digital security frameworks. Once quantum systems reach practical implementation, they could redefine secure communications and digital security strategies on a global scale.

At ETH Zurich, we recognize the importance of anticipating these developments and fostering interdisciplinary collaboration to explore their implications. This book, Quantum Technologies: Trends and Implications for Cyber Defense, offers a timely examination of emerging trends in quantum security, providing valuable perspectives for researchers, industry leaders, and policymakers.

By bringing together expertise from quantum science, cryptography, and cybersecurity, this work serves as a resource for understanding how quantum advancements could influence global security. While many questions remain, engaging in these discussions today will help shape a more secure digital future.

Executive Director, Quantum Center
at ETH Zurich, Zurich, Switzerland
February 2025

Anupama Unnikrishnan

Preface

Quantum technologies are poised to transform various industries, from cybersecurity and communication to finance and pharmaceuticals. The increasing development of quantum computers, quantum communication systems, and hybrid quantum-classical solutions represents not just a technological revolution but also a significant strategic shift in global cybersecurity efforts. This book brings together comprehensive trends, research, and insights from more than 40 leading experts from around the globe to provide a deep understanding of the opportunities, challenges, and implications of quantum technologies for cyber defense.

Each chapter underwent a rigorous single-blind peer-review process, involving both feedback from fellow authors and evaluations by external experts. This thorough review process was crucial to ensure the highest quality and scientific rigor, reinforcing the credibility and depth of the presented content.

Divided in three parts, the book examines core advancements in various types of quantum technologies, addressing the key obstacles that limit progress. It also explores the potential disruptions to current cryptographic standards alongside potential solutions, as well as global quantum strategies and tools designed to monitor trends in quantum technologies.

This book is intended to serve as a resource for researchers, policymakers, cybersecurity specialists, and industry leaders navigating the rapidly evolving quantum landscape. It aims to foster informed decision-making and encourage collaboration across sectors to ensure that quantum technologies contribute to a secure and prosperous future.

Lausanne, Switzerland	Julian Jang-Jaccard
Lausanne, Switzerland	Philippe Caroff
Lausanne, Switzerland	Evan Blezinger
Lausanne, Switzerland	Valentin Mulder
Lausanne, Switzerland	Alain Mermoud
Lausanne, Switzerland	Vincent Lenders
December 2024	

Acknowledgments

We extend our heartfelt gratitude to all the authors of this book for voluntarily dedicating their time and expertise to contribute insightful chapters on various quantum topics. Your willingness to share knowledge has been instrumental in shaping the quality and depth of this work.

We also express our sincere appreciation to the following additional reviewers—Dr. Bernhard Tellenbach, Dr. Gérôme Bovet, Dr. Martin Burkhart, Paul Bagourd (all Cyber-Defence Campus), Johann Richard (European Space Association), Dr. Killian Wasmer (armasuisse), and Prof. Dr. Vincenzo Savona (École Polytechnique Fédérale de Lausanne, EPFL)—as well as other reviewers who wished to remain anonymous, for generously offering their time to provide valuable feedback, helping us refine and enhance each chapter. Special thanks go to the many quantum and cybersecurity professionals whose insights greatly influenced the key topics presented in this book. Their guidance allowed us to connect with experts across relevant fields.

We are particularly grateful to Dr. Andreas Masuhr, Director of the Swiss Quantum Initiative (SQI), for providing an overview of the Swiss quantum ecosystem and strategies. Prof. Dr. Kirsten Moselund, Head of Laboratory of Nano and Quantum Technologies (LNQ) at Paul Scherrer Institut (PSI), offered invaluable insights into quantum research conducted at Swiss federal institutes of technology and facilitated connections with her colleagues at PSI.

Our thanks also extend to Prof. Andreas Wallraff and Dr. Anu Unnikrishnan from ETH Zurich, who shared an overview of ETH's quantum research and connected us with its quantum experts. We thank Dr. Heike Riel and Dr. Marc Stoeklin for linking us with IBM's quantum and security research team. Additionally, we thank Dr. Almudena Carrera Vazquez and Michael Osborne from IBM for their insightful conversations, which enriched our understanding of critical quantum topics relevant to national security. Dr. Frederic Floether of QuantumBasel helped us connect with researchers at QuantumBasel, further broadening our network.

Lastly, we thank Martin Sand, who diligently coordinated this book project during his internship at the Cyber-Defence Campus.

This book is a testament to the collaborative spirit of the quantum community, and we are immensely grateful for everyone's contributions.

Contents

Part I Quantum Computing

1. **Superconducting Qubits** 3
    Stefano Poletto and Angela Q. Chen

2. **Trapped-Ion Quantum Computers** 15
    Cornelius Hempel

3. **Quantum Computing with Neutral Atoms** 25
    Tommaso Macrì

4. **Quantum Computing with Semiconductor Spin** 33
    Santhanu Panikar Ramanandan and Anna Fontcuberta i Morral

5. **Quantum Error Control and Mitigation Strategies** 45
    Nathan Shammah

6. **Quantum Optimization** 57
    Daniel J. Egger, Heike Riel, Stefan Woerner, and Christa Zoufal

7. **Quantum Annealing** 65
    Michael Tsesmelis

8. **Quantum Machine Learning** 73
    Muhammad Usman

9. **Enabling and Accelerating Quantum Computing with AI Supercomputing** 85
    Mark Wolf

Summary Part I

Part II Quantum Communication

10 Quantum Threats 95
Rajiv Krishnakumar

11 Quantum Random Number Generators (QRNG) 107
Bruno Huttner and Gilles Trachsel

12 Trends in Quantum Key Distribution (QKD) 119
Sebastian Kish, Josef Pieprzyk, and Seyit Camtepe

13 Migrating to Quantum Key Distribution 133
Bruno Huttner

14 Post-Quantum Cryptography 143
Steven Galbraith

15 Quantum Readiness: Recommendations for Enterprises 155
Martin Burkhart and Bernhard Tellenbach

16 Perspective on the QKD Versus PQC Debate 163
Renato Renner and Ramona Wolf

17 Quantum Technologies for Space Applications 171
Davide Venturelli and Filip Wudarski

Summary Part II

Part III Quantum Technology Ecosystem Analysis

18 Global Quantum Strategies 185
Brendan Karch

19 Investment Trends in Quantum Computing 197
Loïc Maréchal

20 Analysis of Quantum Trends in Open Software Repositories and Financial News 209
Thomas Berkane, Evgueni Rousselot and Julian Jang-Jaccard

21 Bibliometric Analysis of Convergence of Quantum Technologies 219
Alexander Sternfeld, Andrei Kucharavy and Dimitri Percia David

22 Quantum Ecosystem of Switzerland 231
Brendan Karch

Summary Part III

Glossary

Asymmetric Encryption   A cryptographic method using a public key for encryption and a private key for decryption. It enables secure communication without the need to share private keys in advance.

Atom Interferometry   A measurement technique that uses the wave-like behavior of atoms to detect tiny changes in forces, fields, and accelerations, with applications in navigation, gravity sensing, and fundamental physics.

BB84   A quantum key distribution protocol that uses photon polarization to securely exchange keys. Introduced in 1984, it was the first to demonstrate quantum cryptography and detect eavesdropping via measurement disturbance.

Chaotic Process   A system highly sensitive to initial conditions, producing complex and unpredictable behavior. Its unpredictability makes it useful for applications like cryptographic protocols.

CMOS (Complementary Metal Oxide Semiconductor)   A widely used semiconductor technology for integrated circuits such as microprocessors, memory chips, and image sensors. Known for low power consumption and high noise immunity.

CNOT gate (Controlled-Not Operation)   A fundamental two-qubit quantum gate that flips the target qubit only when the control qubit is in state $|1\rangle$. It is crucial for entanglement and implementing quantum algorithms.

CRQC (Cryptographically Relevant Quantum Computers)   Quantum computers powerful enough to break classical cryptographic schemes such as RSA and ECC.

Cryogenic   Relating to extremely low temperatures (below 120 K), essential for operating many quantum systems by minimizing thermal noise and maintaining quantum coherence.

CV-QKD (Continuous Variable QKD)   A QKD protocol that uses continuous variables, like amplitude and phase of light, to enable secure key exchange.

Diffie-Hellman   A cryptographic protocol for secure key exchange over untrusted channels. It forms the basis of many secure communication systems.

ESA (European Space Agency) An intergovernmental organization focused on space exploration, scientific research, and the development of space-related technologies.

FRQI (Flexible Representation for Quantum Images) A method for encoding classical image data into quantum states, enabling image processing on quantum computers.

GG02 A continuous-variable QKD protocol using Gaussian-modulated coherent states to enable secure quantum communication.

GMCS (Gaussian-Modulated Coherent State) A quantum state used in CV-QKD, where information is encoded in Gaussian-distributed variables like amplitude and phase.

Hamiltonian An operator in quantum mechanics that represents a system's total energy and governs its evolution via Schrödinger's equation.

HSP (Hidden Subgroup Problem) A mathematical problem central to several quantum algorithms, including Shor's algorithm, with implications for cryptography.

ISS (International Space Station) A modular space station serving as a platform for scientific research and international collaboration in space.

JJ (Josephson Junction) A superconducting device made of two superconductors separated by a thin insulator, used in quantum computers and precision sensors.

LEO (Low-Earth Orbit) A near-Earth orbital region, typically within 2,000 km altitude, used for satellites, Earth observation, and communications.

Logical Qubits Error-corrected qubits formed by grouping multiple physical qubits, enabling stable and reliable quantum computation.

LPAI (Light-Pulse Atom Interferometry) A precision measurement technique that uses light pulses to manipulate the wave-like behavior of atoms for detecting forces, accelerations, and fields.

MEMS (Micro-Electromechanical Systems) Miniaturized devices that integrate mechanical and electronic components, commonly used in sensors, actuators, and precision systems.

ML-DSA (Module-Lattice-Based Digital Signature Standard) A post-quantum cryptographic standard based on lattice problems, designed to remain secure against quantum attacks.

NISQ (Noisy Intermediate Scale Quantum) Refers to the current generation of quantum computers with limited qubit counts and high noise levels, yet capable of performing some useful computations.

NIST (National Institute of Standards and Technology) A US government agency responsible for setting technology and cryptographic standards, including those for post-quantum security.

NP-Hard Problem (Nondeterministic Polynomial) A class of problems considered among the most computationally difficult; no known polynomial-time algorithms exist to solve all instances.

NSA (National Security Agency) A US government agency tasked with signals intelligence and cryptographic security for national defense.

PEC (Probabilistic Error Cancellation) A noise mitigation technique in quantum computing that statistically corrects errors by reversing their effects in measurement results.

Physical Qubits The hardware-level qubits (e.g., trapped ions, superconducting circuits) that represent quantum bits but are prone to errors and decoherence.

PIC (Photonic Integrated Circuit) A chip that integrates optical components for use in telecommunications and quantum technologies, enabling compact and scalable systems.

PM-QKD (Phase Matching Quantum Key Distribution) A QKD protocol that improves distance and security by matching the phase of quantum signals between sender and receiver.

PNT (Position, Navigation, and Timing) A set of technologies that provide precise location, movement tracking, and time synchronization. PNT systems are critical for navigation, communication networks, military operations, and infrastructure coordination.

PQC (Post-Quantum Cryptography) Cryptographic methods designed to remain secure against quantum attacks, using classical hardware and techniques like lattice-, code-, and multivariate-based algorithms to ensure long-term digital security.

QAOA (Quantum Approximate Optimization Algorithm) A hybrid quantum-classical algorithm designed to solve combinatorial optimization problems by using parameterized quantum circuits and classical optimization loops to find approximate solutions.

QCCD (Quantum Charge Coupled Device) A device that uses charge coupling to manipulate and transfer quantum information, often employed in trapped-ion quantum computing architectures.

QDS (Quantum Digital Signatures) Protocols that provide secure and authenticated communication by using quantum mechanics to prevent forgery and tampering.

QEC (Quantum Error Correction) A set of techniques that protect quantum information by encoding it across multiple physical qubits, enabling error detection and correction without measuring the quantum state directly.

QEM (Quantum Error Mitigation) Methods that reduce the impact of noise in quantum computations without full error correction, using calibration, statistical filtering, or circuit-level adjustments, suitable for NISQ devices.

QGG (Quantum Gravity Gradiometer) A device that measures gravitational field variations using quantum principles, offering high sensitivity for geophysical and navigation applications.

QKD (Quantum Key Distribution) A method for secure key exchange using quantum mechanics, where any eavesdropping attempt disturbs the quantum states and becomes detectable, enabling unbreakable cryptographic security.

QML (Quantum Machine Learning) The integration of quantum computing with machine learning, leveraging phenomena like superposition and entanglement to improve computational performance and learning accuracy.

QPU (Quantum Processing Unit) A specialized quantum processor designed to execute quantum algorithms by manipulating qubits according to the rules of quantum mechanics.

QRNG (Quantum Random Number Generators) A device that uses quantum phenomena, such as the inherent unpredictability of particle behavior, to generate truly random numbers. QRNGs offer high entropy and security, making them ideal for cryptographic and security-critical applications.

QSC (Quantum-Safe Cryptography) Cryptographic methods that resist quantum attacks, including post-quantum algorithms and quantum-based techniques like QKD, to secure future digital systems.

QSI (Quantum-Secure Identifiers) Cryptographic identifiers that remain secure against threats posed by quantum computing, used for authentication and identity protection.

Quantum Hall Effect A quantum phenomenon where a 2D electron system in a strong magnetic field shows quantized conductance, offering insights into topological phases of matter.

Qubits The fundamental units of quantum information, capable of existing in superposition, meaning they can represent both 0 and 1 simultaneously.

Qubits Gates Quantum operations that manipulate qubit states, forming the basic building blocks of quantum algorithms, analogous to logic gates in classical computing.

Rydberg Interactions Strong, long-range interactions between atoms in highly excited (Rydberg) states, used in quantum computing to create entanglement and perform quantum gates.

SLI (Shaken Lattice Interferometry) A quantum sensing technique that uses atoms in shaken optical lattices to achieve high-precision measurements.

Symmetric Encryption An encryption method that uses the same key for both encryption and decryption. It is fast but requires secure key distribution.

TRL (Technology Readiness Levels) A scale from 1 to 9 used to assess a technology's maturity, from concept (TRL 1) to operational deployment (TRL 9), helping organizations plan development and integration.

ZNE (Zero Noise Extrapolation) A quantum error mitigation technique that estimates ideal results by running circuits at varying noise levels and extrapolating a noiseless outcome, improving accuracy without full error correction.

Part I
Quantum Computing

Part I introduces the foundational concepts, advancements, and emerging trends in quantum computing. It begins with an exploration of key quantum hardware technologies—superconducting qubits, trapped ions, neutral atoms, and semiconductor spins—-highlighting their unique strengths and challenges as researchers strive to develop scalable and reliable quantum systems. The critical role of error correction, essential for achieving robust and large-scale quantum computing, is also discussed as a promising but still developing area.

Building on this foundation, the part delves into the potential of quantum optimization and machine learning, two areas that could transform problem-solving and data analysis as quantum computing evolves. Quantum optimization is presented as a tool for addressing complex decision-making challenges that are difficult or infeasible for classical computers, with a focus on quantum annealing—a specialized approach that shows promise for solving certain optimization problems more efficiently, despite current experimental limitations.

The part concludes with an exploration of quantum machine learning, examining its potential to improve data analysis and pattern recognition by leveraging quantum computing's unique capabilities. While acknowledging its current limitations and challenges, the discussion offers a forward-looking perspective on how quantum machine learning might evolve to unlock new possibilities. Throughout, Part I emphasizes the exploratory nature of these technologies and the ongoing efforts to understand their future impact.

Chapter 1
Superconducting Qubits

Stefano Poletto and Angela Q. Chen

Abstract Superconducting qubits are multilevel micro-fabricated artificial atoms based on superconducting materials. They are mainly operated in the low microwave frequency range (2–8 GHz) and require to be cooled below 20 mK to maintain quantum coherence. They enable precise engineering of transition frequencies and coupling strengths, facilitating advancements in quantum information processing and light-matter interactions. The field has evolved from early devices, characterized by short coherence times, to modern architectures with improved noise resilience, scalability, and fidelity. Better performances have been achieved through innovations in materials, fabrication, control electronics, and circuit design, enabling qubits with millisecond coherence times and gate fidelities exceeding 99.9%. However, challenges remain in mitigating two-level system defects, scaling devices, and addressing the cryogenic and infrastructure needs of larger quantum processing units. Current research focuses on modular and scalable architectures, error correction, and application. The field's progress highlights the potential for superconducting qubits to drive advancements in quantum computation.

1.1 Introduction

Qubits are the quantum counterpart of the classical bit, and they are defined by two quantum states. However, the field of superconducting qubits encompasses more than the study of these two levels. Instead, it is a broad field involving multilevel artificial atoms fabricated on-chip using superconducting materials and defined through standard microfabrication techniques.

On-chip artificial atoms gained popularity due to the ability to design quantum systems with specific energy levels and coupling strengths. This flexibility opened doors for exploring interactions between multiple quantum elements, such as qubit-

---

S. Poletto (✉) · A. Q. Chen
Rigetti Computing, Berkeley, CA, USA
e-mail: stefano@rigetti.com; achen@rigetti.com

qubit coupling, or between atoms and propagating electromagnetic fields, known as light-matter interaction, in various regimes. Exploration ranges from the dispersive coupling, where the interaction is much smaller than the frequency detuning between the quantum elements, to the ultra-strong regime, where the coupling strength approaches the frequency detuning and can result in highly nonlinear effects.

Superconducting artificial atoms are designed to operate in the low microwave spectrum, typically between several hundred MHz to tens of GHz, with most devices designed to function in the 2–8 GHz range. Because there is a wide availability of microwave components in the gigahertz frequency range, including active elements like signal sources and passive components like wiring, the field of superconducting qubits benefits from this frequency spectrum of operation. Furthermore, it is a convenient choice because the on-chip inductances and capacitances needed to reach this frequency range have reasonable size dimensions. To maintain quantum behavior, superconducting artificial atoms must be cooled below 20 mK, minimizing thermal noise and ensuring the system remains in its ground state.

When operated on the first two energy levels, the artificial atom behaves like a two-level system, thus adhering to the strict definition of a *qubit*. Because of the multilevel structure of these artificial atoms, there have been theoretical and experimental works on encoding and processing quantum information using these extra energy levels. The terms *qutrit* and *qudit* refer, respectively, to three-level and multilevel systems.

In 1999, the first coherent oscillation in an artificial atom, the Cooper-pair box, was observed [1], marking a milestone in superconducting quantum device development. Due to the system's short lifetime and high noise, the authors of the paper used control pulses with picosecond resolution to detect coherent oscillations between states $|0\rangle$ and $|1\rangle$, with oscillations shorter than 2 ns. Over the past 25 years, the field has advanced rapidly. Today, coherence time in isolated qubits has approached and surpassed the record value of 1 ms [2–4], two-qubit gate fidelity exceeds 99.9% [5, 6], readout fidelities have reached 99.1% with 40 ns measurement time [7], and processors hold hundreds of qubits [8].

1.2 Analysis

Achieving today's performance levels in superconducting qubits has required solving numerous challenges over the past two decades, like enhancing fabrication processes, improving quantum and classical hardware, and developing new manipulation schemes.

Research continues to focus on advancing these technologies, as superconducting devices remain an active and evolving field. Rather than relying on a single qubit type, diverse architectures are being explored. While the transmon is the most widely used superconducting qubit, promising results are also emerging from fluxonium and other designs.

Today, devices with hundreds of qubits are produced by leading companies and institutions, with many of those devices accessible via cloud services for broad usage. These large devices enable researchers to explore algorithms that harness quantum properties, guiding new strategies toward realizing quantum utility. Although a conclusive demonstration of quantum advantage or utility remains forthcoming, significant progress continues to bring the field closer to that goal.

The following sections delve into the key aspects of superconducting qubit technology, with an overview of current trends and innovations.

1.2.1 Definition

1.2.1.1 Types of Superconducting Qubits

Superconducting qubits are constructed from fundamental components: capacitors, inductors, and nonlinear inductors all made from superconducting materials. The nonlinear inductance is implemented by the Josephson junction (JJ), a thin insulating layer between two superconducting pads. The JJ behaves as an inductor, with its value dependent on the amplitude of the supercurrent passing through it. The specific circuit configuration and values of these three core elements define the type of qubit and the quantum variable used as qubit base for storing and processing information. In most cases, this quantum variable determines the name of the qubit.

The Cooper-pair box was the first superconducting circuit in which coherent oscillations were observed [1]. This type of qubit consists of a superconducting island connected to a "reservoir" via one or more Josephson junctions. The tunneling of Cooper pairs, a pair of bound electrons, through the JJ is controlled by gate voltages. The qubit's computational states are defined by the number of Cooper pairs on the island. Due to its high sensitivity to charge noise, the Cooper-pair box qubit has a short coherence time, and although it played a pivotal role in advancing the field, it is now rarely used as a qubit.

The phase qubit is another superconducting device that played a foundational role in the development of superconducting qubits [9]. In this device, quantum information is stored in the phase difference across the JJ. The system's energy profile resembles a tilted washboard, with the inclination and depth of the local minimum defined by the selected capacitance and inductance. The $|0\rangle$ and $|1\rangle$ states correspond to the first two energy levels of a local minima, and coherent transitions between them are controlled by applying microwave pulses to the device. The phase qubit is less sensitive to charge noise than the Cooper-pair box, but it is susceptible to flux noise and critical current noise in the JJ. For many years, the phase qubit was the best-performing superconducting qubit and was central to several landmark discoveries. One such milestone was the observation of interactions between the qubit and two-level systems in the oxide material used in its parallel plate capacitor, a factor that significantly limited coherence and relaxation times. Advances such as cleaner materials, improved surface processing, and the avoidance of lossy materials in parallel plate capacitors can be attributed to these early discoveries.

The flux qubit consists of a superconducting loop typically interrupted by three or more Josephson junctions [10]. The energy profile of the system is controlled by magnetic flux through the loop, and it resembles a symmetrical double well when biased at specific flux values. The two energy states localized in each well correspond to supercurrents circulating in opposite directions in the loop. An externally applied flux is used to adjust the symmetry of the two wells, while the separation between them is defined by the JJ. Under specific design conditions, the states in the left and right wells become hybridized, allowing coherent oscillations. The qubit states are manipulated with microwave pulses to induce the coherent evolution between $|0\rangle$ and $|1\rangle$, while flux pulses are used to control the phase. The flux qubit is particularly sensitive to flux noise, resulting in relatively short coherence times. Various design improvements, such as flux-insensitive operating points and the addition of shunt capacitances, have enhanced the performance of flux qubits over the years.

The transmon qubit is a modification of the original Cooper-pair box [11]. With the goal to reduce sensitivity to charge noise, one of the major limitations of the Cooper-pair box, a large shunting capacitance is added in series to the JJ. In its simplest form, the transmon qubit consists of either two superconducting islands connected by a JJ (i.e., the "floating" qubit) or a single island connected to ground by a JJ (i.e., the "grounded" qubit). The large shunting capacitance is implemented with planar in-line structures, which makes the transmon one of the qubits with the biggest footprints. The transmon qubit is typically defined by a high ratio of energy stored in the JJ to that in the shunting capacitance, generally exceeding 50. This high ratio makes the $|0\rangle$ and $|1\rangle$ energy profile nearly flat with respect to charge, making it insensitive to charge fluctuations. The two quantum states are manipulated with microwave pulses, but due to the system's low anharmonicity (i.e., the difference between energy gaps of consecutive levels), careful pulse shaping is required to prevent transitions outside the computational subspace. Due to its simple design, long coherence and relaxation times, and scalability, the transmon is one of the most widely used superconducting qubits.

Just as the transmon was developed from the charge qubit to reduce charge noise sensitivity, the fluxonium qubit is a modified version of the flux qubit, designed to reduce sensitivity to flux noise [12]. It consists of a superconducting loop with a Josephson Junction and a large inductance, similar in concept to the large capacitance used in the transmon. Since a practical planar inductance with minimal parasitic capacitance would be unfeasibly large, the large inductance is realized using a chain of hundreds of smaller JJs. This extra inductance modifies the energy profile of the flux qubit while preserving its basic operating principles. The fluxonium achieves maximum coherence and relaxation time when biased at half a flux quantum, also known as the sweet spot, where the qubit states correspond to currents circulating in opposite directions. At this sweet spot, the energy gap between the first two levels can be as low as hundreds of MHz, presenting unique challenges for initialization and operation compared to higher-frequency qubits.

Nevertheless, specialized techniques and two-qubit gates involving higher-energy states in the GHz range have been successfully employed to achieve high operational fidelities [6, 13, 14].

1.2.1.2 Two-Level Systems

Two-level systems (TLS) are quantum objects with only two well-defined energy states. They are typically found in materials and interfaces that make and support the qubit and quantum processors. There is not a unique quantum system that can be identified as TLS but rather a large set of possibilities [15]. In the field of superconducting qubits, TLS are of significant interest because they can severely impact device performance and, in some cases, render the device unusable.

TLS can couple with a qubit either directly or indirectly. Direct coupling occurs when the energy gap of the qubit is close to that of the TLS, allowing them to coherently exchange energy. Depending on the TLS dissipation time, this interaction can lead to a coherent oscillation of excitations between qubit and TLS or a decreased dephasing and relaxation time [16]. TLS can also affect the qubit indirectly. One hypothesis is that the spectral environment experienced by the qubit fluctuates due to unstable TLS or interaction between TLS at different energy scales [17]. These variations may contribute to both frequency fluctuations and reduced coherence times in the qubit.

Research into TLS remains active because a single strongly coupled TLS at the qubit frequency can render the device unusable, while an ensemble of weakly coupled TLS can degrade the coherence and lifetime of individual qubits.

1.2.1.3 Gates

The states of the qubits on a device are manipulated by enacting single-qubit and two-qubit gates on the qubits. From an algorithm point of view, these gates are matrices that perform a state transformation on the qubits in question, such as a rotation when a single-qubit gate is used to excite a qubit from the $|0\rangle$ to $|1\rangle$ state or a SWAP operation when two qubits exchange states.

From the device's point of view, gates consist of pulses that are sent to the qubits that alter the qubit state. Single-qubit gates are performed by applying a microwave pulse at the qubit's frequency. Two-qubit gates, on the other hand, are more complicated and can be implemented in a variety of ways. There is currently no consensus on the best method for implementing a two-qubit gate as it remains an active area of research in the field. The type of two-qubit gate implementation will impact both the design of the qubit device and also the types of unitaries or native gates that are accessible.

An additional consideration for two-qubit gates is how to couple the qubits. In general, the coupling is set by the capacitances or inductances between the qubits on the device, depending on the type of qubits that are used. This means that superconducting qubits generally interact most strongly with their nearest neighbors and are typically coupled to two to three other qubits on a planar device, unlike the case for trapped ion devices, which have all-to-all connectivity between qubits.

In recent years, the field has moved from fixed to tunable qubit-qubit coupling by adding additional elements to the circuit [18]. This has made it possible to modify the interaction strength between qubits, allowing a high on/off coupling ratio. Using this approach, coupling interactions are turned off during single-qubit gates and increased during two-qubit gates.

1.2.1.4 Gate Errors

Like with other qubit modalities, the gate performance of a superconducting qubit is quantified by its fidelity, or 1 − (gate error). The errors are generally classified as:

- Incoherent error: errors coming from the qubit coupling to noise in the environment. The noise can either impact the lifetime of an excited qubit, which is called T_1, or the phase information of the qubit, which is related to T_2. For superconducting qubits, T_1 and T_2 are typically on the order of tens to hundreds of microseconds on multi-qubit devices, with a maximum lifetime of 1-ms on isolated qubits [2–4]. Incoherent error can be a limiting factor for superconducting qubit gates, but it can be reduced by decreasing the ratio of the gate time to T_1 and T_2.
- Coherent error: errors coming from imprecise control over the qubit states. An example of a coherent error is unintentionally allowing some population of the qubit to leave the computational states $|0\rangle$ and $|1\rangle$ and end up in $|2\rangle$, which is possible if the control pulse is not properly calibrated.

1.2.2 Maturity

In the past decade, multiple predictions for the revolutionary impacts of universal quantum computing have been made, including those that would significantly change the cryptography field. However, the physical *quantum processing units* (QPUs) that are essential to these predictions and promises are still in the nascent stages of development, despite the tremendous progress that has been made. To better orient the reader to the current maturity levels of superconducting QPUs and the topics that are at the forefront of researchers' minds, this section provides an overview of the current state of qubit performance and count, practical uses of QPUs, and infrastructure development in the field of superconducting qubits.

As part of this discussion, the following are used as approximate delineations between different QPU sizes: small-scale refers to 1–50 qubits, medium-scale refers to 50–100 qubits, and large-scale refers to 100+ qubits.

1.2.2.1 Performance

One performance metric that sets superconducting qubits apart from other qubit modalities is the speed of their operations, which can be as low as 20–40 ns. Some advances that have made fast two-qubit gate times easier to access include the introduction of tunable couplers and pulse-shaping techniques. Various protocols and designs have been developed to speed up the reset and readout time of superconducting qubits as well.

Besides the speed of operation, the performance of a QPU is also determined by the errors incurred by single-qubit and two-qubit gates. These errors come from both coherent errors, which necessitate improved calibration techniques, and incoherent errors, which come from the fact that superconducting qubits have inherently short lifetimes. In the most generous quantum utility algorithms, such as the surface code, it is expected that the threshold on gate errors for a QPU to start being performant is about 1% [19].

Two-qubit gate fidelity is typically lower than single-qubit gate fidelity since there are more error channels and qubits involved. There is substantial ongoing work into studying different types of two-qubit gates and calibration methods to reduce errors as much as possible. Nowadays, two-qubit gates have reached 99.9% on small-scale devices [20]. On medium- to large-scale devices, the average two-qubit gate fidelity has been reported to be above 99% [8, 21, 22]. A typical fidelity for a single-qubit gate is 99.99%, though this fidelity can decrease when multiple single-qubit gates are operated at the same time.

1.2.2.2 Qubit Count

Small-scale QPUs are a test-bed for optimizing and exploring the superconducting qubit system, but increasing the qubit count on devices—a necessity for future algorithms—presents multiple challenges. In particular, geometry constraints can severely limit the number of qubits that can be practically fabricated on a device given the footprint of the qubits, their corresponding circuit elements, and the placement of signal delivery lines. One of the transitions that made it possible to circumvent some of the geometry restrictions was to transition from a two-dimensional device to a three-dimensional assembly [23]. In this case, qubits and the additional circuit elements are on different layers, which allows for more efficient use of space and signal routing. Three-dimensional assemblies are now routinely used on medium- to large-scale devices.

Besides geometry constraints, another challenge of scaling up qubit count is the practicality of making these large devices in a reproducible manner. As a result, multiple teams have developed methods to tile up small-scale devices to form a larger device, which is possible if high-quality two-qubit gates can be performed across different devices. This has been demonstrated both on the small-scale [24, 25] and medium- to large-scale,[1,2] indicating that modular architectures are a viable path for scaling up qubit count.

1.2.2.3 Applications

The performance and size of current QPUs are in a regime where interesting gate-based algorithms are becoming tenable. As a result, medium-sized QPUs were commercialized by various superconducting qubit companies. Today, companies provide access to QPUs with published gate and pulse calibrations for end-users to use on their desired algorithms, with qubit counts ranging from about 10 to 400. In the ideal situation, device end-users can run gate-based operations without being involved in the details of the calibrations and optimizations of the gates being used. Depending on the algorithm, a tight feedback loop between the deployed gate calibrations and the desired algorithm is still beneficial to optimize algorithm performance and calibrate out undesirable errors.

Another approach taken by research teams is to focus efforts on tailoring multi-qubit device gates and calibrations for specific algorithms, which is necessary when gate sequences become long and multiple gates are operated simultaneously. While this limits the accessibility of the QPUs, tailoring calibrations has resulted in some successful demonstrations of precursors to quantum utility such as quantum supremacy [21] and quantum error correction surface code up to distance-7 [8, 26].

1.2.2.4 Infrastructure

The superconducting qubit field has been moving out of the realm of fundamental research efforts as performance continues to improve and qubit devices grow in size. To support this, the infrastructure available to support superconducting qubit research has needed to evolve and mature as well. One notable example of infrastructure development is the increase in the number of fabrication foundries outside of traditional academic lab settings that are dedicated to making superconducting devices. These fabrication foundries reside in various national labs as well as commercial superconducting qubit companies around the world.

Having quantum-dedicated fabrication facilities accelerates the development of large-scale, high-performing QPUs. Though these facilities can borrow from the

---

[1] Rigetti Computing press release: *Rigetti Computing Announces Next-Generation 40Q and 80Q Quantum Systems.* Available at: https://www.globenewswire.com/news-release/2021/12/15/2352647/0/en/Rigetti-Computing-Announces-Next-Generation-40Q-and-80Q-Quantum-Systems.html (accessed November 2024).

[2] IBM press release: *IBM Debuts Next-Generation Quantum Processor IBM Quantum System Two, Extends Roadmap to Advance Era of Quantum Utility.* Available at: https://newsroom.ibm.com/2023-12-04-IBM-Debuts-Next-Generation-Quantum-Processor-IBM-Quantum-System-Two,-Extends-Roadmap-to-Advance-Era-of-Quantum-Utility (accessed November 2024).

mature techniques used by the semiconductor industry, the processes and techniques still need to be tailored to superconducting qubits. Fabrication processes that are the subject of ongoing research include ones that impact the prevalence of TLS, superconducting surface and interface cleanliness, robustness of multi-stack and multi-chip assemblies, etc.

As the number of qubits on devices increases to 100+, superconducting QPU sizes begin to hit a limit due to the space constraints of cryogenic systems, which consists of the dilution fridges that are needed to cool devices to 20 mK as well as the components inside the fridge that deliver microwave and DC signals down to the devices. Currently, standard cryogenic systems are able to support devices with 10–100 qubits. For large-scale QPUs, one research thrust has been to develop cryogenic components with smaller footprints, resulting in commercial offerings of quantum-tailored, compact cables. At the same time, engineering efforts have been invested into developing larger dilution fridges with sufficient cooling power.

1.2.3 Trends

Although much progress has been made since the first coherent oscillations in a superconducting qubit, the field continues to advance rapidly, with numerous teams and companies now addressing the challenge of scalability and performance. A universal quantum machine may need a million or more qubits, with information encoded and processed by logical qubits rather than physical ones, to solve certain instances of problems of interest [19, 27]. Significant improvements have been made in error-correction codes over the past decade [19, 28, 29], and further advancements are likely.

The primary difficulty ahead involves scaling up the number of qubits and increasing the performance of the QPUs, both of which will involve research from both the quantum and classical spheres. Below is a non-exhaustive list of project themes aimed at addressing upcoming challenges in scaling and performance.

- Quality of the qubits: reduce TLS and TLS impacts on qubits; increase coherence times of qubits; develop fabrication methods to accurately target qubit frequencies; improve control over coupling strengths on the QPUs
- Qubit shapes: develop qubit geometries with smaller footprints; innovate qubit design and materials to increase energy density and coupling strength per unit area
- Qubit manipulation schemes: reduce gate times while maintaining high fidelities; develop novel gate schemes for different algorithms
- Readout improvements: enhance mid-circuit measurement capabilities by increasing fidelity and reducing readout time, minimize readout impacts on performance
- Modular QPU architectures: develop robust methods to tile together small chips in a modular method; maintain gate performance across intra-chip edges

- Multiplexing methods: increase the number of qubits being read out simultaneously (currently limited to fewer than ten qubits); develop methods to control multiple qubits with a single line
- Electronics development: develop quantum-tailored electronics with lower noise; ensure stable electronics performance at scale; enable real-time processing
- Cryogenics fridge capabilities: develop more efficient signal delivery; maintain low temperatures with a large number of cables; develop methods to interconnect multiple quantum processors in separate fridges through optical communication

1.3 Conclusion

Quantum computing represents a paradigm shift in how information is stored and processed, with the potential to revolutionize sectors such as simulations, optimization, cybersecurity, and communications. Among the most promising approaches in the field of quantum computing and quantum technologies, superconducting qubits are a leading candidate as they can be engineered to meet specific operational requirements and are compatible with many standard microfabrication techniques.

However, despite rapid advancements, the field faces a significant talent shortage, as current educational programs struggle to meet the growing demand for highly skilled professionals. This highlights the need for universities, institutions, and governments to invest in educational programs and research initiatives to prepare the next generation of scientists and quantum engineers.

References

1. Y. Nakamura, Y. Pashkin, J. Tsai, Coherent control of macroscopic quantum states in a single-Cooper-pair box. Nature **398**, 786–788 (1999)
2. A. Somoroff et al., Millisecond coherence in a superconducting qubit. Phys. Rev. Lett. **130**, 267001 (2023)
3. M. Tuokkola et al., Methods to achieve near-millisecond energy relaxation and dephasing times for a superconducting transmon qubit (2024). pre-print. arXiv pre-print at arXiv:2407.18778
4. S. Ganjam et al. Surpassing millisecond coherence in on chip superconducting quantum memories by optimizing materials and circuit design. Nat. Commun. **15**, 3687 (2024)
5. R. Li et al., Realization of high-fidelity CZ gate based on a double-transmon coupler (2024). pre-print. arXiv pre-print at arXiv:2402.18926
6. L. Ding et al., High-fidelity, frequency-flexible two-qubit fluxonium gates with a transmon coupler. Phys. Rev. X **13**, 031035 (2023)
7. Y. Sunada et al., Fast readout and reset of a superconducting qubit coupled to a resonator with an intrinsic Purcell filter. Phys. Rev. Appl. **17**, 044016 (2022)
8. R. Acharya et al., Quantum error correction below the surface code threshold (2024). pre-print. arXiv pre-print at arXiv:2408.13687
9. M. Steffen, J.M. Martinis, I.L. Chuang, Accurate control of Josephson phase qubits. Phys. Rev. B **68**, 224518 (2003)
10. J.E. Mooij et al., Josephson persistent-current qubit. Science **285**, 1036–1039 (1999)

11. J. Koch et al., Charge-insensitive qubit design derived from the Cooper pair box. Phys. Rev. A **76**, 042319 (2007)
12. V.E. Manucharyan et al., Fluxonium: single Cooper-pair circuit free of charge offsets. Science **326**, 113–116 (2009)
13. F. Bao et al., Fluxonium: an alternative qubit platform for high-fidelity operations. Phys. Rev. Lett. **129**, 010502 (2022)
14. I.N. Moskalenko et al., High fidelity two-qubit gates on fluxoniums using a tunable coupler. NPJ Quantum Inf. **8**, 130 (2022)
15. C. Müller, J.H. Cole, J. Lisenfeld, Towards understanding two-level-systems in amorphous solids: insights from quantum circuits. Rep. Progr. Phys. **82**(12), 124501 (2019)
16. J. Lisenfeld et al., Electric field spectroscopy of material defects in transmon qubits. NPJ Quantum Inf. **5**, 105 (2019)
17. C. Müller et al., Interacting two-level defects as sources of fluctuating high-frequency noise in superconducting circuits. Phys. Rev. B **92**, 035442 (2015)
18. F. Yan et al., Tunable coupling scheme for implementing high-fidelity two-qubit gates. Phys. Rev. Appl. **10**, 054062 (2018)
19. A.G. Fowler et al., Surface codes: towards practical large-scale quantum computation. Phys. Rev. A **86**, 032324 (2012)
20. V. Negîrneac et al., High-fidelity controlled-z gate with maximal intermediate leakage operating at the speed limit in a superconducting quantum processor. Phys. Rev. Lett. **126**, 220502 (2021)
21. F. Arute et al., Quantum supremacy using a programmable superconducting processor. Nature **574**, 505–510 (2019)
22. L. Abdurakhimov et al., Technology and performance benchmarks of IQM's 20-qubit quantum computer (2024). pre-print. arXiv pre-print at arXiv:2408.12433
23. D. Rosenberg et al., 3d integrated superconducting qubits. NPJ Quantum Inf. **3**, 42 (2017)
24. A. Gold et al., Entanglement across separate silicon dies in a modular superconducting qubit device. NPJ Quantum Inf. **7**, 142 (2021)
25. M. Field et al., Modular superconducting-qubit architecture with a multichip tunable coupler. Phys. Rev. Appl. **21**, 054063 (2024)
26. S. Krinner et al., Realizing repeated quantum error correction in a distance-three surface code. Nature **605**, 669–674 (2022)
27. S.N. Saadatmand et al., Fault-tolerant resource estimation using graph-state compilation on a modular superconducting architecture (2024). pre-print. arXiv pre-print at arXiv:2406.06015
28. L.Z. Cohen et al., Low-overhead fault-tolerant quantum computing using long-range connectivity. Sci. Adv. **8**, eabn1717 (2022)
29. S. Bravyi et al., High-threshold and low-overhead fault-tolerant quantum memory. Nature **627**, 778–782 (2024)

Stefano Poletto is a director of quantum engineering at Rigetti Computing. He has worked with superconducting qubits since earning his physics degree from the University of Padua in 2003. Poletto completed his PhD in physics at the University of RomaTre in 2007 and subsequently held research positions at the Karlsruhe Institute of Technology, IBM T.J. Watson Research Center, and QuTech Research Center at the University of Delft prior to joining Rigetti in 2018. His current research is focused on developing next-generation devices and gates for superconducting quantum computers.

Angela Q. Chen is a quantum engineer at Rigetti Computing. Her current research is focused on exploring qubit-qubit interactions in superconducting quantum devices. Prior to joining Rigetti, she received a BA in physics from Harvard University and a PhD in condensed matter physics from the University of Illinois, Urbana-Champaign.

Open Access This chapter is licensed under the terms of the Creative Commons Attribution 4.0 International License (http://creativecommons.org/licenses/by/4.0/), which permits use, sharing, adaptation, distribution and reproduction in any medium or format, as long as you give appropriate credit to the original author(s) and the source, provide a link to the Creative Commons license and indicate if changes were made.

The images or other third party material in this chapter are included in the chapter's Creative Commons license, unless indicated otherwise in a credit line to the material. If material is not included in the chapter's Creative Commons license and your intended use is not permitted by statutory regulation or exceeds the permitted use, you will need to obtain permission directly from the copyright holder.

Chapter 2
Trapped-Ion Quantum Computers

Cornelius Hempel

Abstract The trapped-ion architecture was the first platform to demonstrate quantum gate operations in 1995 and continues to be a leading candidate for building a fault-tolerant quantum computer. This chapter provides a brief background on common performance metrics and nomenclature, summarizes the state of the art, and places them in context within the larger pursuit of error-corrected quantum computers. Current research thrusts in academia and industry are referenced, and an example roadmap is examined to show where the platform is right now and where it might be headed on the road to realizing a scaled-up device.

2.1 Introduction

The trapped-ion architecture was the first to demonstrate a physical quantum logic gate operation in 1995 [1]. This milestone came shortly after the first practical blueprint [2] on how to build such a machine was written, bringing to life what until then had only been a theoretical concept. The linchpin for this development was the excitement surrounding Peter Shor's discovery of his namesake factoring algorithm [3], and all was made possible by the preceding decade of research on atomic clocks, providing the first ever access to individual quantum objects in the early 1980s. To this day, the trapped-ion architecture continues to show the highest performance, with the lowest error rates among all quantum computing architectures. However, it operates at slower speeds compared to other platforms and faces nontrivial technological challenges in the scaling-up of system size.

Trapped-ion quantum computers store and manipulate information encoded in individual atoms. The devices remove an electron from each atom, turning them into charged particles known as ions that are trapped in a vacuum using electric fields. Which specific atomic element is chosen for this purpose is determined by its

---

C. Hempel (✉)
ETH Zurich - PSI Quantum Computing Hub, Villigen, Switzerland
e-mail: cornelius.hempel@psi.ch

© The Author(s) 2026
J. Jang-Jaccard et al. (eds.), *Quantum Technologies*,
https://doi.org/10.1007/978-3-031-90727-2_2

atomic structure, which in turn dictates which lasers and optical elements have to be used and what levels of performance these have to have. The most common choices to encode trapped-ion quantum bits are barium (Ba), calcium (Ca), or ytterbium (Yb).

Two of the ion's internal atomic energy levels can be used to encode a quantum bit (*qubit*). As the quantum equivalent of a classical bit, which would only take values of 0 *or* 1, a qubit can also allow for superpositions of 0 *and* 1, as well as so-called nonclassical correlations known as entanglement with other qubits. To manipulate the quantum state stored within laser (and/or microwave), pulses are used, which are generated by devices that in current-day machines are still located outside the ion trap. Information is retrieved using laser light, which projects the quantum state to classical one that can be read out easily: if the state is 1, the ion emits light when illuminated by the laser; if the state is 0, the ion remains dark. As in all quantum technologies, quantum superpositions (i.e., values between 0 and 1) are extracted from statistics after repeated runs of the same sequence of operations, yielding probabilities for the respective outcomes.

A unique feature of ion trap quantum computers is their tunable connectivity. Within a given trapped-ion processor region of a size of at most $\sim$50 qubits (i.e., the upper limit for practical reasons), the qubit interactions can be varied between next-neighbor-only and all-to-all, without any change to the hardware. This is possible because the connections between ion qubits are not physical in nature, but rather mediated through their joint motion inside the trapping potential (cf. Newton's cradle), which can be controlled using laser pulses directed at the ion(s). Directly connected to this feature is the ability to natively implement n-qubit gates where n is larger than two, again without any hardware changes. This goes significantly beyond the standard paradigm in quantum computing, which holds that single- and two-qubit gates are sufficient for universal computation [4]. As such, as of now, the practical utility of this feature for algorithms remains underexplored, albeit it is often used to great advantage in analog quantum simulations for scientific exploration run on trapped-ion systems, which already reach beyond what classical computers can access [5].

2.2 Analysis

Qubits in trapped ions can be implemented in different ways using its internal energy levels. Here, the main distinction is between ground-state qubits, where the qubit levels are assigned to states within the lowest atomic energy level, and optical qubits, where a ground-state energy level is combined with a metastable energy level. Metastable states naturally decay (relax) back to the ground state after a certain time. Both encodings have their respective advantages for either storage or operations, and conversions between them are possible, even though not yet commonly used. The most significant difference in terms of qubit manipulation is that in trapped-ion optical qubits the energy splitting between the two qubit levels corresponds to optical frequencies, allowing a single laser beam to manipulate the qubit state of a given ion; for ground-state qubits either microwave frequencies, which cannot be well focused in space, or pairs of laser beams with slight frequency differences can be used for state manipulation. Some elements allow for a specific type of ground-state encoding referred to as hyperfine qubits. These are much less sensitive to external noise, allowing for exceptionally long qubit coherence.

Physical qubit Uniformity and Reliability As fundamental building blocks of matter, atoms and, by extension, ions come at essentially zero cost, are all identical by nature, and can be replenished easily due to the practically infinite supply. This can be an advantage over human-made qubits in terms of reliability and yield, but it also takes away the freedom to design qubits and tailor their properties as desired. If all qubits are identical, concerns over increased cross-talk might arise. However, optical control through laser fields with the option to be combined with deliberate physical displacements of the ions in their trapping potential through shuttling enables exceptionally low cross-talk between qubits.

Logical qubits are formed by the combination of multiple physical qubits with an algorithmic recipe called a quantum error correction (QEC) code. There are a large number of quantum error correction codes, which are characterized by the number of physical qubits required to encode a logical qubit and the codes susceptibility to errors, i.e., how many errors can occur before a failure can no longer be recovered. As quantum error correction encodes information across many physical qubits, connectivity between qubits (e.g., next-neighbor-only vs. all-to-all) determines which codes can efficiently and often effectively be implemented. The performance of a quantum error correction code is then determined by the overall time it takes to detect and correct an error, referred to as the cycle time, in contrast to the time bare physical qubits can usefully store quantum information. At an abstract level, this is captured by the logical error rate.

The two most common types of quantum error correction codes today, the surface code [6] and the color code [7], have been successfully demonstrated on the trapped-ion platform [8, 9]. Compared to surface codes, color codes have more stringent requirements on the physical qubit error rate, i.e., a lower threshold that has to be reached for the code to actually help. However, they require fewer physical qubits and less measurement overhead, making color codes the current quantum error correction code of choice for trapped ions. Very recently, a new type of even more efficient quantum error correction code known as qLDPC has also been demonstrated for the first time [10], which was made possible by the long-range connectivity available in the trapped-ion architecture.

Coherence times describe the effective time throughout which the quantum state stored in a qubit can be maintained to a useful degree. They are the fundamental limitation of all physical qubit architectures and are given in the form of two numbers, T_1 and T_2, referring to the overall lifetime of the quantum state encoding the information and the time it remains accessible for coherent manipulations, respectively. As trapped-ion qubits are well-isolated quantum systems in a vacuum, they exhibit exceptionally long coherence times (cf. Table 2.1 below), which makes

Table 2.1 Summary table of performance metrics of trapped-ion systems. Best case and typical values are given where ranges reflect trade-offs between operation speed and fidelity. QEC stands for quantum error correction

Metric	Values	Comment
T_1 coherence time	Optical: 1 s (Ca), 25 s (Ba); Ground-state: infinite	Depending on the encoding and element chosen
T_2 phase coherence time	Optical: 100–500 ms; Ground-state: 50 s (Ca)	Values for passive memory; >1 hour possible with active stabilization
Single-qubit gate fidelity (time)	99.9999% (1–12 μs)	99.99% in commercial systems
Two-qubit gate fidelity (time)	99.94% (30–100 μs)	99.9% in commercial systems
Number of ion qubits per device	Up to 56	100s can be stored but not operated
QEC scaling demonstrated	Yes	For a range of QEC codes
Real-time QEC with feedback	Yes	The only platform to date

them useful for many proof-of-concept experiments on qubits without quantum error correction. In fact, in ground-state qubits, T_1 can effectively be infinite; hyperfine ground-state qubits passively reach T_2 up to one minute. These coherence properties significantly reduce the resource demand when implementing quantum error correction codes, making them more efficient.

Fidelity quantifies the error rates, more specifically *one minus the error rate* in percent. There are three important measures: (1) the single qubit gate fidelity, which describes how well each qubit can be manipulated on its own, (2) the two-qubit gate fidelity, which describes how well two qubits can interact with one another to create entanglement—the key ingredient of quantum computing—and (3) the read-out fidelity, which describes how well the resulting state of a qubit can be retrieved. In all these metrics, trapped-ion systems perform best, yet there is always a trade-off between the speed of any of these operations and their fidelity. Quoted numbers in the literature or commercial marketing material often tend to give best-case results in small systems, making reliable and holistic benchmarking an important and constantly evolving research area agnostic to the actual choice of quantum computing hardware.

Clock rates are usually stated based on the duration (or speed) of quantum gate operations, excluding initialization and read-out. Gate operations are slower with trapped ions than in other architectures because of the strong isolation from their environment. However, there are proof-of-concept experiments that demonstrate faster gate speeds[1] can be achieved. Eventually, however, the actual clock speed

---

[1] Typical two-qubit quantum gate operations take 10–100 μs corresponding to a clock rate of 10–100 kHz. However, two-qubit gates with 1.6 μs [11] and even 200 ps [12] (∼5 GHz) have been demonstrated.

of a *useful* quantum computer will be entirely determined by the cycle time of the quantum error correction algorithm it runs to maintain a given target error rate or logical qubit fidelity. The execution speed of this added algorithmic layer incorporates the interplay of the above base physical error rates, the code-required number of qubits and measurements per cycle, and the speed of classical electronics generating suitable feedback.

Scaling up to larger system sizes, while maintaining performance, is a challenging task for any quantum computing architecture. For trapped-ion quantum computers, there are two well-established paths for scaling. The first is the quantum charge-coupled device (QCCD) architecture [13], where ions are trapped above the surface of a small microchip in small groups and are moved by electrical signals between designated memory and processing zones. The second approach is based on fiber-optically linked sets of fixed modules with a small number of trapped ions in each [14]. Here, the modules do not necessarily have to be chip-based, simplifying trap design but introducing the additional challenge of requiring lossy optical links. Each of these approaches is pursued both on the academic and commercial side, and it is unclear which one ultimately scales faster and exhibits lower overhead under reliable error correction.

2.2.1 Maturity

With their 40-year history rooted in research on atomic clocks, trapped ions are one of the best-understood and well-characterized systems for the implementation of qubits. Their use as quantum computers in small-scale processors [15, 16] and scaling approaches [13, 14] have been established for more than a decade. Single- and two-qubit gate times have remained in the range of single to tens of microseconds, and while proof-of-concept experiments demonstrated that nanosecond [11] and even picosecond [12] speeds can be realized in principle, there is currently little research on increasing gate speeds. Similarly, current system sizes available for universal quantum computing reach up to $\sim$56 fully connected qubits [17]. This size, combined with all-to-all connectivity, is sufficient to carry out extensive error correction studies that reached significantly below breakeven (i.e., logical qubit error rate < physical qubit error rate) [18], proof-of-concept algorithms on logical qubits [19], and implement meaningful scientific (analog) quantum simulation experiments without error correction.

Trapped-ion systems first demonstrated quantum error correction more than a decade ago [8, 20] in the academic context, and cutting-edge research continues today [9, 21, 22] largely driven by US intelligence and defense research agencies (most prominently Intelligence Advanced Research Projects Activity (IARPA)). The recent establishment of commercial efforts with large teams of engineers and significant capital expenditure allowed the platform to demonstrate the next milestone: real-time error correction [23], which did not break even (i.e., logical fidelity < physical fidelity), but was the first demonstration of actually closing the quantum error correction feedback loop on any platform. This is in stark contrast to the prevailing quantum error correction experiments reported in the literature and press—across all architectures, both commercial and academic—where data is recorded and corrections are applied only in post-processing by removing erroneous data. Although this approach already allows one to reach significantly beyond break-even, real-time feedback will be a definitive requirement when performing calculations at scale.

Due to the complexity of the enabling technology that is required to run trapped-ion quantum computers,[2] their adoption is not as widespread in industry nor is the reporting on them. Nevertheless, significant and steady progress is being made and commercial providers such as AQT[3] in Austria and ionq[4] and Quantinuum[5] in the USA now offer cloud access to their systems either directly or through providers such as Microsoft's Azure or Amazon's Bracket. The differences between the three companies are in their approach to scaling and also in their business model. Quantinuum is pursuing the shuttling-based quantum CCD architecture, while ionq is focused on advancing optically linked modules instead. Both provide a full-stack offering and only complete machines, while the much smaller AQT also offers components for ion trap quantum computers in addition to developing their own devices. More recently, Infineon Technologies, best known for its semiconductor business, is positioning itself as a supplier for ion trap chips. This growing commercial technology base already benefits the research sector and may further accelerate developments in industry. With several more trapped-ion hardware startups[6] having formed in recent years, one can expect accelerated progress and novel ideas fueled by increasing competition.

2.2.2 Trends

Research in trapped-ion quantum computation has largely moved beyond work on improving qubits, gate fidelities, or speeds and follows three main lines: (1) a focus on hardware for scaling up system size, (2) investigations on quantum error correction codes and alternative qubit encoding schemes, and (3) exploring near-term utility for scientific research prior to error correction. In each area, both academic groups and commercial providers are active and complement each other.

Hardware trends include research on the integration and miniaturization of optical components for laser light delivery and detection, the scaling to larger

---

[2] Lasers and other advanced optical systems, ultra-high vacuum enclosures and many custom components, which are not readily available commercially.

[3] Co-founders are luminaries in the field, including the author of the original blueprint from 1995.

[4] Venture capital funded, first startup to be publicly listed.

[5] Hardware built by Honeywell, which is also the main shareholder.

[6] Oxford Ionics, Universal Quantum, eleQtron, QUDORA, Quantum Art, ZuriQ....

Development roadmap

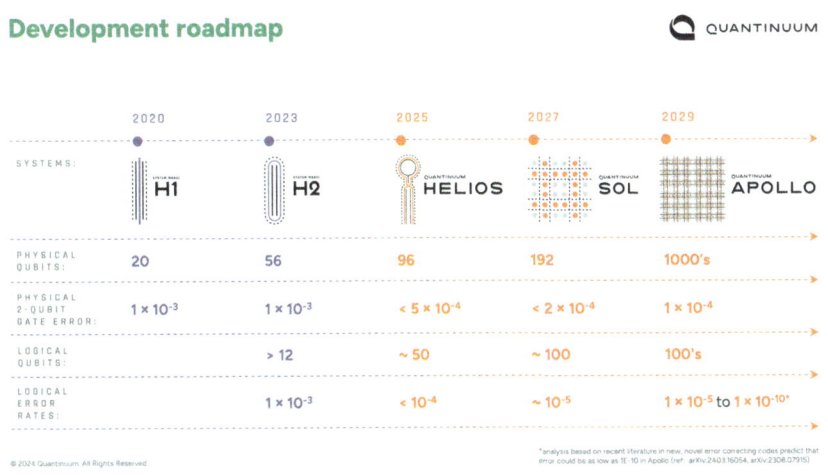

Fig. 2.1 Roadmap of commercial provider Quantinuum, representative of the overall performance goals that are pursued by the trapped-ion field in general, as well as what can (optimistically) be expected over the coming years

processors with surface ion trap chips in the QCCD approach, and investigations on replacing laser-based gate operations with microwave signals.

On the software side, various quantum error correction code families are being tested on high-performance trapped-ion quantum computers. Here, the ability to arbitrarily reconfigure qubit interactions—from all-to-all to next-neighbor only—provides a clear benefit, enabling the direct comparison of codes with significantly different connectivity requirements, without the need for new hardware. In 2024, superconducting qubits provided the strongest evidence yet that the theoretical assumption of error scaling with code size is correct [24]. With fewer physical qubits available on the platform, trapped-ion systems do not (yet) pursue size scaling but rather evaluate the impact of lower error rates on quantum error correction codes.

An example of an industry roadmap[7] is given in Fig. 2.1. It reflects the expectation that the base two-qubit quantum gate fidelity will likely not significantly improve over the coming years and shows that progress in the reliability of qubits has to come from quantum error correction and the development of logical qubits. In particular, there is still significant uncertainty in the eventual performance of quantum error correction, corresponding to a factor of 100,000 in error rate. While this might seem problematic, it is actually a reflection of the tremendous progress made in the theory of quantum error correction over the past 3–4 years, which is bringing such vast improvements into the realm of possibility.

In parallel to these efforts to scale, much of the research on trapped ions today focuses on proof-of-concept science cases with digital quantum computation

---

[7] The only one available in the trapped-ion area at the time of writing.

prior to quantum error correction [25] or analog quantum computation, which is generally captured under the term quantum simulation [26]. These latter efforts are likely going to provide at least qualitative insights into currently computationally demanding or even intractable phenomena, yet will not provide the accuracy and resolution that can be expected from future quantum error correction-based systems.

2.3 Conclusion

Trapped-ion quantum computers remain at the forefront of the quest to build an error-corrected, fault-tolerant quantum computer. Although the systems have not yet reached the large qubit numbers found in other modalities, high fidelities, repeatability, and long-range all-to-all connectivity make up for this shortcoming at the current stage. At the same time, the complex technical infrastructure—mainly composed of optical components—required to scale the technology does have a broad range of other application areas, both in quantum technologies (e.g., sensing) and also outside. The drive toward miniaturization and integration of components does provide benefits for other applications where visible light is used, such as fluorescence microscopy and metrology. Overall, the technological hurdles on the way to a large-scale quantum computer have been identified and are being worked on in both academia and industry, resulting in steady progress in the field.

References

1. C.R. Monroe, D. Meekhof, B. King, W.M. Itano, D.J. Wineland, Demonstration of a fundamental quantum logic gate. Phys. Rev. Lett. **75**(25), 4714–4717 (1995)
2. J.I. Cirac, P. Zoller, Quantum computations with cold trapped ions. Phys. Rev. Lett. **74**(20), 4091–4094 (1995)
3. P.W. Shor, Algorithms for quantum computation: discrete logarithms and factoring, in *Proceedings 35th Annual Symposium on Foundations of Computer Science*, Proceedings 35th Annual Symposium on Foundations of Computer Science (1994), pp. 124–134
4. D.P. DiVincenzo, Two-bit gates are universal for quantum computation. Phys. Rev. A **51**(2), 1015–1022 (1995)
5. A.J. Daley, I. Bloch, C. Kokail, S. Flannigan, N. Pearson, M. Troyer, P. Zoller, Practical quantum advantage in quantum simulation. Nature **607**(7920), 667–676 (2022)
6. A.G. Fowler, M. Mariantoni, J.M. Martinis, A.N. Cleland, Surface codes: towards practical large-scale quantum computation. Phys. Rev. A **86**(3), 032324 (2012)
7. H. Bombin, M.A. Martin-Delgado, Topological quantum distillation. Phys. Rev. Lett. **97**(18), 180501 (2006)
8. D. Nigg, M. Müller, E.A. Martinez, P. Schindler, M. Hennrich, T. Monz, M.A. Martin-Delgado, R. Blatt, Quantum computations on a topologically encoded qubit. Science **345**(6194), 302–305 (2014)
9. L. Egan, et al., Fault-tolerant control of an error-corrected qubit. Nature **598**(7880), 281–286 (2021)

10. Y. Hong, E. Durso-Sabina, D. Hayes, A. Lucas, Entangling four logical qubits beyond break-even in a nonlocal code. Phys. Rev. Lett. **133**(18), 180601 (2024)
11. V.M. Schäfer, C.J. Ballance, K. Thirumalai, L.J. Stephenson, T.G. Ballance, A.M. Steane, D.M. Lucas, Fast quantum logic gates with trapped-ion qubits. Nature **555**(7694), 75–78 (2018)
12. J.D. Wong-Campos, S.A. Moses, K.G. Johnson, C.R. Monroe, Demonstration of two-atom entanglement with ultrafast optical pulses. Phys. Rev. Lett. **119**(23), 230501 (2017)
13. D. Kielpinski, C.R. Monroe, D.J. Wineland, Architecture for a large-scale ion-trap quantum computer. Nature **417**(6890), 709–711 (2002)
14. C. Monroe, R. Raussendorf, A. Ruthven, K. R Brown, P. Maunz, L.M. Duan, J. Kim, Large-scale modular quantum-computer architecture with atomic memory and photonic interconnects. Phys. Rev. A **89**(2), 022317 (2014)
15. P. Schindler et al., A quantum information processor with trapped ions. New J. Phys. **15**(12), 123012 (2013)
16. S. Debnath, N.M. Linke, C. Figgatt, K.A. Landsman, K. Wright, C. Monroe, Demonstration of a small programmable quantum computer with atomic qubits. Nature **536**(7614), 63–66 (2016)
17. M. DeCross et al., The computational power of random quantum circuits in arbitrary geometries (2024). arXiv
18. M.P. da Silva et al., Demonstration of logical qubits and repeated error correction with better-than-physical error rates (2024). arXiv
19. K. Mayer et al., Benchmarking logical three-qubit quantum Fourier transform encoded in the Steane code on a trapped-ion quantum computer (2024). arXiv
20. P. Schindler, J.T. Barreiro, T. Monz, V. Nebendahl, D. Nigg, M. Chwalla, M. Hennrich, R. Blatt, Experimental repetitive quantum error correction. Science **332**(6033), 1059–1061 (2011)
21. A. Erhard et al., Entangling logical qubits with lattice surgery. Nature **589**(7841), 220–224 (2021)
22. L. Postler et al., Demonstration of fault-tolerant universal quantum gate operations. Nature **605**(7911), 675–680 (2022)
23. C. Ryan-Anderson et al., Realization of real-time fault-tolerant quantum error correction. Phys. Rev. X **11**(4), 041058 (2021)
24. R. Acharya et al., Quantum error correction below the surface code threshold. Nature (2024)
25. Y. Alexeev et al., Quantum computer systems for scientific discovery. PRX Quantum **2**(1), 017001 (2021)
26. E. Altman et al., Quantum simulators: architectures and opportunities. PRX Quantum **2**(1), 017003 (2021)

Cornelius Hempel leads the Ion Trap Quantum Computation group at the ETH Zürich-PSI Quantum Computing Hub. Prior to its founding in 2021, he was a senior research fellow and principal investigator at the University of Sydney's Quantum Control Laboratory. Cornelius obtained his PhD in physics in the group of Prof. Rainer Blatt at the University of Innsbruck (Austria) in 2014 and previously obtained Master's and Diploma degrees at the University of Michigan (USA) and Martin Luther University Halle (Germany).

Open Access This chapter is licensed under the terms of the Creative Commons Attribution 4.0 International License (http://creativecommons.org/licenses/by/4.0/), which permits use, sharing, adaptation, distribution and reproduction in any medium or format, as long as you give appropriate credit to the original author(s) and the source, provide a link to the Creative Commons license and indicate if changes were made.

The images or other third party material in this chapter are included in the chapter's Creative Commons license, unless indicated otherwise in a credit line to the material. If material is not included in the chapter's Creative Commons license and your intended use is not permitted by statutory regulation or exceeds the permitted use, you will need to obtain permission directly from the copyright holder.

Chapter 3
Quantum Computing with Neutral Atoms

Tommaso Macrì

Abstract Neutral-atom quantum computers are an emerging platform for scalable quantum computation. This review outlines the fundamental principles, current technologies, and potential future directions of neutral-atom quantum computing. It also highlights key trends and challenges in the field, offering recommendations to strengthen the global quantum ecosystem.

3.1 Introduction

Quantum computing represents a breakthrough technology that harnesses the principles of quantum mechanics to solve problems far beyond the reach of classical computers. Among the many quantum architectures being explored, neutral-atom quantum processors have emerged as a highly scalable and versatile platform.

Neutral atoms, which are manipulated using laser light in optical tweezers or lattices, serve as qubits with long coherence times and low error rates. This architecture offers advantages over superconducting qubits and trapped ions due to the natural scalability of atomic systems and their ability to support various quantum simulations and algorithmic tasks.

First, atoms are nature's perfect qubits: they are identical, robust, and naturally immune to many sources of noise that affect other qubit systems. This intrinsic stability leads to lower error rates during computation, making them suitable for large-scale quantum processors.

Additionally, neutral atoms operate at room temperature, avoiding the need for complex cryogenic systems required by other quantum computing platforms, like superconducting qubits. This significantly reduces the operational overhead and allows for more accessible and scalable quantum systems.

T. Macrì (✉)
QuEra Computing Inc., Boston, MA, USA
e-mail: tmacri@quera.com

© The Author(s) 2026
J. Jang-Jaccard et al. (eds.), *Quantum Technologies*,
https://doi.org/10.1007/978-3-031-90727-2_3

Moreover, the use of optical tweezers allows these qubits to be easily reconfigurable, meaning they can be dynamically arranged to optimize problem encoding and error correction. This versatility enhances both the system's scalability and its ability to tackle various quantum algorithms,

By utilizing Rydberg interactions—where neutral atoms are excited to high-energy states—the platform facilitates entangling gates between distant qubits, making it suitable for implementing quantum algorithms at scale. This architecture has already demonstrated promising applications in NISQ devices and beyond, providing a pathway to fault-tolerant quantum computing.

3.2 Analysis

Neutral-atom quantum computers operate by trapping individual atoms in arrays created by optical tweezers. These atoms are used as qubits, where their internal states—such as hyperfine levels—encode quantum information. Interactions between qubits are mediated through Rydberg excitations, which enable two-qubit gates. The advantage of this system lies in its scalability; hundreds or even thousands of qubits can be arranged in regular patterns, with precise control over their position and state.

Neutral-atom platforms have demonstrated significant versatility in both digital and analog quantum computing. In digital quantum computing, qubits are used to execute algorithms in the form of circuits to be compiled through a set of native gates.

In analog quantum computing, the qubit basis states are encoded in a ground state and an excited Rydberg state. The dynamics is then enabled by engineering pulses that control the microscopic parameters of the underlying Hamiltonian. This versatility positions neutral-atom platforms as key players in both scientific quantum simulations and near-term commercial quantum applications.

One of the most compelling applications of neutral-atom platforms is quantum simulation, where these systems are employed to model the behavior of complex quantum phenomena that are otherwise intractable on classical computers. Notably, they have been used to simulate quantum phases of matter, including spin liquids and topological insulators. Through precise control of atomic interactions, researchers can probe the physics of strongly correlated systems in ways that remain beyond the reach of traditional computational methods.

Another key capability of neutral-atom systems is their ability to execute quantum algorithms. Recent advancements in achieving high-fidelity quantum gates have expanded their applicability, enabling researchers to explore quantum optimization algorithms, quantum chemistry simulations, and other computational tasks that leverage quantum speedups to solve problems more efficiently than classical approaches.

3.3 Maturity

Neutral-atom quantum processors have emerged as a highly promising architecture for scalable quantum computation due to their unique capability to manipulate large arrays of qubits with high spatial and temporal precision. Recent advancements by leading companies such as QuEra Computing have demonstrated practical implementations of neutral-atom systems that surpass the capabilities of classical computers in specific tasks. For instance, QuEra's "Aquila" quantum processor, featuring a 256-qubit architecture, has shown the potential to perform complex quantum simulations of materials and tackle optimization problems with real-world applications across industries such as finance, logistics, and chemistry [1].

Despite their scalability advantages, neutral-atom platforms face significant challenges in achieving fault tolerance, a critical requirement for large-scale, error-corrected quantum computation. Currently, these systems predominantly operate within the Noisy Intermediate-Scale Quantum (NISQ) regime, where the presence of errors limits the depth and accuracy of computations. Although fault-tolerant quantum computing remains many years away, the demonstrated capabilities of neutral-atom processors in NISQ applications highlight their growing importance in the quantum ecosystem in the short to medium term. These platforms are particularly well-suited for exploring quantum algorithms and simulations that are otherwise infeasible on classical hardware.

A key factor for advancing neutral-atom quantum processors toward fault-tolerant quantum computing is the improvement of gate fidelity. Recent breakthroughs have significantly enhanced the fidelity of two-qubit gates, bringing them closer to the thresholds required for implementing quantum error correction codes. However, achieving the performance levels necessary for fault-tolerant computation will require further advancements in both hardware and control algorithms. Techniques such as parallel transversal gates, which allow multiple qubits to be manipulated simultaneously to boost processing speed, and zoned architectures, which optimize qubit connectivity while reducing noise, are currently being explored to address these challenges. These innovations are expected to improve both the stability and efficiency of neutral-atom quantum processors.

The development of quantum control systems and supporting software infrastructure is another crucial element in the advancement of neutral-atom platforms. Achieving scalable, high-performance quantum processors requires collaboration between hardware developers and supply chain partners to drive innovation in several key areas. These include the development of precise laser systems for qubit manipulation, advanced control electronics for delivering accurate pulse sequences, and middleware solutions that optimize the performance of quantum algorithms across different hardware configurations. Such partnerships are essential to addressing existing bottlenecks related to system stability, gate fidelity, and overall computational performance. By overcoming these challenges, neutral-atom quantum processors are poised to play a critical role in the future of quantum computing.

3.4 Trends

The future of neutral-atom quantum computing will likely emphasize hybrid quantum-classical systems, where quantum processors complement classical high-performance computing (HPC) infrastructures. In such models, quantum processors handle specialized tasks benefiting from quantum speedup, while classical systems manage broader computational workloads. This synergistic approach enables more efficient solutions to complex problems that are otherwise intractable for classical computers.

Cloud-based quantum computing services have become a key tool for democratizing access to quantum processors. Platforms such as AWS Braket, IBM Quantum, and Microsoft Azure Quantum provide users with the ability to experiment with quantum algorithms without significant investment in hardware. These platforms support a range of quantum hardware, including neutral-atom processors, and integrate seamlessly with classical computing resources, facilitating the development of hybrid algorithms. Notably, QuEra's Aquila, a 256-qubit analog quantum processor, is currently the only neutral-atom quantum system available via cloud services. Access through AWS Braket allows users to explore advanced quantum simulations and optimization techniques, accelerating innovation across various industries.

The integration of quantum computing with HPC centers is another critical area of focus, allowing quantum processors to act as accelerators for specific tasks within classical systems. Countries like Japan and members of the European Union are pushing forward with initiatives to embed quantum systems into their supercomputing infrastructures. The European High-Performance Computing Joint Undertaking (EuroHPC JU) initiative aims to enhance Europe's supercomputing capabilities by integrating quantum processors into existing HPC centers to address industrial, scientific, and societal challenges [2]. Similarly, Pasqal's delivery of a quantum processor to GENCI and IBM's collaboration with Pasqal on creating quantum-centric supercomputers highlight the growing global momentum toward hybrid architectures [3, 4]. Outside of Europe, QuEra Computing has secured a contract with Japan's National Institute of Advanced Industrial Science and Technology (AIST) to deploy a neutral-atom quantum computer alongside AIST's AI-focused supercomputing infrastructure, including the AI Bridging Cloud Infrastructure-Quantum (ABCI-Q) system, further highlighting the practical potential of integrating classical and quantum systems [5].

Distributed Quantum Computing (DQC) offers a novel approach to overcoming scalability limitations by interconnecting smaller quantum processors to work collectively on larger problems. Neutral-atom systems are particularly well-suited for this architecture due to their long coherence times and flexible connectivity. However, DQC is still in its early stages, with challenges related to communication overhead, error correction, and efficient entanglement generation [6]. Continued research in quantum networking, better control of distributed entanglement, and the integration of classical systems for coordination will be essential for advancing this paradigm.

Together, these developments point to a future in which neutral-atom quantum processors play an important role in hybrid and distributed quantum computing, enabling new breakthroughs in scientific research and industrial applications.

3.5 Recommendations

Neutral-atom quantum processors are a vital component of the broader quantum computing ecosystem, offering unique capabilities that complement other quantum platforms and classical high-performance computing (HPC) systems. The development of this ecosystem depends on strong partnerships between national laboratories, academic institutions, and industry players. Such collaborations are critical to driving innovation, creating public policies that foster quantum advancement, and ensuring the development of a skilled quantum workforce. As this ecosystem continues to evolve, neutral-atom quantum processors are expected to play an increasingly important role in hybrid quantum-classical systems.

Efforts to integrate neutral-atom quantum processors into classical supercomputing infrastructures are already underway in various regions. These initiatives aim to maximize the potential of quantum systems by pairing them with established HPC centers to solve complex problems more efficiently. Alongside hardware development, the creation of programs focused on workforce development and broader access to quantum technologies is essential to ensure sustainable growth in the quantum sector.

For example, in the UK, the National Quantum Computing Centre (NQCC), in partnership with UK Research and Innovation (UKRI), has launched a £30 million initiative to support the development of quantum computing testbeds. These testbeds aim to accelerate the country's quantum capabilities by fostering the development of prototype quantum computers. Scheduled to be operational by 2025, the testbeds will help identify the most promising quantum architectures for various applications while addressing bottlenecks in current technology readiness. This initiative involves multiple quantum hardware companies, including neutral-atom providers, such as QuEra Computing and Cold Quanta UK, and aims to drive innovation, create high-tech jobs, and boost economic growth.

In the USA, the Quantum Computing User Program (QCUP), led by Oak Ridge National Laboratory (ORNL), offers researchers access to advanced quantum computing resources through cloud-based platforms. By the end of 2023, QCUP supported over 80 projects and 271 active users, making it one of the most prominent quantum user programs globally. QCUP enables users to explore quantum algorithms, optimize scientific workflows, and experiment with quantum-classical hybrid systems by integrating quantum processors with ORNL's high-performance computing capabilities. These programs provide vital opportunities for researchers and industries to access cutting-edge quantum technologies without the need for significant infrastructure investments.

To further advance the global quantum ecosystem, it is essential to focus on key areas such as increasing R&D investment, strengthening industry-academia collaborations, and building comprehensive national strategies. Increased funding for research institutions and startups will accelerate innovation and support the translation of quantum breakthroughs into practical applications. Partnerships between academia and industry are crucial for bridging the gap between research and commercialization, enabling faster adoption of quantum technologies. Additionally, developing a national strategy that integrates neutral-atom quantum processors into existing HPC infrastructures will help nations stay competitive in the evolving quantum landscape.

By prioritizing investment, collaboration, and infrastructure development, countries can accelerate the growth of their quantum ecosystems. These efforts will foster a quantum-ready workforce, drive economic growth, and ensure that emerging quantum technologies continue to play a pivotal role in solving complex global challenges across various scientific and industrial domains.

3.6 Conclusion

Neutral-atom quantum computers have emerged as a promising platform for scalable quantum computing, with notable advancements in recent years. Their ability to leverage Rydberg interactions for entanglement, combined with inherent scalability, positions them as key players in both near-term and long-term quantum technologies. The versatility of neutral atoms in quantum simulations, optimization, and other computational tasks opens up a broad range of applications that can drive scientific discovery and industrial innovation.

Despite these advancements, challenges such as gate fidelity and error rates remain significant obstacles. Achieving fault-tolerant quantum computing will require continued innovation in hardware, control systems, and error correction techniques. Addressing these challenges through increased R&D investment, fostering industry-academia collaborations, and developing comprehensive quantum strategies will be essential for advancing neutral-atom quantum platforms and realizing their full potential across various sectors.

References

1. J. Wurtz, A. Bylinskii, B. Braverman, J. Amato-Grill, S.H. Cantu, F. Huber, A. Lukin, F. Liu, P. Weinberg, J. Long, S.-T. Wang, N. Gemelke, A. Keesling, Aquila: QuEra's 256-qubit neutral-atom quantum computer (2023)
2. HPCQS, HPCQS: high-performance computer and quantum simulator hybrid (2024). https://www.hpcqs.eu/

3. Quantum Computing Report, Pasqal delivers first advanced quantum processing unit to GENCI and CEA, enhancing Europe's hybrid high-performance computing capabilities (2024). https://quantumcomputingreport.com/pasqal-delivers-first-advanced-quantum-processing-unit-to-genci-and-cea-enhancing-europes-hybrid-high-performance-computing-capabilities/
4. IBM and Pasqal, IBM and Pasqal initiate collaboration to define classical-quantum integration for quantum-centric supercomputers (2024). https://www.hpcwire.com/off-the-wire/ibm-and-pasqal-initiate-collaboration-to-define-classical-quantum-integration-for-quantum-centric-supercomputers/
5. Inside Quantum Technology, QuEra lands deal to deploy quantum computer alongside supercomputer in Japan (2024). https://www.insidequantumtechnology.com/news-archive/quera-lands-42m-deal-to-deploy-quantum-computer-alongside-supercomputer-in-japan/
6. J. Ramette, J. Sinclair, Z. Vendeiro, A. Rudelis, M. Cetina, V. Vuletić, Any-to-any connected cavity-mediated architecture for quantum computing with trapped ions or Rydberg arrays. PRX Quantum **3**, 010344 (2022)

Dr. Tommaso Macrì works as an executive account manager at QuEra Computing, where he aligns quantum technology innovations of neutral-atom quantum computers with commercial needs. Before this, he was Professor of Physics at the Federal University of Rio Grande do Norte (UFRN), where he joined in 2015. He holds a PhD from the International School for Advanced Studies (SISSA) in Trieste, Italy. His research interests focus on quantum simulation with neutral atoms and the development of numerical algorithms for quantum many-body physics. He is the author of more than 50 research papers, including a recent review of modern physics on the physics of long-range interacting quantum systems.

Open Access This chapter is licensed under the terms of the Creative Commons Attribution 4.0 International License (http://creativecommons.org/licenses/by/4.0/), which permits use, sharing, adaptation, distribution and reproduction in any medium or format, as long as you give appropriate credit to the original author(s) and the source, provide a link to the Creative Commons license and indicate if changes were made.

The images or other third party material in this chapter are included in the chapter's Creative Commons license, unless indicated otherwise in a credit line to the material. If material is not included in the chapter's Creative Commons license and your intended use is not permitted by statutory regulation or exceeds the permitted use, you will need to obtain permission directly from the copyright holder.

Chapter 4
Quantum Computing with Semiconductor Spin

Santhanu Panikar Ramanandan and Anna Fontcuberta i Morral

Abstract Developing a universal quantum computer that can solve complex problems beyond the reach of classical computers is an open challenge. Achieving this requires integrating a large number of qubits into a quantum processor, much like integrating millions of transistors in a silicon chip. Among the available quantum computing approaches, semiconductor spin qubit technology has a unique advantage in scaling up to larger quantum systems as it builds on well-established semiconductor chip processing technology. This chapter aims to provide a comprehensive overview of semiconductor spin qubit technology for nonspecialists. The chapter begins by explaining the operational principles of spin qubit systems. It then introduces different types of spin qubits and commonly used terminologies, assesses the performance metrics, and compares them with other quantum computing technologies. Active research activities in academia and industry are also discussed. Finally, the chapter reviews recent trends in spin qubit research and offers practical recommendations.

4.1 Introduction

Quantum computing is a rapidly advancing field of research with several promising technological approaches. The most promising technologies involve superconducting qubits, photonics, trapped ion or atom qubits, and semiconductor spin qubits. A list of start-ups and established companies working in these areas can be found in The Quantum Insider [1]. This chapter focuses on semiconductor spin qubit technology and provides an overview of the field for a nonspecialist. Unlike superconducting qubits, used by IBM [2] and Google [3], or trapped ion technology, employed by Quantinuum [4] and IonQ [5], semiconductor spin qubit technology utilizes the well-established semiconductor chip fabrication process.

S. P. Ramanandan (✉) · A. Fontcuberta i Morral
Laboratory of Semiconductor Materials - EPFL, Lausanne, Switzerland
e-mail: santhanu.ramanandan@epfl.ch; anna.fontcuberta-morral@epfl.ch

© The Author(s) 2026
J. Jang-Jaccard et al. (eds.), *Quantum Technologies*,
https://doi.org/10.1007/978-3-031-90727-2_4

This compatibility with existing industrial infrastructure renders semiconductor spin qubits particularly attractive for building large-scale quantum processors.

To understand the working principle of semiconductor spin qubits, the reader is invited to imagine an isolated electron in a semiconductor as a tiny compass needle. The spin state of an electron can be visualized as the direction in which the electron "spins" around its axis. Much like a compass needle that can point north or south, an electron's spin can also point "up" or "down" in a magnetic field. These two orientations represent the possible states of a qubit, analogous to how classical computers use 0 and 1 to store information. Unlike a compass needle, quantum mechanics allows the spin of an electron to be in a superposition of both states.

Extending from the success of the semiconductor transistor, the concept of semiconductor spin qubit quantum computing was first introduced by Daniel Loss (University of Basel, Switzerland) and David P. DiVincenzo (RWTH Aachen, Germany) in 1998 [6]. In this theoretical work, they proposed using the spin of an electron confined within a semiconductor quantum dot to define a quantum bit (qubit).

Electrons in semiconductors are negatively charged particles, and their movement can be controlled electrostatically by applying a voltage. For example, in transistors used in semiconductor chips, the polarity of the voltage applied to the gate electrode switches the transistor on or off, as shown in Fig. 4.1. A positive gate voltage attracts electrons into the semiconductor, turning the device on (Fig. 4.1a), while a negative gate voltage removes electrons, turning it off (Fig. 4.1b).

Similarly, in a semiconductor quantum dot device, multiple nanoscale gate electrodes are placed next to each other, as shown in Fig. 4.1c. By applying appropriate voltages to these gates, a single electron is trapped in a small region under one of them. These localized regions are called quantum dots, and they isolate electrons from the rest of the material.

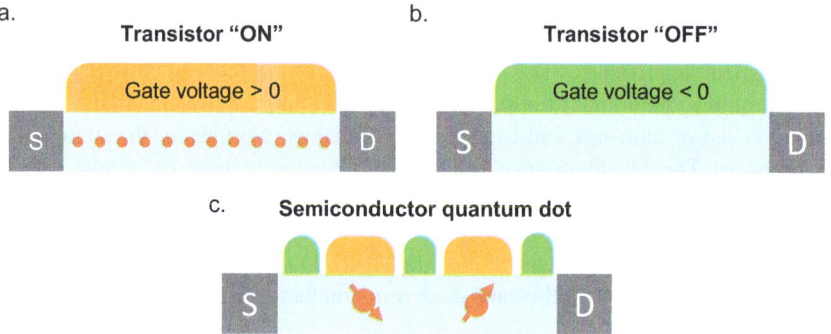

Fig. 4.1 (**a**) Schematic of a transistor in the "on" state: a positive voltage applied to the gate attracts electrons into the semiconductor channel, turning the transistor on. (**b**) Schematic of the "off" state: a negative gate voltage removes electrons, emptying the semiconductor channel and turning the transistor off. (**c**) Schematic of a semiconductor quantum dot, where a series of local gate electrodes are used to isolate a single electron

Once an electron is trapped, a static magnetic field is applied to split the energy levels of the spin-up and spin-down states. A transverse alternating magnetic or electric field is then applied to rotate the spin states, allowing precise manipulation of the qubit's spin state. After each operation, the final state of the qubit is read out by monitoring the current flowing out of the quantum dot. A measurable current is produced if the electron is in the spin-up state, whereas no current flows if the electron remains in the spin-down state.

4.2 Analysis

Today, several types of semiconductor-based spin qubits exist. They all share the same fundamental physical principles for initializing, manipulating, and reading quantum information. This section provides an overview of various spin qubit systems, introduces key terminologies and performance metrics, and concludes with a comparison of these metrics.

4.2.1 Types of Semiconductor Spin Qubits

The initial concept of a spin qubit involved a single electron trapped in a semiconductor quantum dot. Over time, other spin qubit types have emerged that involve other kinds of particles, such as holes or nuclear particles, and that use diverse semiconductor material systems.

- **Electron spin qubits**: These qubits utilize the spin states of an electron to represent a quantum bit.
- **Hole spin qubits**: These qubits use the spin states of a hole, the positively charged counterpart of an electron, to define a quantum bit.
- **Nuclear spin qubits**: These qubits rely on the spin states of an atomic nucleus to define a quantum bit.

Among the available systems, the most promising today correspond to electron spin qubits in silicon [7] and hole spin qubits in germanium [8]. The rest of this chapter will focus on these two systems.

4.2.2 Physical Qubit Yield, Reliability, and Connectivity

Semiconductor spin qubit systems are fabricated using state-of-the-art semiconductor fabrication technology, identical to the one that produces transistors in silicon chips. The maturity of this fabrication process greatly impacts the yield and reliability of physical qubits. As a result, spin qubits fabricated in university cleanrooms may suffer from large device-to-device variations, which limit the yield. Much faster progress is to be made by the application of industrial-standard processes for device fabrication to increase wafer-scale yield and reliability of spin qubits. In this regard, Intel Corporation, in collaboration with QuTech, has recently demonstrated the fabrication of electron spin qubits in silicon, utilizing their 300 mm semiconductor manufacturing facility [9]. The Interuniversity Microelectronics Centre (IMEC) in Belgium has also adapted its 300 mm silicon wafer fabrication flow specifically for electron spin qubits [10]. Additionally, ongoing research at CEA-Leti's Institute in Grenoble, France [11], and IBM Research Zurich [12] also aims to leverage industrial-scale processing to realize qubits.

Nevertheless, building a scalable quantum processor requires not only increasing the number of qubits but also achieving high qubit connectivity. Common approaches to establishing connectivity between nearby qubits depend on a close proximity of 100–200 nanometers (nm). The large number of metallic gates needed to surround each qubit for precise control makes scaling beyond small arrays challenging. Maintaining high qubit connectivity continues to be a significant hurdle, and various strategies are being explored to enable connectivity between qubits spaced 10–250 micrometers (μm) apart. Recently, a crucial milestone was reached in this area with the demonstration of long-distance qubit connectivity using virtual photons [13, 14]. However, further development is necessary to improve the accuracy and reliability of such long-distance qubit operations.

QuTech Delft has made notable advancements in the field by demonstrating a four-qubit quantum processor using hole spin qubits [15] and a six-qubit quantum processor utilizing electron spin qubits [16]. While these achievements are significant, these numbers are still modest compared to other qubit technologies. For instance, IBM has recently announced their 1121 superconducting qubit quantum processor "Condor" [2]. Quantinuum has also launched its 56-qubit quantum processor based on trapped-ion technology [4].

4.2.3 Coherence Times

The coherence time is a measure of how long the quantum information can be retained by the spin states. Semiconductor spin qubits have two relevant coherence times, T_1 and T_2.

- T_1, *or energy relaxation time*, is the time a spin qubit can stay in the high-energy state (spin up) before relaxing to the ground state (spin down).
- T_2, *or dephasing time*, refers to the time taken to fully randomize a qubit's initial state. T_2 also defines the duration over which a spin qubit can be coherently manipulated. Typically, T_2 is shorter than T_1 and is the limiting factor for many quantum operations. For electron spin qubits, T_2 can reach nearly 100 microseconds [17], while for hole spin qubits, the record T_2 is 17.6 microseconds [18]. For comparison, state-of-the-art superconducting qubits

reach coherence times exceeding 1 millisecond [19], and trapped-ion qubits have the highest coherence time, reaching up to 50 seconds [20].

Sources of qubit Decoherence Spin qubits are extremely fragile and sensitive to local electric and magnetic fluctuations within the host semiconductor material. This leads to qubit decoherence, or the loss of quantum information. The two primary sources of decoherence in spin qubits are charge noise and hyperfine noise. Charge noise results from local fluctuation in the electric field, often caused by defects and impurities in the device. Improving the quality of semiconductor materials and refining fabrication processes can help to reduce charge noise. Hyperfine noise arises from interactions between the spin state of the qubit and magnetic fluctuations caused by nearby atomic nuclei. Isotopically enriching the host semiconductor material with nuclear spin-free isotopes can suppress hyperfine noise and extend coherence times. As an illustration of this effect, the switch from a nuclear spin-rich GaAs semiconductor system to an isotopically purified ^{28}Si system for electron spin qubits resulted in four orders of magnitude increase in coherence time [17].

4.2.4 Fidelity

Fidelity measures how closely an actual qubit operation matches the desired result. The two commonly reported metrics for fidelity values are single-qubit gate fidelity and two-qubit gate fidelity.

- **The single qubit gate fidelity** indicates the accuracy of an operation involving a single qubit. For electron spins in silicon, these values have already surpassed 99.9% [21]. Recently, hole spin qubits in germanium have also achieved a single-qubit gate fidelity of 99.9% [22]. The reported fidelity values for single-qubit operation are comparable to those achieved in superconducting and trapped ion qubits.
- **The two-qubit fidelity** values for electron spin qubit typically range from 92% to 98%. Recently, the Australian company Diraq Quantum and a few other research groups [23, 24] have reported two-qubit gate fidelity exceeding 99%. While these values obtained for electron spin qubits in silicon are comparable with those on superconducting qubits, they still lag behind those reported for trapped ion qubits. There are no reports on the two-qubit gate field for hole spin qubits.

4.2.5 Operational Speed

In a spin qubit system, the operational speed (or gate time) typically refers to how quickly a gate operation can be executed. A faster operational speed means a large number of operations can be performed before the qubits lose their quantum information. Spin qubits benefit from relatively high operational speeds, enabling them to compete with superconducting qubits in gate times. Single-qubit operations typically occur within tens of nanoseconds, and two-qubit operations take between hundreds of nanoseconds to a few microseconds [25].

4.2.6 Scaling up to Larger Systems

Semiconductor quantum dots have an exceptionally small footprint, with a single electron qubit typically occupying an area of about 20 nm × 20 nm [7]. This small size enables the potential integration of billions of qubits, similar to the billions of transistors on a silicon chip. However, scaling up to larger systems also requires the establishment of quantum links between distant qubits to improve qubit connectivity and enable quantum entanglement throughout the system.

The current strategy for scaling up involves creating a two-dimensional array, similar to the crossbar technology used in display screens. The qubits in the 2D array are coupled via exchange interaction. This method is expected to increase the number of interconnected qubits up to 1024 [26]. Further scaling requires the connection of distant 2D arrays of qubits over long distances using quantum links. One of the most promising approaches for long-distance quantum links is using a microwave photon in a superconducting resonator, the so-called quantum bus [26]. Research groups from TU Delft [27], Princeton University [28], and ETH Zurich [29] have demonstrated strong spin-photon coupling for electron spin qubits. Recently, this milestone was achieved by a research group from EPFL for hole spin qubits in germanium [30].

4.2.7 Maturity

While the spin-based semiconductor platform shows strong potential for large-scale integration due to its compatibility with silicon semiconductor technology, the field remains in its early stages. Over the past 25 years, the spin qubit technology has shown steady progress in the fabrication of the semiconductor quantum dots, control and manipulation of the spin qubits, and readout. A primary factor limiting their progress has been the development of suitable semiconductor materials to host spin qubits. Recent advancements in isotopically enriched host semiconductor material have sharply increased the prospect of semiconductor spin qubit technology. Table 4.1 summarizes the state-of-the-art spin qubit performance.

The next steps involve scaling up the number of qubits, which are primarily constrained by the maturity of the device fabrication process and the inherent challenges of achieving high qubit connectivity. Collaborations between academia and industry are expected to address these challenges. With these advances, the spin qubit platform will expand significantly over the next decade.

Table 4.1 Performance metrics for electron spin qubits in silicon and hole spin qubits in germanium based on data from [25].

Electron spin qubits		
Metric	Value	Comment
T_1 relaxation time	1 ms–1 s	Isotopically enriched ^{28}Si
T_2 dephasing time	10 µs–1 ms	Obtained using Hahn echo
Single-qubit fidelity (gate time)	99.9% (100 ns–1 µs)	
Two-qubit fidelity (gate time)	99% (100 ns–1 µs)	Recently achieved
Number of spin qubits	6	
Hole spin qubits		
Metric	Value	Comment
T_1 relaxation time	1 µs–10 ms	In natural Ge
T_2 dephasing time	10 µs	Obtained using Hahn echo
Single-qubit fidelity (gate time)	99.9% (20 ns)	
Two-qubit fidelity (gate time)	75 ns	No report on fidelity yet
Number of spin qubits	4	

4.3 Trends in Semiconductor Spin Qubit Research

Research in semiconductor spin qubits is evolving in three main directions. First, the improvement of the qubit performance remains a central focus. Second, efforts are being made to improve qubit connectivity and to create larger spin qubit systems. Third and in parallel to the above, the community continues the development of cryogenic CMOS electronics.

Improving Qubit Performance As mentioned previously, spin qubit technology is still in its early stages. Current research primarily focuses on enhancing two-qubit gate fidelity by increasing the purity of the host semiconductor material and improving the device quality. To achieve high-quality devices with low charge noise, universities are increasingly partnering with industry. These collaborations enable high-throughput testing and benchmarking of qubit devices. Notable partnerships include collaborations between QuTech Delft and Intel [9], the University of Basel, ETH Zurich, and IBM Research Zurich [31], as well as HRL Laboratories and the University of California, Los Angeles (UCLA). A serious challenge is with the accessibility of isotopically purified host materials. Only a few major suppliers exist worldwide. Depending on geopolitical developments, this limited supply chain could hinder further progress.

Scaling to Larger Qubit Systems Efforts to scale up qubit systems are advancing in two primary directions. The first approach involves utilizing the industrial standard silicon semiconductor process to enable wafer-scale integration of qubit devices. Intel and IMEC have demonstrated the fabrication of electron spin qubits using their 300 mm industrial-scale technology in this direction [9, 31]. Research groups are also investigating different strategies to achieve two-qubit operations over large distances, which could improve qubit connectivity and facilitate more complex quantum architectures [14, 32, 33]. An additional strategy focuses on operating qubits at higher temperatures. These so-called hot qubits can operate above 1 K [31]. Higher operating temperatures reduce the cooling requirements and could make quantum computing systems more practical and cost-effective.

Cryogenic CMOS Electronics The initialization, control, and readout of qubits currently rely on bulky high-frequency electronics. Most electronic systems operate at room temperature and are connected to quantum chips maintained at a temperature of 20 mK via long coaxial cables and attenuators, collectively referred to as interconnects. As the number of qubits scales up, the interconnects required for qubit operation also increase. This will lead to a large thermal noise and increase the system's complexity. The ongoing research in cryogenic CMOS electronics addresses these challenges by enabling circuits to operate at cryogenic temperatures, typically around 4.2 K instead of room temperature [34]. Since spin qubits in silicon can operate above 1 K, cryo-CMOS technology allows for the co-integration of spin qubits and control electronics on the same chip. This approach reduces thermal noise and simplifies the design.

4.4 Recommendations

Scientific advancement strongly relies on cooperation with partners who have complementary skills and knowledge. Strengthening collaboration between industry and academia is crucial for advancing quantum technologies, including semiconductor-based spin qubit technology. In addition, schemes facilitating international cooperation are essential for researchers to stay at the forefront of science.

4.5 Conclusion

In summary, it can be said that semiconductor spin qubit technology presents a promising way to realize a universal quantum computer. The small size of spin qubits, their fast operational speeds, and compatibility with existing semiconductor manufacturing processes make this technology particularly attractive for scaling up to larger systems. Additionally, the possibility of operating spin qubits at temperatures close to 1 K provides a unique advantage. However, compared to superconducting and trapped ion qubits, semiconductor spin qubits are still at an early stage of development. An important technological hurdle lies in improving the spin qubit yield and connectivity. Ongoing research addresses these challenges and has led to steady progress in qubit performance. Finally, there is an emerging trend for collaboration between industry and academia that offers favorable prospects for the further development of the technology.

References

1. The Quantum Insider, Quantum computing companies (2023). https://thequantuminsider.com/2023/12/29/quantum-computing-companies/. Accessed 5 Jan 2025
2. J. Gambetta, IBM's roadmap for scaling quantum technology. IBM Research Blog (September 2020) (2020)
3. F. Arute, K. Arya, R. Babbush, D. Bacon, J.C. Bardin, R. Barends, R. Biswas, S. Boixo, F.G.S.L. Brandao, D.A. Buell et al., Quantum supremacy using a programmable superconducting processor. Nature **574**(7779), 505–510 (2019)
4. M. DeCross, R. Haghshenas, M. Liu, E. Rinaldi, J. Gray, Y. Alexeev, C.H. Baldwin, J.P. Bartolotta, M. Bohn, E. Chertkov et al., The computational power of random quantum circuits in arbitrary geometries (2024). arXiv preprint arXiv:2406.02501
5. N.M. Linke, D. Maslov, M. Roetteler, S. Debnath, C. Figgatt, K.A. Landsman, K. Wright, C. Monroe, Experimental comparison of two quantum computing architectures. Proc. Natl. Acad. Sci. **114**(13), 3305–3310 (2017)
6. D. Loss, D.P. DiVincenzo, Quantum computation with quantum dots. Phys. Rev. A **57**(1), 120 (1998)
7. L.M.K. Vandersypen, M.A. Eriksson, Quantum computing with semiconductor spins. Phys. Today **72**(8), 38–45 (2019)
8. G. Scappucci, C. Kloeffel, F.A. Zwanenburg, D. Loss, M. Myronov, J.-J. Zhang, S. De Franceschi, G. Katsaros, M. Veldhorst, The germanium quantum information route. Nat. Rev. Mater. **6**(10), 926–943 (2021)
9. A.M.J. Zwerver, T. Krähenmann, T.F. Watson, L. Lampert, H.C. George, R. Pillarisetty, S.A. Bojarski, P. Amin, S.V. Amitonov, J.M. Boter et al., Qubits made by advanced semiconductor manufacturing. Nat. Electron. **5**(3), 184–190 (2022)
10. R. Li, N.I. Dumoulin Stuyck, S. Kubicek, J. Jussot, B.T. Chan, F.A. Mohiyaddin, A. Elsayed, M. Shehata, G. Simion, C. Godfrin et al., A flexible 300 mm integrated Si MOS platform for electron- and hole-spin qubits exploration, in *2020 IEEE International Electron Devices Meeting (IEDM)* (IEEE, Piscataway, 2020), pp. 38–3
11. T. Bédécarrats, B. Cardoso Paz, B. Martinez Diaz, H. Niebojewski, B. Bertrand, N. Rambal, C. Comboroure, A. Sarrazin, F. Boulard, E. Guyez et al., A new FDSOI spin qubit platform with 40nm effective control pitch, in *2021 IEEE International Electron Devices Meeting (IEDM)* (IEEE, Piscataway, 2021), pp. 1–4
12. A. Fuhrer, M. Aldeghi, T. Berger, L.C. Camenzind, R.S. Eggli, S. Geyer, P. Harvey-Collard, N.W. Hendrickx, E.G. Kelly, L. Massai et al., Spin qubits in silicon FinFET devices, in *2022 International Electron Devices Meeting (IEDM)* (IEEE, Piscataway, 2022), pp. 14–1
13. J. Dijkema, X. Xue, P. Harvey-Collard, M. Rimbach-Russ, S.L. de Snoo, G. Zheng, A. Sammak, G. Scappucci, L.M.K. Vandersypen, Cavity-mediated iswap oscillations between distant spins. Nat. Phys. **21**(1), 168–174 (2025)
14. F. Borjans, X.G. Croot, X. Mi, M.J. Gullans, J.R. Petta, Resonant microwave-mediated interactions between distant electron spins. Nature **577**(7789), 195–198 (2020)
15. N.W. Hendrickx, W.I.L. Lawrie, M. Russ, F. van Riggelen, S.L. de Snoo, R.N. Schouten, A. Sammak, G. Scappucci, M. Veldhorst, A four-qubit germanium quantum processor. Nature **591**(7851), 580–585 (2021)

16. S.G.J. Philips, M.T. Mądzik, S.V. Amitonov, S.L. de Snoo, M. Russ, N. Kalhor, C. Volk, W.I.L. Lawrie, D. Brousse, L. Tryputen et al., Universal control of a six-qubit quantum processor in silicon. Nature **609**(7929), 919–924 (2022)
17. M. Veldhorst, J.C.C. Hwang, C.H. Yang, A.W. Leenstra, B. de Ronde, J.P. Dehollain, J.T. Muhonen, F.E. Hudson, K.M. Itoh, A.T. Morello et al., An addressable quantum dot qubit with fault-tolerant control-fidelity. Nat. Nanotechnol. **9**(12), 981–985 (2014)
18. N.W. Hendrickx, L. Massai, M. Mergenthaler, F.J. Schupp, S. Paredes, S.W. Bedell, G. Salis, A. Fuhrer, Sweet-spot operation of a germanium hole spin qubit with highly anisotropic noise sensitivity. Nat. Mater. **23**, 920–927 (2024)
19. A. Krasnok, P. Dhakal, A. Fedorov, P. Frigola, M. Kelly, S. Kutsaev, Advancements in superconducting microwave cavities and qubits for quantum information systems (2023). arXiv preprint arXiv:2304.09345
20. C.D. Bruzewicz, J. Chiaverini, R. McConnell, J.M. Sage, Trapped-ion quantum computing: progress and challenges. Appl. Phys. Rev. **6**(2), 021314 (2019)
21. J. Yoneda, K. Takeda, T. Otsuka, T. Nakajima, M.R. Delbecq, G. Allison, T. Honda, T. Kodera, S. Oda, Y. Hoshi et al., A quantum-dot spin qubit with coherence limited by charge noise and fidelity higher than 99.9%. Nat. Nanotechnol. **13**(2), 102–106 (2018)
22. C.-A. Wang, V. John, H. Tidjani, C.X. Yu, A.S. Ivlev, C.Déprez, F. van Riggelen-Doelman, B.D. Woods, N.W. Hendrickx, W.I.L. Lawrie et al., Operating semiconductor quantum processors with hopping spins. Science **385**(6707), 447–452 (2024)
23. T. Tanttu, W.H. Lim, J.Y. Huang, N. Dumoulin Stuyck, W. Gilbert, R.Y. Su, M. Feng, J.D. Cifuentes, A.E. Seedhouse, S.K. Seritan et al., Assessment of the errors of high-fidelity two-qubit gates in silicon quantum dots. Nat. Phys. **20**, 1804–1809 (2024)
24. A.R. Mills, C.R. Guinn, M.J. Gullans, A.J. Sigillito, M.M. Feldman, E. Nielsen, J.R. Petta, Two-qubit silicon quantum processor with operation fidelity exceeding 99%. Sci. Adv. **8**(14), eabn5130 (2022)
25. P. Stano, D. Loss, Review of performance metrics of spin qubits in gated semiconducting nanostructures. Nat. Rev. Phys. **4**(10), 672–688 (2022)
26. L.M.K. Vandersypen, H. Bluhm, J.S. Clarke, A.S. Dzurak, R. Ishihara, A. Morello, D.J. Reilly, L.R. Schreiber, M. Veldhorst, Interfacing spin qubits in quantum dots and donors—hot, dense, and coherent. NPJ Quantum Inform. **3**(1), 34 (2017)
27. N. Samkharadze, G. Zheng, N. Kalhor, D. Brousse, A. Sammak, U.C. Mendes, A. Blais, G. Scappucci, L.M.K. Vandersypen, Strong spin-photon coupling in silicon. Science **359**(6380), 1123–1127 (2018)
28. X. Mi, M. Benito, S. Putz, D.M. Zajac, J.M. Taylor, G. Burkard, J.R. Petta, A coherent spin–photon interface in silicon. Nature **555**(7698), 599–603 (2018)
29. A.J. Landig, J.V. Koski, P. Scarlino, U.C. Mendes, A. Blais, C. Reichl, W. Wegscheider, A. Wallraff, K. Ensslin, T. Ihn, Coherent spin–photon coupling using a resonant exchange qubit. Nature **560**(7717), 179–184 (2018)
30. F. De Palma, F. Oppliger, W. Jang, S. Bosco, M. Janík, S. Calcaterra, G. Katsaros, G. Isella, D. Loss, P. Scarlino, Strong hole-photon coupling in planar Ge for probing charge degree and strongly correlated states. Nat. Commun. **15**(1), 10177 (2024)
31. L.C. Camenzind, S. Geyer, A. Fuhrer, R.J. Warburton, D.M. Zumbühl, A.V. Kuhlmann, A hole spin qubit in a fin field-effect transistor above 4 kelvin. Nat. Electron. **5**(3), 178–183 (2022)
32. P. Scarlino, D.J. Van Woerkom, A. Stockklauser, J.V. Koski, M.C. Collodo, S. Gasparinetti, C. Reichl, W. Wegscheider, T. Ihn, K. Ensslin et al., All-microwave control and dispersive readout of gate-defined quantum dot qubits in circuit quantum electrodynamics. Phys. Rev. Lett. **122**(20), 206802 (2019)
33. G. Burkard, T.D. Ladd, A. Pan, J.M. Nichol, J.R. Petta, Semiconductor spin qubits. Rev. Mod. Phys. **95**(2), 025003 (2023)
34. E. Charbon, F. Sebastiano, A. Vladimirescu, H. Homulle, S. Visser, L. Song, R.M. Incandela, Cryo-CMOS for quantum computing, in *2016 IEEE International Electron Devices Meeting (IEDM)* (IEEE, Piscataway, 2016), pp. 13–5

Santhanu Panikar Ramanandan is a PhD student in the Laboratory of Semiconductor Materials (LMSC) within the Material Science Department at École Polytechnique Fédérale de Lausanne (EPFL) since August 2020. His research centers on creating a scalable material platform based on Germanium nanowires for implementing hole spin qubit logic.

Anna Fontcuberta i Morral is the President of the École Polytechnique Fédérale de Lausanne (EPFL). She earned her physics degree from the University of Barcelona (1997) and a PhD in materials science from École Polytechnique, France (2001). She then moved to the Harry Atwater group at Caltech, where she worked on multijunction solar cells and co-founded Aonex Technologies. In 2005, she became a team leader at the Walter Schottky Institute at Technische Universität München, where she earned a habilitation in experimental physics in 2009. Since 2008, she has led the Laboratory of Semiconductor Materials at EPFL. Her research focuses on novel semiconductor structures for next-generation energy harvesting and computing applications. She has received several prestigious awards, including the Marie Curie Excellence Grant, an ERC Starting Grant, the SNF Consolidator Grant, and the EPS Emmy Noether Prize. Since 2025, she has served as the President of EPFL.

Open Access This chapter is licensed under the terms of the Creative Commons Attribution 4.0 International License (http://creativecommons.org/licenses/by/4.0/), which permits use, sharing, adaptation, distribution and reproduction in any medium or format, as long as you give appropriate credit to the original author(s) and the source, provide a link to the Creative Commons license and indicate if changes were made.

The images or other third party material in this chapter are included in the chapter's Creative Commons license, unless indicated otherwise in a credit line to the material. If material is not included in the chapter's Creative Commons license and your intended use is not permitted by statutory regulation or exceeds the permitted use, you will need to obtain permission directly from the copyright holder.

Chapter 5
Quantum Error Control and Mitigation Strategies

Nathan Shammah

Abstract Quantum error control and mitigation techniques help improve how quantum computers handle errors, making algorithms run more efficiently despite noisy hardware. These strategies work at the software level and are built into programs before they run on quantum machines. Unlike quantum error correction, which actively detects and fixes errors during computation, error mitigation does not use real-time corrections but instead reduces the impact of errors after computations. Error mitigation can also help reduce the extra resources needed for full error correction. This chapter explains how these techniques relate to each other, provides an overview of key error mitigation methods and their limitations, and highlights leading academic and technological players in this field. It also covers current trends, such as integrating error-aware programming, benchmarking performance, and ensuring access to quantum hardware for testing. To advance quantum computing, it is recommended that research ecosystems support specialized centers and contribute to key strategic areas in the field.

5.1 Introduction

The occurrence of errors in quantum computer operation hampers their usefulness. Errors arise because of the interaction of the qubits on which the information is encoded with the environment—they have various microscopic reasons and effects, from microscopic defects in materials at fabrication to the tiniest wobbles in the control pulses of the device operation, and cannot be removed completely, as they go down to fundamental reasons. All these factors are collectively referred to as noise, from a physics perspective, and depending on the qubit architecture one source may contribute more than others, such as qubit crosstalk, decoherence time, qubit lifetime, etc. Developing better quantum computers, with low noise hardware, is of

---

N. Shammah (✉)
Unitary Foundation, San Francisco, CA, USA
e-mail: nathan@unitary.foundation

© The Author(s) 2026
J. Jang-Jaccard et al. (eds.), *Quantum Technologies*,
https://doi.org/10.1007/978-3-031-90727-2_5

paramount importance, but it has been shown not to be sufficient, since, eventually, errors accumulate and, just like in normal computer operations, these errors need to be controlled and corrected with some protocols to reliably execute the logical operations that, concatenated, compose different algorithms.

To some extent, one could summarize the issue saying that the key problem lies in the hardware—but can the software help solve it? One promising solution has been found with the development of protocols for quantum error correction (QEC). These algorithms are entailed with detecting, during the program run, whether noise-induced errors are occurring, and they correct their effect on the fly, exploiting some physical properties that also emerge at the information processing level on the so-called logical qubits. Below some noise thresholds, QEC algorithms improve the error budget balance as the size of the quantum chip increases. However, these protocols require additional qubits to operate and very low noise level to start from in order to be applied to quantum algorithms and remove errors at scale and have only recently started to be explored in small- to medium-scale experiments.

Quantum error mitigation (QEM) [1] is an umbrella term adopted to describe various techniques that aim at reducing the impact of errors in quantum computing without the active feedback correction of QEC. Indeed, QEM is compared to QEC as an alternative set of techniques to mitigate, rather than actively protect or effectively remove at scale, the effect of this noise on quantum information processing. QEM is mainly applied to quantum computing, although extensions have been proposed for other applications, from quantum simulation to quantum sensing. QEM as a distinct field has emerged in the past 10 years in quantum computing, although several ideas and even full-fledged techniques have been widely adopted for a long time, generally with other names, or used by slightly different communities, such as in quantum optics, or with elements coming from the classical world, such as in signal processing.

It is important to note that besides QEM, other error control strategies are employed when a program is compiled into lower-level machine-readable code, using information on how the noise affects the quantum chip.

An important debate has ensued on the fundamental limitations of QEM strategies, that is, what can be said of their overhead and effectiveness for given amounts of noise. Indeed, mitigating errors has a cost, and the save in qubit overhead from QEC comes at the cost of increased sampling cost—since you need to run more and more quantum programs—which in the worst case can nullify the benefit of running a quantum algorithm in the first place. Some boundaries have even been rigorously proved theoretically [2]. Some of the limits found for QEM are even broader and affect the advantage that variational quantum algorithms can produce, and the topic is under active research. Still, QEM provides a platform for ideas to test and verify how to reduce the impact of errors in quantum computers with strategies that can be applied today and in the near future and also to reduce overheads of QEC codes themselves. Prof. John Preskill from Caltech has recently argued, in a keynote speech at the 2024 Q2B conference in Silicon Valley, how QEM and error control strategies will keep being employed together with QEC algorithms as we transition from the early noisy-intermediate-scale quantum computing regime (NISQ) up to that below the million error-free operations with QEC.

This regime is valuable for many scientific explorations, with an emphasis on those relying on quantum simulation, in which easy-to-use QEM techniques can help resolve fuzzy results. Moreover, exploring the response to noise in the structure of quantum programs is of paramount importance in the discovery of new quantum codes that exhibit resilience to noise due to intrinsic properties that are encoded in their operation and practical compilation.

5.1.1 Definition

While QEM has emerged as a distinct field of research quite recently, it benefits from knowhow coming from well-established fields and areas of expertise in quantum physics and technology, which include the theory of open quantum systems (and quantum noise and quantum optics), variational quantum algorithms, optimal control theory and quantum control, quantum characterization verification and validation, and quantum error correction.

A more general terminology for error control management accounts for strictly QEM techniques as well as techniques that are more closely inherent to the noise-aware compilation of programs on quantum processing units (or quantum chips). These umbrella terms can also comprise quantum control, which refers to the capability of controlling the operation of qubits, at the pulse level, in ways that take into account the unwanted effects of the environment. Hence, quantum optimal control acts closer to the quantum chip, at the level of pulses with pulse shaping and can include feedback loops, and borrows concepts and strategies from optimal control theory, sometimes readapting existing algorithms to the quantum technology case. This is the case, for example, notably, for the Krotov method, initially devised to control spaceship landing on the Moon in the 1950s, which is used in quantum computing for pulse shaping of qubit control so that gates are optimized.

In the following, we refer to QEM in broad terms, including also the adjacent error control strategies also referred to as error suppression [3]. QEM can be divided into two main steps:

- The first step consists of changing the original program into different ones.
- The second step consists of an analysis, or extrapolation, of the results of each program.

Each quantum error mitigation can be mapped to this schema, and each technique is different in the way it compiles the programs (first step) and in the way it post-processes the noisy results (second step). In general, we can imagine the first step in QEM as learning the noise landscape. By sending different programs to the quantum computer, which should bring similar results, one is able to test how such results are different. The second step consists of extrapolating the best guess for the zero-noise (or lower-noise) result, based on the collection of the different noisy results. These two steps are decoupled and do not require an active feedback loop as in QEC, where real-time error decoding is needed. Indeed, the first step can be seen as a quantum sampling step, while the second one can borrow purely classical (as in non-quantum-specific) methods from a large toolbox of statistical techniques for inference and extrapolation.

5.2 Analysis

The most active centers for academic research on error control expertise have been Germany, the USA, the UK, and Australia, with startups including Q-CTRL (Australia) and Qruise (Germany). For QEM, the USA, UK, and Japan stand out, and specifically entities like IBM, Google, Oxford University, NTT, LANL, and the Unitary Foundation, while startups include QEDMA (Israel) and Algorithmiq (Finland).

Since error control strategies and QEM are comprised of a variety of independent techniques, we list the main ones (or main families) here, briefly explaining the working principles and analyzing some of their key points. Readers who are not interested in technical information can simply skip to the next section.

Zero Noise Extrapolation (ZNE) This is the most popular technique in QEM in terms of adoption. The technique was first proposed in two independent papers in 2017 [4, 5]. The first most evident application in an experiment, on a superconducting quantum chip, was obtained in 2019 [6] by IBM on two qubits, paving the way to increased interest in the wider QEM field. It is notable that the follow-up work on quantum utility by IBM and collaborators published in 2024 [7] remains a milestone from the QEM perspective, as it expands its reach to 127 qubits and thousands of gates. A field study on ion and superconducting architectures accessed from the cloud has been performed in Russo et al. [8], showing overall improvements for the use of ZNE even with no or minor knowledge of the noise model of the specific quantum chip.

In essence, ZNE works as follows: Based on the realization that operating the quantum chip without noise is not possible for the user, it tries to learn how to extrapolate the value for the zero-noise result by operating it at different noise intensities. When the original program is run on the quantum chip, one obtains a result that is affected by an error, due to the base level of the noise. It is possible to scale, i.e., increase, the noise to which the qubits are exposed. This is counterintuitive but is the key ingredient to obtaining more data points at different levels of noise. This noise scaling can be done by adjusting the control pulses operating the qubit operations on the quantum chip and making them last longer. This gives the user a result that is twice as noisy or three times as noisy, and so a zero-noise result can be extrapolated. Crucially, all the values for less than the base noise, including zero noise, are not accessible directly and need to be extrapolated. Moreover, there is no theoretical guarantee that the fit obtained from values at one or greater noise will apply to lower values of noise. There could be a phase transition, or the initial value could be so noisy that the extrapolation is not meaningful, so this method is effective when the magnitude of the noise is small enough not to already spoil the sampled values completely. Knowledge of the noise sources affecting the device, both qualitatively and quantitatively, is not per se required to apply ZNE but ends up being crucial to avoid the intrinsic bias in the extrapolation of the error-free value giving wrong results.

Despite the limitations, ZNE is possibly the most widely explored QEM technique to date, due to its ease of implementation. To overcome limitations, it has been hybridized in various ways, including by applying its key concept of noise scaling to QEC, exploring how to scale noise for logical qubits, as well as hybridizing it with probabilistic components to limit the bias.

Probabilistic Error Cancellation (PEC) The main idea behind PEC [5] is as follows: In order to make an estimate of the correct expectation value, we can reconstruct, or extrapolate, the zero-noise result by learning how the actual gates operated on the quantum chip differ from the ideal, noiseless gates. Indeed, in PEC one learns information about the noise landscape of the quantum chip by intentionally modifying the original program to programs that have some probabilistically injected differences or randomization in the gate parameters. PEC is different from ZNE for it reconstructs the ideal gates with an unbiased estimation, which eventually, with enough measurements, guarantees correct results, although this comes at a sampling cost that can make it impractical to apply PEC for any relevant computations in a straightforward way. As the learning of noise affecting the quantum gates is particularly quantum computationally expensive, as it scales exponentially with the number of qubits, proposals have been made to reduce the overhead by hybridizing it with ZNE and performing less demanding noise characterization methods [9].

Dynamical Decoupling and Optimized Control The key idea behind dynamical decoupling is that a qubit that is kept idle can be more prone to decohere [10]. In a quantum program, not all qubits are actively rotated at all times. Thus, these idle windows can expose a given program to more noise from the environment. This basic concept has been extended to apply to pulse shaping and decoupling among qubits whose control signals may interfere with each other. The art of effectively applying dynamical decoupling is often very closely related to knowledge about the specific hardware characteristics of the quantum chip and its operation. Other techniques based on this kind of noise-aware compilation have been developed, such as gate twirling, and are used in conjunction with other QEM or QEC algorithms, and can take the name of error suppression.

Learning-Based Simulation Methods There is a family of QEM methods that generally works with learning the response to noise of the quantum program, by simulating a different, but similar, set of programs classically and then applying the information gained on that set to the actual quantum program to be run on the quantum chip. Such methods generally rely on the fact that quantum circuits containing only, or mostly only, the so-called Clifford gates are efficiently simulatable on a classical computer and can be used as a training set to learn to correct the noise in the original quantum program. These methods have also been employed with the help of machine learning, neural networks, and usage of classical ways to approximately simulate parts of the quantum computation, including with high-performance computing and theoretical approximation methods.

Symmetry-Based Methods There is a full set of QEM methods that exploit the expected symmetries in the structure of the algorithm and/or of the final quantum state to be measured in order to remove. To its lowest degree of complexity, this approach can consist of a post-selection of bitstrings, sequences of 0s and 1s, of a quantum computation, based on a symmetry that the final sequence is supposed to have, even if the actual disposition of 0s and 1s in the bitstring is unknown. The measurements that do not preserve such parity are hence discarded.

These kinds of measurement-based QEM or post-selection processes can be made more complex, generally at the cost of adding additional ancillary qubits. The underlying assumptions are similar to the working principles of quantum error-correcting codes, in which a bit flip or other error is detected by a change in the symmetry or parity of that portion of the quantum chip. In these QEM methods, which are different from QEC, there is no active correction, but rather a projection.This family of methods includes techniques known as quantum subspace expansion and virtual distillation.

Other Methods It is also worth noting that QEM is a very active field of research, and new approaches keep surfacing, each with a possible new ingredient or take on the basic task. In general, each technique can be described in terms of the two parts outlined in the Definition section.

5.2.1 Maturity

QEM has a low-to-moderate maturity, having coalesced as a field only in the past 10 years, with a fast incubation time before being tested in experiments. As outlined, general concepts predate the field definition by several decades, in specific instances. In fields related to error control like quantum optimal control, the maturity is higher as the concepts, borrowing results, and numerical methods from standard optimal control theory predate QEM by several decades.

Somewhat siloed environments of specific know-how exist in research laboratories or industrial players, especially on the experimental side, for specific quantum chip architectures. The field, especially on the theory side, is bolstering with new ideas. As we progressively move from the noisy intermediate-scale quantum computing era (NISQ) to a time where small or medium-sized QEC codes can be run on quantum chips, harnessing QEM to reduce the qubit and code distance budget could become an important factor to determine the actual capability in performing quantum chip experiments.

5.2.2 Trends

Current trends in QEM include:

- **Hybridization of QEC with QEM.** While QEM is generally presented as an alternative approach to QEC, the two frameworks can be hybridized. In fact, QEM subroutines can be used to reduce QEC's overhead. In this way, an effectively approximate QEC algorithm can be designed, such as reducing the qubit resources for the gates required in QEC or by performing ZNE in the logical qubit space, rather than in the physical noise space.
- **Stacking of multiple QEM techniques together.** Some quantum error mitigation techniques and error control strategies can be stacked together, or hybridized. This is the case, for example, of dynamical decoupling can, in general, be added to other techniques, as well as together with QEC, as in the most recent Google experiment with the Willow quantum chip [11]. Other examples include combining ZNE with readout error mitigation.
- **Co-development with hardware architectures and noise models.** QEM can get much further if one knows the main source of errors. That is, if there is an accurate noise model for the quantum processing unit that runs the algorithm. For example, ZNE can work even without knowledge of the underlying noise mechanism, but it can be much more effective if the noise model is known. Studies have shown that frequency-dependent or time-dependent noise, which is less trivial than uncorrelated (white) noise, can be more effectively counteracted with one or another choice of strategies in ZNE. Moreover, one could even select the most appropriate QEM technique based on the properties of the hardware, or even make hardware design choices based on estimates of the algorithm (or algorithmic family) to run on the quantum chip. For this reason, in the design stack for quantum hardware, open-source tools and shared facilities could be used [12] to accelerate experimentation and sharing of promising results (or dead ends).
- **Integration of error control and QEM into compilation stack.** The quantum computing software ecosystem relies on open-source, as a global community uses, provides feedback, tests, maintains, and contributes to open-source projects. This is the case for compilers, and it is also the case for QEM features, be they standalone or integrated in compilers or software development kits (SDKs). Mitiq [13] is the most popular tool and provides a large collection of QEM techniques, all available at the gate level to enhance cross-platform compatibility with both different SDKs and different quantum chips as back-ends. Another specific toolkit is Qermit, while major SDKs like Qiskit contain some specific QEM capabilities. On the other hand, QEM is being developed also in closed-source toolkits and closer to the quantum chip, such as with proprietary software as provided by specialized startups like Australian Q-CTRL or Israeli Qedma, or directly integrated by quantum hardware providers themselves at the low level of the stack. Quantum compilers need to be able to adopt, either internally or by integrating with specific QEM and error control management tools, in

order to really get the best out of a quantum chip performance or algorithmic synthesis. Further integration with high-performance computing infrastructure is needed together with resource estimation of the related compilation stack [14]. Open-source and transparent error control operations and QEM techniques on cloud-accessible quantum chips from providers are particularly valuable to QEM and QEC researchers, who need low-level control to test how tinkering with different new solutions has an impact on their computations.

- **Benchmarks.** The role of benchmarks in quantum computing (and quantum technology in general) is of paramount importance, since the field is progressing only as fast as it can demonstrate. In the context of quantum computing benchmarks, it is important to discern between quantum chip benchmarks, focusing on properties of the hardware and benchmarks that take into account the use of QEM also for inference—which can and should be tested too, but highlighting their usage. For this reason, open-source methods are to be preferable in QEM benchmarking. In order to evaluate the best strategies, some of the important elements to consider include a standardized and transparent benchmarking of the whole compilation chain, a definition of hardware-related specifics for compilers, and the inclusion of noise characterization information to adapt QEM and compilation passes. Some first studies for QEM benchmarking have been performed, but we are still far from a wide adoption of common practices from the field, which should be accelerated instead.
- **Integration with noise characterization.** QEM techniques can really increase the impact they have in cases in which the noise model of the system is known. Generally, there are many contributing factors to noise in quantum chips, and their budget is carefully studied to mitigate the impact also with hardware choices—from gapped quantum chips for superconducting circuit chips prone to limit the disruption of cosmic rays, to other classical sources of noise in control pulses. Understanding the error budget and thus characterizing noise efficiently becomes an important step to obtain better results when applying QEM, from choosing which technique is best suited to controlling the free parameters of its implementation.

In addition to the current trends in the field, this author identifies the following areas as promising avenues for research and development, which may not yet have been sufficiently explored:

- **QEM beyond qubit systems.** There are only a few examples of QEM methods explored in practice beyond qubit systems, such as for qudits, adapted for bosonic systems, or explored in photonics-based quantum computing platforms. In the case of bosonic qubits, this is due to the fact that QEC is somewhat implemented at the single qubit level, with so-called cat qubits or autonomous QEC.
- **QEM beyond quantum computing.** There are only a few initial studies on the use of QEM beyond quantum computing, used to enhance the signal-to-noise ratio in quantum sensing and quantum communication. This seems a promising area of development.

5.3 Recommendations

Quantum computing research and quantum science, in general, have seen significant advancements globally, with numerous countries boasting vibrant scientific and technological communities active across various domains.

Key centers of activity include leading academic institutions with dedicated quantum research centers, often populated by researchers working in quantum error mitigation (QEM) and related fields. Experimental contributions to QEC demonstrations and error control management from labs specializing in superconducting circuit qubits and trapped ions, for example, highlight the importance of experimental validation. Research groups focusing on quantum noise, variational quantum algorithms, and neural network-based quantum systems are driving advancements in these areas, alongside a growing emphasis on quantum software development.

Industrial research centers also play a pivotal role, with major companies conducting research on quantum hardware and software. Seminal results in QEM hybridization and the development of core quantum software platforms are examples of how these institutions contribute to the ecosystem. Companies specializing in supply chain technologies for quantum devices further support the integration of theoretical and experimental research.

Error control and QEM strategies require validation on quantum hardware. Access to a diverse array of hardware architectures, coupled with a breadth of experimental and theoretical expertise, is a significant advantage for fostering innovation. Streamlining cloud-based access to quantum hardware for researchers, whether through credits from existing providers or by bringing new hardware online, could enhance collaboration and broaden the reach of quantum research. Open access initiatives could benefit the global scientific community, much like the initiatives seen at the Open Quantum Institute, which emphasize inclusivity and societal impact in quantum technology development.

The growing focus on benchmarking presents another key opportunity. Independent verification and benchmarking of quantum computing technologies, including the impact of QEM techniques and resource estimation tools, could build trust and advance the field. Neutral and collaborative frameworks for benchmarking could further strengthen international cooperation.

The open-source software community also plays a critical role in advancing quantum computing. Open-source projects amplify the impact of research by distributing tools and infrastructure widely across the industry. As QEM and error control strategies increasingly integrate into the quantum computing compilation stack, supporting open-source initiatives through workshops, hackathons, and maintenance funding can foster collaboration, scrutiny, and iterative improvements.

From a technology transfer perspective, the tasks involved in error control and QEM are highly interdisciplinary but also require focused development. Industrial environments and startups are particularly suited to streamline processes and accelerate research and development. Co-design centers for application-specific problems can catalyze impactful outcomes, especially when aligned with mature industrial players targeting real-world applications.

Finally, QEM is inherently interdisciplinary, often benefiting from insights and techniques repurposed from adjacent fields. Continued funding for basic research is essential, empowering investigators with independent research ideas to explore novel concepts that drive innovation.

By adopting these strategies, the global quantum ecosystem can further advance QEM and error control strategies, ensuring a collaborative, open, and application-oriented future for quantum computing.

5.4 Conclusion

Quantum error mitigation and adjacent error control strategies beyond pure QEC are a relatively new fields of research that have found quick application in experiments, with important input both from academic groups and in the quantum industry. It is important that this field provides a playground to test ideas with input and collaboration across industry and academia—as well as some healthy competition. One of the most important features of QEM may indeed be the fact that it has brought two research communities closer for a true cross-pollination for the faster advancement (or at least understanding) of quantum computing in the presence of noise. These two communities are those of quantum computing experts, including quantum error correction experts, and that of quantum noise experts, generally coming from quantum optics and the theory of open quantum systems. Here, "open" refers to systems that are subject to external influences in their dynamics, resulting in noise and, consequently, errors. Over a relatively short period of time, this newly minted community has learned to borrow existing knowledge to distill creative ideas and practical results even beyond what may have seemed initially quite saturated areas of knowledge, such as quantum optics theory. In the current landscape, both in pure research and industry, one approach cannot ignore the other anymore. Noise models need validation and adherence to hardware characteristics, even when the ultimate goal is correcting errors with QEC approaches.

While useful quantum computing may still be quite far away for general applications, our collective understanding of how to operate these new machines is benefiting from the learning obtained from QEM and other error control strategies. Scientific discovery is already benefiting from the use of these techniques, such as in quantum dynamics simulations that can shed light on new phenomena in physics, chemistry, and biology.

References

1. Z. Cai, R. Babbush, S.C. Benjamin, S. Endo, W.J. Huggins, Y. Li, J.R. McClean, T.E. O'Brien, Quantum error mitigation. Rev. Mod. Phys. **95**, 045005 (2023)
2. Y. Quek, D. Stilck França, S. Khatri, J.J. Meyer, J. Eisert, Exponentially tighter bounds on limitations of quantum error mitigation. Nat. Phys. **20**(10), 1648–1658 (2024)
3. M. Steffen, What's the difference between error suppression, error mitigation, and error correction? (2022)
4. Y. Li, S.C. Benjamin, Efficient variational quantum simulator incorporating active error minimization. Phys. Rev. X **7**, 021050 (2017)
5. K. Temme, S. Bravyi, J.M. Gambetta, Error mitigation for short-depth quantum circuits. Phys. Rev. Lett. **119**, 180509 (2017)
6. A. Kandala, K. Temme, A.D. Córcoles, A. Mezzacapo, J.M. Chow, J.M. Gambetta, Error mitigation extends the computational reach of a noisy quantum processor. Nature **567**(7749), 491–495 (2019)
7. Y. Kim, A. Eddins, S. Anand, K.X. Wei, E. van den Berg, S. Rosenblatt, H. Nayfeh, Y. Wu, M. Zaletel, K. Temme, A. Kandala, Evidence for the utility of quantum computing before fault tolerance. Nature **618**(7965), 500–505 (2023)
8. V. Russo, A. Mari, N. Shammah, R. LaRose, W.J. Zeng, Testing platform-independent quantum error mitigation on noisy quantum computers. IEEE Trans. Quantum Eng. **4**, 1–8 (2023)
9. E. van den Berg, Z.K. Minev, A. Kandala, K. Temme, Probabilistic error cancellation with sparse Pauli–Lindblad models on noisy quantum processors. Nat. Phys. **19**(8), 1116–1121 (2023)
10. D.A. Lidar, I.L. Chuang, K.B. Whaley, Decoherence-free subspaces for quantum computation. Phys. Rev. Lett. **81**, 2594–2597 (1998)
11. Google Quantum AI and Collaborators, Quantum error correction below the surface code threshold. Nature (2024)
12. N. Shammah et al., Open hardware solutions in quantum technology. APL Quantum **1**(1), 011501 (2024)
13. R. LaRose et al., Mitiq: a software package for error mitigation on noisy quantum computers. Quantum **6**, 774 (2022)
14. M. Mohseni et al., How to build a quantum supercomputer: scaling challenges and opportunities (2024)

Nathan Shammah is a physicist, technologist, and entrepreneur specializing in quantum technology, open-source software, and deep tech transfer. As Chief Technology Officer of Unitary Foundation, he leads research and open-source projects like Mitiq and Metriq in quantum computing. He is also Chief Strategy Officer at Quantum Italia, fostering startup creation and acceleration in the quantum tech ecosystem, and co-founder of Metis, a legaltech AI startup. He is also Chief Strategy Officer at Quantum Italia, a startup studio fostering startup creation in the quantum tech ecosystem. With a PhD in physics from the University of Southampton, Nathan was a postdoctoral researcher at RIKEN in Japan, contributing to theoretical quantum physics, scientific open-source software, and deep tech transfer.

Open Access This chapter is licensed under the terms of the Creative Commons Attribution 4.0 International License (http://creativecommons.org/licenses/by/4.0/), which permits use, sharing, adaptation, distribution and reproduction in any medium or format, as long as you give appropriate credit to the original author(s) and the source, provide a link to the Creative Commons license and indicate if changes were made.

The images or other third party material in this chapter are included in the chapter's Creative Commons license, unless indicated otherwise in a credit line to the material. If material is not included in the chapter's Creative Commons license and your intended use is not permitted by statutory regulation or exceeds the permitted use, you will need to obtain permission directly from the copyright holder.

Chapter 6
Quantum Optimization

Daniel J. Egger, Heike Riel, Stefan Woerner, and Christa Zoufal

Abstract Quantum computing is a new computational paradigm with the prospect of outperforming classical computing on many tasks. Optimization is frequently mentioned as a promising area for achieving a quantum advantage, i.e., solving a problem faster, more accurately, or more efficiently than classical computers. This chapter gives a brief summary of the potential benefits the state of the art and recommends possible directions to further progress.

6.1 Introduction

Optimization problems arise in almost every industry and scientific discipline, e.g., finance, logistics and supply chain management, manufacturing, material design, and biology, just to name a few. However, for many optimization problems, it is known that it generally requires a runtime that scales exponentially in the problem size to find a provably optimal solution. While for some problem instances, approximations or heuristics may provide good solutions quickly, there are many other problems that remain challenging with significant room for improvement. Thus, enhancing state-of-the-art optimization algorithms to deliver solutions of better quality, with shorter runtimes, or at reduced cost can have a huge impact.

Optimization has been identified early as a potential application area for quantum computers [1]. Algorithms like Grover Search [2] and Quantum Adiabatic Annealing [3, 4] theoretically offer (up to) a quadratic speed-up over brute force search for combinatorial optimization. Depending on the problem, various alternative classical approaches exist that are superior to brute force search. Nevertheless, quantum algorithms sometimes can be used as algorithmic sub-routines, which may allow them to achieve an overall quadratic speed-up compared to the classical state of the art [5]. However, they typically require fault-tolerant error-corrected quantum

---

D. J. Egger · H. Riel · S. Woerner (✉) · C. Zoufal
IBM Quantum - IBM Research Europe, Zurich, Switzerland
e-mail: deg@zurich.ibm.com; hei@zurich.ibm.com; wor@zurich.ibm.com; ouf@zurich.ibm.com

© The Author(s) 2026
J. Jang-Jaccard et al. (eds.), *Quantum Technologies*,
https://doi.org/10.1007/978-3-031-90727-2_6

computers due to the depth of the required quantum circuits.[1] Further, a quadratic speed-up over an algorithm with an exponential runtime still implies an exponential runtime.

In general, i.e., including the *worst-case*, we do not expect more than quadratic quantum speedups for **NP**-hard problems.[2] However, there is hope for better performance and larger quantum advantage for *specific* problem instances. For example, the famous Shor's algorithm for factoring large numbers [6], which can also be translated into optimization problems [7, 8], implies that quantum algorithms can achieve even an exponential speedup for special instances of problem classes, although such optimization problem instances are unlikely to occur in practice. In addition, most complexity theoretic results apply only to the *worst-case*. If we consider the *average-case* instead, the situation is much less clear, and is the topic of ongoing theoretical research.

The previous discussion considers algorithms that result in a provably optimal solution. In contrast, approximation algorithms provide solutions that might not be optimal but that come with an a priori performance guarantee, i.e., a guaranteed approximation ratio. Here, quantum computers can achieve the same guarantees in a shorter time or better guarantees than the best known classical approximation [9].

In practical applications of classical combinatorial optimization, we mostly rely on heuristics, i.e., algorithms without any theoretical a priori performance guarantees that may work well for many problem instances but not for all. Algorithms can be heuristic by nature, such as simulated annealing, or they can be more structured algorithms, such as branch-and-bound-and-cut algorithms that are terminated before convergence to provable optimality [1].

These heuristics are developed and tested at scale on complex problem instances, which allows to build intuition on what works well and what does not and to further improve them. While quantum computing offers opportunities to develop new heuristics that may outperform classical ones in some cases, testing them at scale is still difficult due to the limited availability of reliable large-scale quantum hardware. Recently, the first quantum computing experiments have been performed for system sizes that are beyond exact classical simulation capabilities [10, 11]. This marks the beginning of the era of *quantum utility* where using real quantum computers helps to advance science on the path toward a practically relevant quantum advantage. While these quantum computers may not yet provide a quantum advantage for the

---

[1] Quantum circuits, similar to classical logical circuits, describe programs executable by a quantum computer. Quantum circuits are composed of qubits as well as the gates that are applied to them. The depth of a quantum circuit reflects the number of gates that have to be applied sequentially, i.e., that cannot be applied in parallel.

[2] **NP** stands for *nondeterministic polynomial time* and refers to the complexity class of problems that in general require an exponential runtime to solve on a classical computer. **NP**-hard problems are the hardest problems in that class, since all other problems in **NP** can be translated into those problems with only polynomial overhead. Many combinatorial optimization problems turn out to be **NP**-hard. In contrast, the complexity class **P** for *polynomial time* includes all problems that can be efficiently solved on a classical computer. It is widely believed that $\mathbf{P} \neq \mathbf{NP}$.

considered problem—since alternative approaches may still outperform quantum algorithms—they enable the testing of heuristics for interesting problems. Quantum utility allows to augment theoretical pen-and-paper research by empirical trial-and-error research to advance our understanding and accelerate the progress toward quantum advantage.

6.2 Analysis

In this section, we analyze the current maturity of quantum optimization as well as its current trends. We first discuss the maturity of quantum hardware and put it in relation to the state of the art in quantum optimization algorithm development. Then, we dive into current trends in quantum optimization research and the respective opportunities to generate practically relevant quantum advantage.

6.2.1 Maturity

Quantum hardware is progressing rapidly. A decade ago, state-of-the-art quantum computing hardware featured only a few qubits, typically hosted by university research groups. These devices required constant human attention to be calibrated, experiments were manually run by researchers, and devices were inaccessible to the broader community working on theory, algorithms, and applications.

Today, multiple hardware vendors offer quantum computing platforms that are easily accessible through the cloud and have high availability. This requires automated qubit calibration protocols to compensate for drifts in the system. Furthermore, the scale of quantum computers has drastically increased. For example, IBM Quantum offers 156-qubit devices through its cloud platform [12]. The largest single-chip superconducting qubit processor that has been demonstrated is the IBM Quantum Condor device with 1121 qubits. Achieving this scale and going beyond it requires the development of several technologies, including multilevel wiring, packaging, and dedicated control and readout electronics[3]—also at cryo-temperature.[4] These technical advances are crucial to scale quantum computing and fabricate components more cost-effectively.

Crucially, qubit count is not the only important metric for quantum computers. Indeed, current quantum computers are noisy; each gate has a non-negligible

---

[3] It refers to the systems and circuits used to measure, process, and convert signals from a device or sensor into a readable format, often for analysis or further processing. In quantum computing, they are used to detect and interpret the quantum states of qubits without disrupting their operation.

[4] It refers to extremely low temperatures, typically below—150°C (123 K), where unique physical properties, such as superconductivity, can occur.

probability of inducing an error. For example, in superconducting qubit hardware, these errors are on the order of 0.1% to 1% per two-qubit gate [12]. These errors limit the depth of the quantum circuits that can be executed before the errors mask the result. Today, though we cannot fully correct the errors appearing, we can apply error mitigation and noise suppression methods. These methods do not fully remove the noise and their cost is exponential in the noise strength. Therefore, they only extend the reach of noisy hardware. For example, simulations based on the Ising model have been reported, utilizing 127 qubits with up to 60 layers of CNOT gates[5] [10].

Quantum utility does not imply a quantum advantage, which is only attained once a quantum computer outperforms all classical methods for a given valuable problem. Nevertheless, the quantum utility era will speed up the development and implementation of new quantum heuristics, for example, to tackle combinatorial optimization problems. Indeed, being able to faithfully execute circuits on quantum hardware beyond what classical computers can simulate opens the possibility of faster algorithmic progress. Here, the Quantum Approximate Optimization Algorithm (QAOA) [13] and its variants have seen a lot of interest in recent years. QAOA, in general, is a quantum optimization heuristic for Quadratic Unconstrained Binary Optimization (QUBO). In special cases there are known performance guarantees, which make the QAOA an approximation algorithm. QAOA constructs a problem-specific parametrized quantum circuit, inspired by adiabatic annealing, and leverages classical continuous optimization to find good parameters. The development of such heuristic algorithms is key to advance quantum optimization, and many variants of QAOA have been proposed to further improve its performance. For example, recursive QAOA can produce better approximation ratios than standard QAOA [14] while warm-start methods increase solution quality and reduce hardware costs [15]. Another promising direction to explore is to encode multiple decision variables into a single qubit [16]. Such algorithms must then be executed and benchmarked on hardware and at utility scale [1].

Going forward, quantum computing hardware must scale to a size where quantum error correction is possible. Indeed, this will allow one to execute extremely deep quantum circuits making it possible to run algorithms such as quantum phase estimation [17] or QAOA with high depth. For example, the IBM Quantum Roadmap foresees that the first error-corrected hardware may be available in 2029 with a capability to execute 100 million quantum gates. Beyond 2033, the IBM Quantum Roadmap targets error-corrected hardware capable of executing one billion quantum gates. Reaching such a scale will only be possible with modular hardware in which individual quantum chips are connected through couplers. Crucially, the software stack must continuously evolve to accommodate

---

[5] A CNOT gate is a two-qubit gate that entangles two qubits by applying a controlled-NOT operation, i.e., it applies a NOT gate to the target qubit conditioned on the state of the control qubit.

the increasing size of the hardware. For example, circuit compilation into pulse-level payloads must remain efficient as circuit sizes scale.

In summary, quantum computers are not yet capable of outperforming classical hardware on business valuable tasks. This is also true for combinatorial optimization where classical heuristics have benefited from decades of research and development. However, the hardware and algorithmic progress over the last decade is tremendous, and the pace of this advances does not appear to be slowing down.

6.2.2 Trends

In the following, we present a short discussion on several trends in quantum optimization. They cover identifying practically relevant applications that may profit from quantum optimization, empirical studies and systematic benchmarking to test algorithms on real quantum computers, and theoretical research on limitations and potential of quantum computers for optimization in general and of concrete quantum algorithms more specifically. For a more detailed overview of these topics, we refer the interested reader to [1].

There is an ongoing effort to identify problems that are truly challenging classically, while having the potential of a significant (business) impact in case of finding better solutions or achieving reduced runtimes or cost. While it is not guaranteed that quantum computers can solve such problems, it is a necessary condition to justify the need for a new technology. This requires to find the best classical state-of-the-art solver for a problem, which is not always easy. However, a quantum advantage is only possible if there is no known classical alternative to achieve similar performance.

In addition, we need to identify application-agnostic problems, possibly artificial and hand-crafted, where we can demonstrate the potential of a quantum advantage. This helps to drive the algorithmic research as well as to guide the search for promising applications. Since many quantum optimization algorithms are heuristics, a systematic benchmarking of algorithms on real hardware is key. Being able to test ideas on real hardware at a scale beyond what can be simulated classically enables us to augment the mostly theoretical algorithmic research with empirical research.

Nevertheless, theoretical research remains important, to understand potential and limitations of concrete quantum algorithms and quantum computing in general, identifying new quantum algorithms, and analyzing situations beyond what we can empirically test today.

6.3 Recommendations

Quantum optimization provides a field with various opportunities to be analyzed and benchmarked by researchers all over the world in the upcoming years. To stay on top of and contribute to these developments, it is essential to have access to quantum hardware and to facilitate quantum research on application areas such as optimization. Thus, the number of groups that have the required access and expertise to investigate, test, and benchmark quantum algorithms respectively applications thereof needs to be grown further. Further, it is of great importance to foster collaboration to expand the competence in quantum algorithms and applications. Furthermore, quantum optimization research can strongly benefit from the expertise on classical optimization that exists, e.g., at established academic institutes and industrially relevant companies. Collaborating with universities and research organizations can help to identify specific optimization models where a quantum advantage could be achieved. Furthermore, the input from the industry might facilitate identifying optimization problems where a potential quantum advantage could have a practically relevant impact. The latter identification is particularly interesting for sectors such as finance and banking [18, 19], insurance [20, 21], logistics [22, 23], and pharmaceuticals [24, 25]. Finally, quantum optimization advantages could also help in the quest of reducing energy usage [26–28] or the realization of renewable energy resources [29–31] and, hence, assist in driving sustainable energy transition—a topic of great significance.

6.4 Conclusion

In this chapter, we summarized the state of the art in quantum optimization, current trends, and promising directions. Achieving a practically relevant quantum advantage requires a holistic interdisciplinary approach involving academia and industry as well as theoretical and empirical research in addition to systematic benchmarking. Since applications of optimization are found almost everywhere, it is likely that any advantage demonstrated on problems of mostly academic interest will shortly after also have a practically relevant impact.

References

1. A. Abbas et al., Challenges and opportunities in quantum optimization. Nat. Rev. Phys. **6**, 718–735 (2024)
2. L.K. Grover, A fast quantum mechanical algorithm for database search (1996)
3. T. Kadowaki, H. Nishimori, Quantum annealing in the transverse Ising model. Phys. Rev. E **58**(5), 5355 (1998)
4. E. Farhi, J. Goldstone, S. Gutmann, M. Sipser, Quantum computation by adiabatic evolution (2000)
5. R. Shaydulin et al., Evidence of scaling advantage for the quantum approximate optimization algorithm on a classically intractable problem (2023)
6. P.W. Shor, Algorithms for quantum computation: discrete logarithms and factoring, in *Proceedings 35th Annual Symposium on Foundations of Computer Science* (1994), pp. 124–134

7. N. Pirnay, V. Ulitzsch, F. Wilde, J. Eisert, J.-P. Seifert, An in-principle super-polynomial quantum advantage for approximating combinatorial optimization problems (2023)
8. M. Szegedy, Quantum advantage for combinatorial optimization problems, Simplified (2022)
9. S.P. Jordan, N. Shutty, M. Wootters, A. Zalcman, A. Schmidhuber, R. King, S.V. Isakov, R. Babbush, Optimization by decoded quantum interferometry (2024)
10. Y. Kim, A. Eddins, S. Anand, K.X. Wei, E. van den Berg, S. Rosenblatt, H. Nayfeh, Y. Wu, M. Zaletel, K. Temme, A. Kandala, Evidence for the utility of quantum computing before fault tolerance. Nature **618**(7965), 500–505 (2023)
11. S. Anand, K. Temme, A. Kandala, M. Zaletel, Classical benchmarking of zero noise extrapolation beyond the exactly-verifiable regime (2023)
12. IBM Quantum, https://quantum.ibm.com/. Accessed 13 Aug 2024
13. E. Farhi, J. Goldstone, S. Gutmann, A quantum approximate optimization algorithm (2014)
14. S. Bravyi, A. Kliesch, R. Koenig, E. Tang, Obstacles to variational quantum optimization from symmetry protection. Phys. Rev. Lett. **125**, 260505 (2020)
15. D.J. Egger, J. Mareček, S. Woerner, Warm-starting quantum optimization. Quantum **5**, 479 (2021)
16. M. Sciorilli, L. Borges, T. L. Patti, D. García-Martín, G. Camilo, A. Anandkumar, L. Aolita, Towards large-scale quantum optimization solvers with few qubits (2024)
17. M.A. Nielsen, I.L. Chuang, *Quantum Computation and Quantum Information* (Cambridge University Press, Cambridge, 2000)
18. D. Herman, C. Googin, X. Liu, Y. Sun, A. Galda, I. Safro, M. Pistoia, Y. Alexeev, Quantum computing for finance. Nat. Rev. Phys. **5**(8), 450–465 (2023)
19. D.J. Egger, C. Gambella, J. Marecek, S. McFaddin, M. Mevissen, R. Raymond, A. Simonetto, S. Woerner, E. Yndurain, Quantum computing for finance: state-of-the-art and future prospects. IEEE Trans. Quantum Eng. **1**, 1–24 (2020)
20. M. Tamturk, Quantum computing in insurance capital modelling. Mathematics **11**(3), 658 (2023)
21. P. Schulte, D. Chuen, *AI & Quantum Computing for Finance & Insurance: Fortunes and Challenges for China and America* (World Scientific, Singapore, 2019)
22. P. Gachnang, J. Ehrenthal, T. Hanne, R. Dornberger, Quantum computing in supply chain management state of the art and research directions. Asian J. Logist. Manag. **1**(1), 57–73 (2022)
23. F. Hernández, K. Díaz, M. Forets, R. Sotelo, Application of quantum optimization techniques (QUBO method) to cargo logistics on ships and airplanes, in *2020 IEEE Congreso Bienal de Argentina (ARGENCON)* (2020)
24. A. Robert, P. K.L. Barkoutsos, S. Woerner, I. Tavernelli, Resource-efficient quantum algorithm for protein folding. NPJ Quantum Inform. **7**(1), 38 (2021)
25. R. Santagati et al., Drug design on quantum computers. Nat. Phys. **20**(4), 549–557 (2024)
26. S. Koretsky, P. Gokhale, J.M. Baker, J. Viszlai, H. Zheng, N. Gurung, R. Burg, E.A. Paaso, A. Khodaei, R. Eskandarpour, F.T. Chong, Adapting quantum approximation optimization algorithm (QAOA) for unit commitment, in *Proceedings of the 2021 IEEE International Conference on Quantum Computing and Engineering (QCE)* (2021), pp. 181–187
27. M. Takahashi, H. Nishioka, M. Hirai, H. Takano, A study of the optimization problem on the combination of sectionalizing switches in power grid with quantum annealing (2023)
28. T. Morstyn, Annealing-based quantum computing for combinatorial optimal power flow. IEEE Trans. Smart Grid **14**(2), 1093–1102 (2023)
29. M.S. Zini, A. Delgado, R. dos Reis, P.A.M. Casares, J.E. Mueller, A.-C. Voigt, J.M. Arrazola, Quantum simulation of battery materials using ionic pseudopotentials. Quantum **7**, 1049 (2023)
30. A. Delgado et al., Simulating key properties of lithium-ion batteries with a fault-tolerant quantum computer. Phys. Rev. A **106**, 032428 (2022)
31. D. Claudino, B. Peng, K. Kowalski, T.S. Humble, Modeling singlet fission on a quantum computer. J. Phys. Chem. Lett. **14**(24), 5511–5516 (2023)

Dr. Daniel J. Egger is a senior research scientist in the Quantum Computational Science group at IBM Quantum, IBM Research Europe–Zurich. He received his PhD with distinction in physics from the University of Saarland in 2014. In addition, he has a background in financial risk management and a decade of experience in quantum computing. He has published seminal work in quantum finance, quantum control, and quantum optimization.

Dr. Heike Riel is an IBM fellow and head of the Science of Quantum and Information Technology Department, IBM Research Europe–Zurich. She is a distinguished scientist aiming at achieving scientific and technological breakthroughs in quantum computing and technologies, physics of artificial intelligence, nanoscience and nanotechnology, and exploring new avenues in data processing.

Dr. Stefan Woerner is a principal research scientist and manager of the Quantum Computational Science group at IBM Quantum, IBM Research Europe–Zurich. He holds a Doctor of Science in Operations Management from ETH Zurich. Stefan is renowned for his work in quantum finance, optimization, and machine learning. He has authored key papers, supervised PhD students, and given invited talks at major conferences and institutions.

Dr. Christa Zoufal is a quantum applications researcher in the Quantum Computational Science group at IBM Quantum at IBM Research Europe–Zurich. In 2021 she received her PhD in physics from ETH Zurich for a thesis focused on Generative Quantum Machine Learning. In her current research she focuses on advancing algorithmic and verification methods for quantum machine learning and quantum simulation—both from a theoretical and from an empirical point of view.

Open Access This chapter is licensed under the terms of the Creative Commons Attribution 4.0 International License (http://creativecommons.org/licenses/by/4.0/), which permits use, sharing, adaptation, distribution and reproduction in any medium or format, as long as you give appropriate credit to the original author(s) and the source, provide a link to the Creative Commons license and indicate if changes were made.

The images or other third party material in this chapter are included in the chapter's Creative Commons license, unless indicated otherwise in a credit line to the material. If material is not included in the chapter's Creative Commons license and your intended use is not permitted by statutory regulation or exceeds the permitted use, you will need to obtain permission directly from the copyright holder.

Chapter 7
Quantum Annealing

Michael Tsesmelis

Abstract Quantum annealing is a quantum optimization approach designed to solve complex problems that require finding the optimal solution among a vast number of choices. These problems are often difficult or impossible for classical computers to handle efficiently. This chapter examines the role of quantum annealing in addressing such challenges, showcasing its potential through existing applications and discussing the opportunities and limitations of these systems. It also presents a strategic roadmap for applying quantum annealing technologies in the defense sector, highlighting their importance and potential for solving intricate optimization tasks.

7.1 Introduction

Optimization problems appear in wide-ranging fields such as physics and finance. In the defense sector specifically, optimization is mostly being investigated as a means to improve logistics, supply chain efficiency, and mission planning. The parameter space of modern optimization problems is intractable even for high-performance computers, and most research in classical optimization looks at speeding up the optimization process by trying out new heuristics[1] and solution-converging algorithms. Quantum optimization on the other hand attempts to solve different classes of optimization problems by leveraging the new hardware and computing paradigms that are quantum superposition, entanglement, and tunneling.

Optimization algorithms explore the solution space of a problem and in doing so attempt to find the solution that maximizes or minimizes an objective function

---

[1] Heuristic methods are fast problem-solving algorithms, which usually converge to an approximate instead of the optimal solution.

M. Tsesmelis (✉)
Centre for Quantum Technologies - National University of Singapore, Singapore, Singapore
e-mail: michael.tsesmelis@u.nus.edu

© The Author(s) 2026
J. Jang-Jaccard et al. (eds.), *Quantum Technologies*,
https://doi.org/10.1007/978-3-031-90727-2_7

[1]. The solution space is characterized by a set of parameters that an optimizer tunes iteratively until a solution is found. In classical optimization, many different approaches exist to solve a problem exactly for a global solution or partially for a local solution. Quantum optimization is being explored as a method to solve optimization problems of type NP-hard—nondeterministic polynomial hard[2] [1, 2]. Two major paradigms exist to solve such optimization problems on quantum hardware: quantum annealing and variational quantum circuits [1]. The first is a physics-based approach to quantum optimization which relies on natural quantum processes to solve the problem. The second uses mathematical optimization principles to sequentially tune the parameters of a quantum system according to some given rules. Both approaches are being explored as efficient solvers of NP-hard problems, and it is yet unclear whether one of the two methods will prove definitively superior to the other.

7.2 Analysis

7.2.1 Theory

Quantum annealing is the preferred method for combinatorial optimization, where an optimization protocol must select the optimal set among a list of allowed, discrete parameters. The typical example is the traveling salesman problem, in which a salesman is tasked with optimizing his route to different cities while minimizing the total travel distance. Here, the cities represent a discrete set of possible destinations. Quantum annealing often works in conjunction with a classical computer, such as a high-performance computer, which pre- or postprocesses part of the optimization problem before delegating subtasks to the quantum processing unit. The classical processor is often tasked with deciding on the next set of parameters that is encoded into the quantum processing unit.

The quantum processing unit in quantum annealing operates based on principles derived from adiabatic quantum computing [3, 4]. To understand adiabatic quantum computing, we must first present a fundamental law of physics. Physical systems always tend to the lowest possible energy state; an apple detaching itself from a branch will fall to the ground, where its gravitational potential energy is lowest. The physical description of the system's behavior is encoded within a mathematical formalism called a Hamiltonian (i.e., a mathematical operator representing the

---

[2] Optimization problems of type nondeterministic polynomial time (NP) are difficult to solve but easy to verify. An example thereof would be an optimization process to search a delivery route shorter than some distance D. For a given solution, it is usually easy to verify whether the total distance is lower or higher than D. A problem of type NP-hard, on the other hand, is difficult to verify as well. Is the same delivery route optimal? Answering this would require comparing all possible solutions.

7 Quantum Annealing

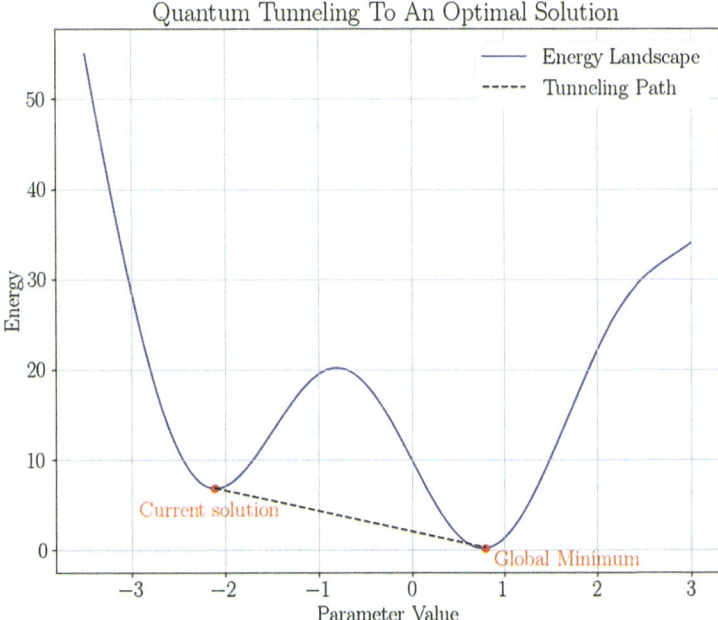

Fig. 7.1 Every Hamiltonian has an associated energy landscape, which maps all possible solutions of the problem to their corresponding energies. For a given Hamiltonian and energy landscape, the aim is to find the solution that minimizes the energy, also called the global minimum. Without external intervention, quantum systems can transition from a local minimum to an improved/global minimum by tunneling through hills of higher energy

total energy of the system), and the system configuration with the lowest energy associated with that Hamiltonian is called the ground state.

Adiabatic quantum computing initializes a quantum system made up of many qubits in the ground state of an easy-to-solve Hamiltonian H_0. This Hamiltonian does not usually bear any relation to the optimization problem that needs solving, which is encoded in a second, target Hamiltonian H_t. By slowly tuning the electromagnetic fields in the hardware, the initial Hamiltonian H_0 can be updated. Every new Hamiltonian usually has associated with it a different ground state of the qubit system, and as the Hamiltonian of the system evolves, so does its ground state. The whole process relies on quantum tunneling, which helps the system find a lower energy state by probabilistically tunneling its way through areas of high energy to arrive at areas of lower energy (see explanation in Fig. 7.1).[3] By slowly evolving the Hamiltonian from the initial Hamiltonian H_0 to the target Hamiltonian H_t, the ground state of the qubit system converges to the ground state

---

[3] This tunneling effect occurs naturally at the quantum mechanical level of the physical qubits and does not cost the hardware any additional operations.

of the target Hamiltonian; this final ground state is the solution to the original optimization problem [1, 3]. Quantum annealing broadly mimics this process and relaxes some constraints to allow for the practical implementation of adiabatic quantum computing on quantum hardware.

7.2.2 Hardware and Applications

The most popular commercial quantum annealing platform is D-Wave's Advantage system, which comprises over 5000 qubits and boasts a qubit connectivity of 15, allowing each qubit to couple to 15 neighboring qubits [4, 5]. D-Wave's computers rely on superconducting qubits to encode the problem. Other platforms exist that try to mimic the physics of quantum annealing, including Fujitsu's Digital Annealer and Hitachi's CMOS Annealing Machine. These systems, however, rely on classical computing technology to solve combinatorial problems and, therefore, cannot be classified as quantum computers per se.

Some notable scientific and engineering optimization problems solved with quantum annealing deal with condensed matter physics [6], protein design [7], quantum chemistry [8], and electronic circuit fault diagnosis [9]. Moreover, as quantum machine learning gains popularity on gate-based quantum computers, there has been a growing effort to implement machine learning algorithms on quantum annealers. For instance, machine learning classifiers have been implemented on quantum annealers to solve problems in particle physics and biology [10, 11]. Several studies have also explored image recognition algorithms on quantum annealers [5]. Finally, combinatorial optimization plays a central role in the management sciences as a way to optimize constrained resource-management problems. Thus, several attempts at solving resource-constrained combinatorial problems have been implemented on quantum annealers, including power network optimization [12], logistics [13], and job scheduling [14].

7.2.3 Challenges

While numerous studies have explored current applications of quantum annealing, they have yet to demonstrate a definitive advantage or speedup over all possible classical algorithms. These investigations typically rely on small-scale quantum algorithm implementations, quantum computer simulation tools, and mathematical analyses to determine whether the time and resources required to solve a problem scale differently for quantum annealers and classical algorithms. An example of this difference in scaling is depicted in Fig. 7.2. Some studies have shown that quantum annealing is competitive with some of the preferred classical solvers for a given problem [6, 15–17], though these findings do not consider the possibility that the classical solvers are suboptimal and their performance could be improved as well.

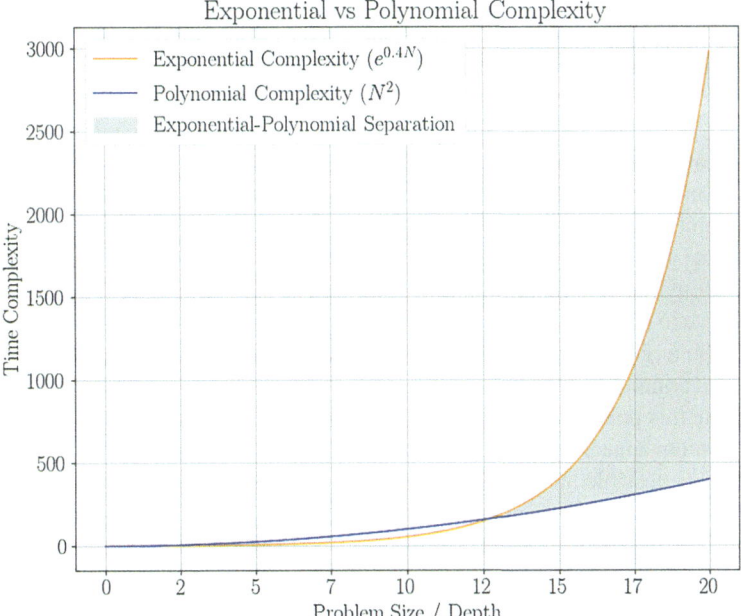

Fig. 7.2 Many optimization problems require exponentially growing time to solve on a classical computer. Some quantum algorithms (not related to quantum annealing) theoretically promise polynomial scaling of time required to solve such problems [18]. Above are plotted both an exponential function e^N and a polynomial function N^2, where N is the problem size. Their curves only separate at larger problem sizes; therefore, a polynomially scaling quantum algorithm only becomes useful for problems of large size N

It is thus too early to tell whether quantum annealing solvers will offer provable and considerable speedups over their classical variants [1].

To improve the performance of quantum annealers and run large-scale problems where the separation in performance between quantum annealers and classical solvers would be made apparent if it exists, significant hardware improvements must be engineered. Remaining hardware imperfections continue to introduce noise into the quantum state of the qubit system, which hinders the convergence to optimal solutions [10]. The short coherence time of the superconducting qubits also limits the size of the problems that can be tested [4].

Most combinatorial tasks also require all-to-all qubit connectivity, in which we want all possible combinations of the discrete parameter space to be allowed in the search for an optimal solution. If the traveling salesman were located in some city, full connectivity means all cities can be possible destinations in the next leg of his travels. Qubit connectivity is limited in current systems, however [4, 14]. Researchers resort to different solutions to get around this problem. One possibility is to break down the full parameter space into subsets that fit into current hardware. The quantum processing unit then iteratively solves the problem for each subset before generating a solution in the original full parameter space. Embedding methods are another solution to the qubit connectivity problem [4]. To connect two disconnected qubits, we encode one logical qubit in several physical qubits, such that we create a continuous chain between the two disconnected qubits at the endpoints. This chain allows for interaction between the two distant qubits, with the trade-off that the physical qubits forming the chain are no longer available to represent independent quantum states, as they are collectively used to encode the logical qubit.

One final significant challenge facing quantum annealing is the growing evidence that, as the parameter space expands, the evolution of the qubit system from one ground state to another requires increasingly longer evolution times [4, 18]. The time to reach the target Hamiltonian thus grows, erasing the quantum advantage relative to classical computers [18, 19]. If we consider the traveling salesman problem again to illustrate this point, we would therefore say that if the number of cities grows too large, quantum annealing might not find the optimal solution in a reasonable amount of time. This possible hurdle will only be confirmed once large-scale combinatorial problems are accessible to quantum annealers.

7.3 Outlook for the Defense Industry

Applications of combinatorial optimization in the defense industry often involve the analysis of paths in a graph. For instance, [20] considers the problem of finding the optimal refueling stops for military aircraft. Another paper [21] considers the maintenance workload problem, wherein parts or vehicles in need of repair must be assigned to different repair facilities in order to minimize the turnover time and operating cost. These examples show that optimization can play a crucial role in military decision-making. These classical optimization problems, however, have not yet been mapped to their quantum computing counterparts. Perhaps a more pertinent example, [22] uses a quantum annealer to optimize satellite constellations. The aim here is to minimize the overhead cost and latency of a communication link across a cluster of satellites.

One important consideration in determining the value of quantum annealing for the defense industry is the scale of the optimization parameter space. It is well supported that quantum computers, if they ever do display significant speedups over classical computers, will only do so at large problem sizes, where the exponential and polynomial cost curves separate (see Fig. 7.2). This critical size is potentially larger than the current network size of many standing armies; the maintenance workload problem remains solvable on a classical computer if there are only a few repair facilities and thus a restricted problem size. Possible applications would, therefore, have to be carefully selected. Examples include: route planning, where the cost of traveling on difficult terrain could be encoded in the Hamiltonian; supply-logistics planning for many small and separated units, wherein one supply vehicle is tasked with delivering supplies to as many units as possible in one supply run; and optimal target selection, where the most crucial nodes in a network can be targeted according to certain priorities, again encoded into the Hamiltonian.

7.4 Conclusion

Although several possible quantum optimization use cases have emerged in recent years, the current era of quantum computing is one of research and development. Based on current findings, several combinatorial optimization tasks have been successfully carried out on the current generation of quantum annealers, but few are relevant to the defense industry. Also, current evidence does not yet support the fact that quantum annealers are better at solving optimization problems than classical solvers. As a possible roadmap for the defense industry's strategy in quantum annealing, an important first step would be to identify key optimization problems that are intractable on classical computers but could theoretically be solved on quantum annealers. A further step could try to encode such problems into a Hamiltonian and run a restricted-size version of the original task on a cloud-accessible quantum annealer to test the feasibility of the idea. If future quantum annealers deliver improved performance, these combinatorial optimization problems could then be scaled up to find solutions to problems that were previously intractable on classical computers.

References

1. B.C.B. Symons, D. Galvin, E. Sahin, V. Alexandrov, S. Mensa, A practitioner's guide to quantum algorithms for optimisation problems (2023). arXiv:2305.07323
2. A. Abbas et al., Quantum optimization: potential, challenges, and the path forward (2023). arXiv:2312.02279
3. A. Perdomo-Ortiz, S.E. Venegas-Andraca, A. Aspuru-Guzik, A study of heuristic guesses for adiabatic quantum computation. Quantum Inform. Process. **10**(1), 33–52 (2011)
4. P. Hauke, H.G. Katzgraber, W. Lechner, H. Nishimori, W.D. Oliver, Perspectives of quantum annealing: methods and implementations. Rep. Progr. Phys. **83**(5), 054401 (2020)
5. R.K. Nath, H. Thapliyal, T.S. Humble, A review of machine learning classification using quantum annealing for real-world applications. SN Comput. Sci. **2**(5), 365 (2021)
6. A.D. King et al., Scaling advantage over path-integral Monte Carlo in quantum simulation of geometrically frustrated magnets. Nat. Commun. **12**, 1113 (2021)
7. A. Irbäck, L. Knuthson, S. Mohanty, C. Peterson, Using quantum annealing to design lattice proteins. Phys. Rev. Res. **6**(1), 013162 (2024)
8. R. Babbush, P.J. Love, A. Aspuru-Guzik, Adiabatic quantum simulation of quantum chemistry. Sci. Rep. **4**(1), 6603 (2014)
9. A. Perdomo-Ortiz, A. Feldman, A. Ozaeta, S.V. Isakov, Z. Zhu, B. O'Gorman, H.G. Katzgraber, A. Diedrich, H. Neven, J. de Kleer, B. Lackey, R. Biswas, Readiness of quantum optimization machines for industrial applications. Phys. Rev. Appl. **12**(1), 014004 (2019). arXiv:1708.09780 [quant-ph]

10. A. Mott, J. Job, J.-R. Vlimant, D. Lidar, M. Spiropulu, Solving a Higgs optimization problem with quantum annealing for machine learning. Nature **550**(7676), 375–379 (2017)
11. R.Y. Li, R. Di Felice, R. Rohs, D.A. Lidar, Quantum annealing versus classical machine learning applied to a simplified computational biology problem. NPJ Quantum Inform. **4**(1), 1–10 (2018)
12. T. Morstyn, Annealing-based quantum computing for combinatorial optimal power flow. IEEE Trans. Smart Grid **14**(2), 1093–1102 (2023)
13. S.J. Weinberg, F. Sanches, T. Ide, K. Kamiya, R. Correll, Supply chain logistics with quantum and classical annealing algorithms. Sci. Rep. **13**(1), 4770 (2023)
14. L.F.P. Armas, S. Creemers, S. Deleplanque, Solving the resource constrained project scheduling problem with quantum annealing. Sci. Rep. **14**(1), 16784 (2024)
15. F.A. Quinton, P.A.S. Myhr, M. Barani, P.C. del Granado, H. Zhang, Quantum annealing versus classical solvers: applications, challenges and limitations for optimisation problems (2024). arXiv:2409.05542 [quant-ph]
16. J. King, S. Yarkoni, M.M. Nevisi, J.P. Hilton, C.C. McGeoch, Benchmarking a quantum annealing processor with the time-to-target metric (2015). arXiv:1508.05087
17. T. Albash, D.A. Lidar, Demonstration of a scaling advantage for a quantum annealer over simulated annealing (2018). arXiv:1705.07452
18. A. Abbas et al., Challenges and opportunities in quantum optimization. Nat. Rev. Phys. **6**(12), 718–735 (2024)
19. A. Das, B.K. Chakrabarti, *Colloquium* : quantum annealing and analog quantum computation. Rev. Mod. Phys. **80**(3), 1061–1081 (2008)
20. T.E. Kannon, S.G. Nurre, B.J. Lunday, R.R. Hill, The aircraft routing problem with refueling. Optim. Lett. **9**(8), 1609–1624 (2015)
21. R.R. Squires, K.L. Hoffman, A military maintenance planning and scheduling problem. Optim. Lett. **9**(8), 1675–1688 (2015)
22. S.M. Venkatesh, A. Macaluso, M. Nuske, M. Klusch, A. Dengel, Quantum annealing-based algorithm for efficient coalition formation among LEO satellites (2024). arXiv:2408.06007

Michael Tsesmelis earned a master's degree in applied computational science and engineering in 2023 from Imperial College London. He previously worked as a researcher in Technology Monitoring at CYD Campus, a Quantum computer scientist at CERN, and a cybersecurity software developer for the Swiss Armed Forces. Currently, he is pursuing a PhD in quantum physics at the Centre for Quantum Technologies of the National University of Singapore. His past work focused on measuring security development in IT and identifying future cyber defense technologies through text mining. His current research focuses on quantum photonic chips, quantum chemistry, and theoretical quantum physics.

Open Access This chapter is licensed under the terms of the Creative Commons Attribution 4.0 International License (http://creativecommons.org/licenses/by/4.0/), which permits use, sharing, adaptation, distribution and reproduction in any medium or format, as long as you give appropriate credit to the original author(s) and the source, provide a link to the Creative Commons license and indicate if changes were made.

The images or other third party material in this chapter are included in the chapter's Creative Commons license, unless indicated otherwise in a credit line to the material. If material is not included in the chapter's Creative Commons license and your intended use is not permitted by statutory regulation or exceeds the permitted use, you will need to obtain permission directly from the copyright holder.

Chapter 8
Quantum Machine Learning

Muhammad Usman

Abstract The rapid advancement of artificial intelligence has made machine learning (ML) methods central to modern science, technology, and industry. At the same time, the emergence of programmable quantum computers, along with the anticipation of large-scale fault-tolerant machines in the future, has generated interest in the potential of quantum machine learning (QML)—a field that explores quantum properties to enhance ML tasks. While QML is often considered a promising application for quantum computing, its practical advantages over classical methods remain an area of active research and exploration. In recent years, QML has garnered significant global attention, with researchers investigating its potential and limitations. In this chapter, we introduce the fundamentals of QML and provide an overview of recent developments and future trends in the field. We outline potential opportunities where quantum properties might offer advantages in ML tasks while also addressing the open challenges that QML faces in terms of scalability, implementation, and practical utility. We also explore the potential applications of QML in defense and security-sensitive domains. Here, researchers speculate that integrating quantum computing into ML could lead to the development of systems capable of resisting sophisticated threats, such as data manipulation and poisoning. However, realizing these possibilities requires further advancements in both quantum hardware and algorithmic design, making QML a promising yet still evolving field.

M. Usman (✉)
Data61 - CSIRO, Eveleigh, NSW, Australia

School of Physics, The University of Melbourne, Parkville, VIC, Australia

Monash University, Clayton, VIC, Australia
e-mail: muhammad.usman@data61.csiro.au

© The Author(s) 2026
J. Jang-Jaccard et al. (eds.), *Quantum Technologies*,
https://doi.org/10.1007/978-3-031-90727-2_8

8.1 Introduction

Quantum computing is an emerging field of research which promises immense computational power to solve challenging computational problems which are otherwise intractable by classical computing methods. Recently, researchers from Google have shown that their quantum processor could perform a computational task in less than five minutes, which a conventional classical computer would take septillion years [1]. Although a remarkable result, their work showed the supremacy of the quantum processor only for a contrived task, and a general-purpose quantum advantage for real-world applications will still require significantly more development on both quantum hardware and software fronts. Nevertheless, the anticipated revolutionary impact of quantum computing has led to intense research on identifying its applications in many fields of research and technologies, including quantum chemistry [2], drug discovery [3], financial optimization [4], and transport [5]. The key aim of quantum computing research is to develop fundamentally new algorithms and computing methods which can outperform conventional classical approaches. Among those, integrating the power of quantum computing in machine learning (ML) is quite intrinsic as the associate computational power from quantum computing is anticipated to lead to significant speed-up, enhanced accuracy, and/or superior robustness of ML models [6]. This has led to the birth of a new field of research, namely quantum machine learning (QML)—the development and benchmarking of ML models that explicitly rely on the unique properties of quantum mechanics, such as superposition and entanglement, to outperform their classical counterparts [7–10]. The field of QML is currently a rapidly advancing area of research, with quantum versions of almost all classical ML algorithms being actively developed and benchmarked on the existing near-term noisy quantum processors.

An important line of research within the field of QML pertains to its application in security-sensitive applications such as intelligence, security, surveillance, reconnaissance, and targeting systems [8]. Despite high efficiency and accuracy of classical ML algorithms, it has been found that they can be readily fooled by an adversary through manipulation or spoofing of data also known as adversarial attacks [11], which poses serious security threat for applications where reliability is the key parameter of interest. This has raised an important question: whether QML algorithms are also as vulnerable as classical ML models [12–14]. Recent preliminary work has theoretically shown that QML algorithms are remarkably robust against adversarial attacks [12], which is attributed to the fact that classical adversarial attacks are ineffective on QML models due to fundamentally lacking quantum resources such as quantum entanglement which is the hallmark of quantum systems [15]. This offers a unique opportunity to leverage quantum computing, specifically its unique properties like superposition and entanglement, to develop highly resistant QML-based autonomous systems, leading to a new area of research known as quantum adversarial machine learning (QAML).

Despite significant progress in algorithmic development and benchmarking of QML and QAML models, their experimental implementation on quantum processors is still in its infancy [16, 17]. Further advancements in the capabilities of quantum models toward practical-scale applications, in particular their experimental implementation, can lead to an end-to-end QAML capability to secure, e.g., future autonomous Intelligence Surveillance and Reconnaissance (ISR) systems for military and defense purposes.

8.2 Analysis

Classical ML is not a new field of research. The progress in classical ML methods has undergone decades of development; however, it is only quite recently that the state-of-the-art classical ML such as deep neural networks, large language models, and natural language processing have found remarkable applications in nearly all fields of research and industrial workflows. A key reason for such tremendous rapid progress in ML in recent days is due to the availability of tremendous computational capabilities which have enabled efficient training and testing of ML models on very large datasets. The fundamental requirement of ML for computational power indicates that it is ideally poised to benefit from quantum computing, which promises tremendous computational advantage over classical supercomputers.

It has been reported that many of the ML algorithms rely on linear algebra routines such as the Fast Fourier transform, matrix inversion or finding the Eigen values of a large matrix, which a quantum computer might be able to solve more efficiently than a classical computer, thereby providing a speed-up to the QML models over their classical counterparts [6]. However, in order for such benefit to be practically achieved, the loading of classical data into a quantum state has to be efficient so that the exponential cost of the data loading step does not overcome any benefit of the QML model. Indeed, recent work has focused on efficient quantum state preparation for QML models [16].

Apart from training speed-up, it is also important to explore other possibilities of quantum advantage for ML tasks such as robustness against adversarial attacks. Finally, the application of QML to quantum data is considered a promising pathway to achieve quantum advantage which circumvents the exponential cost of encoding classical data [18].

The vulnerability of ML algorithms has been well known in the classical literature as data spoofing and manipulation attacks can be designed which can easily fool even very powerful classical ML models. This has given birth to a new field of research known as adversarial ML [19, 20], an area of research that deals with attacks and defense of ML models. Although there have been numerous attacks and defense methods designed for classical ML models with varying degrees of success, there is no clear resolution if a universal defense method exists which can overcome the vulnerabilities of ML models. An important finding in this context is related to the high transferability of attacks from one ML model to other ML models, *i.e.*, attacks designed for one specific ML model are found to be highly effective on other independently trained ML models [12]. This leads to serious security concerns for ML applications in security-sensitive applications such as in defense and military systems, as one adversary could design an attack on their models and transfer to models working in highly sensitive applications causing serious damage.

With the integration of quantum computing into ML in recent years, researchers have started to investigate the important question of whether QML will suffer from similar vulnerabilities [8]. Recent work has focused on the analysis of QML models, in particular with the context of transferability of attacks between classical and quantum ML architectures [12]. It has been discovered that while the attacks from classical ML models do not transfer to QML models, contrarily the attacks from QML models were easily able to fool classical ML algorithms. This is an important finding which describes a dual advantage for early adopters of quantum computing technologies. On the one hand, quantum computing could generate highly effective attacks, easily fooling classical ML systems, while, on the other hand, being very robust against any adversarial attack. The study also reported that QML networks remain vulnerable against quantum attacks, and more work is needed to ensure the complete safety of ML system in post-quantum era where an adversary may also have access to quantum computers.

8.2.1 Definition

A typical QML model, such as quantum neural network, consists of three major building blocks [8]: data encoding, feature learning, and measurement outcome (see Fig. 8.1). For classical datasets, the data encoding step loads a classical dataset into a quantum state by using an appropriate encoding scheme. The common encoding schemes are amplitude encoding [21], phase encoding [21], and flexible

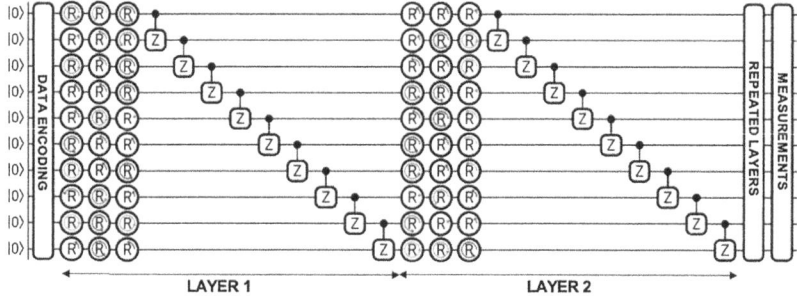

Fig. 8.1 Schematic illustration of a standard quantum variational architecture that has been trained in the literature to perform QML tasks. The circuit consists of a data encoding layer, followed by multiple layers of trainable variational gates and two-qubit CNOTs. The final measurement layer reveals the outcome of the trained QML network

representation for quantum images (FRQI) [22]. The second building block is generally a variational quantum circuit consisting of single-qubit rotation gates and two-qubit entangling gates such as control-phase gates. The classical optimization of single-qubit rotation gates during the training process allows the learning of features from the input data, whereas the two-qubit gates introduce entanglement. The final step is measurement which for any test data instance reveals the outcome of the quantum machine learning model. While the data loading and measurement steps remain the same, the implementation of the feature learning block could vary based on the architectural design of a particular quantum machine learning model.

QAML is a field of research in which new QML models are developed and benchmarked to investigate their robustness against adversarial attacks. An adversarial attack is defined as a careful manipulation of the input dataset such that it is able to flip the outcome of a well-trained ML model, whether quantum or classical. For example, a well-trained ML model on the photos of cats and dogs will correctly label previously unseen photos of cats and dogs. However, an effective adversarial attack will carefully manipulate a photo of a cat by selectively changing some pixels in the image such that the ML model will label it incorrectly as the photo of a dog. There are two kinds of adversarial attack settings: black-box attack and white-box attack. In a black-box attack, the attack is generated without any knowledge of the ML model being attacked. This is also known as transferability of an attack, as the attack is usually generated on one model and then transferred to a different target model. Contrarily, a white-box attack is generated with complete knowledge of the ML model being attacked. Several attacks have been developed in the literature to trick ML models such as PGD [23], FGSM [24], and Auto [25], which offer varying degrees of effectiveness.

8.2.2 Maturity

The field of QML is very nascent at this stage, with new algorithmic developments rapidly emerging, and their testing on the available quantum hardware is presently an active area of research. Despite significant progress and promising results, the application of QML models has been primarily to simple proof-of-concept datasets, whereas its implementation on datasets from real-world applications would require significant future research and new scientific breakthroughs in the coming years. There are still several key challenges associated with various components in the QML pipeline, such as efficient loading of classical data into quantum states, overcoming barren plateaus in the training of QML models, mitigating or canceling the impact of noise or errors in quantum hardware, and optimization of QML architectures to achieve accuracies at par with classical counterparts. However, recent work reported in the literature [8] has shown significant progress on all fronts which incites the excitement around the prospect of QML for practical problems in the coming years.

Likewise, on the theoretical front, a few recent studies have shown that the integration of quantum computing in ML has a clear potential to enhance their robustness against adversarial attacks (see, for example, Ref. [8] and references therein). The experimental implementation is still challenging due to intensive resource requirements and the relatively limited capabilities of the current generation of quantum processors. Nevertheless, a couple of initial proof-of-concept experimental demonstrations of QAML models have already been reported [16, 17], confirming the potential for quantum-enhanced robustness of ML models.

8.2.3 Trends

QML and QAML are relatively new areas of research that have gained momentum only in the last few years. Given its strong implications for security-sensitive applications, QAML has recently been a subject of strong attention, particularly within the defense and military communities. QML and QAML are closely related fields of research, and they share many common trends. Below, we highlight a few active areas of research in the context of QML and QAML development:

1. **Optimization of encoding circuits.** Data encoding is presently one of the biggest issues toward the practical implementation of QML and QAML, particularly in the era of near-term quantum devices. Two usual approaches are amplitude and phase encoding [21], both coming with their own advantages and overheads. For example, amplitude encoding is efficient by exploiting the exponentially (in the number of qubits) large Hilbert space of the quantum computer, but its main limitation is that it requires exponentially deep encoding quantum circuits—a significant overhead for the implementation on near-term quantum devices where noise severally limits the fidelity of deep quantum circuits. Contrarily, phase encoding, in which data is encoded into the angles of single-qubit rotations, is more efficient in regard to circuit depths, but it demands a large number of qubits, which seriously limits its ability to implement on the current quantum hardware where only a handful number of qubits are available. There are other encoding schemes, such as interleaved data encoding strategy, which consists of alternating layers of data encoding and variational gates. Such a strategy allows for a user-controlled trade-off between number of qubits and circuit depth, making it particularly suitable for the current generation of quantum computers. Notably, a recent experimental implementation of QAML employed this encoding scheme [17]. Nevertheless, the development of efficient data encoding schemes remains an active area of research for both QML and QAML. While the current implementation of QML is primarily focused on simple proof-of-concept datasets such as MNIST and FMNIST, its scalability toward complex real-world data sets will inevitably require new and more efficient data encoding schemes. An alternative line of research is to apply data reduction schemes by classical pre-processing or using novel methods for

approximate state preparation, which drastically reduce the overhead associated with data encoding [16, 26].
2. **Architecture design.** Central to the conventional approaches to QML and QAML is an optimizable variational quantum circuit sandwiched between a data encoding circuit and a set of measurements to determine the prediction of the classifier. A quantum variational circuit is made up of a repeated sequence of a number of parameterized single-qubit rotation gates followed by two-qubit gates generating entanglement. The parameters of single-qubit gates are classically optimized to learn input data features, which is conceptually similar to tuning of classical neuron weights in traditional neural networks. Although the variational quantum circuit approach has been quite successful for simple image datasets, its performance for larger and complex data is already facing challenges such as trainability, barren plateaus, and expressibility. As an example, the presence of barren plateaus in the training loss landscape leads to a serious impediment to the training of deep quantum circuits. Although it is not entirely clear what form the large-scale quantum classifiers of the future will take, it has already started to become evident that future QAML models will require much more sophisticated architectures if they are to train on highly complex datasets relevant for practical applications. Recent work has already started, which is focusing on developing quantum convolutional networks [27] and quantum RESNET [28]—a quantum version of a powerful and sophisticated classical architecture.
3. **Noise mitigation and error correction.** The current generation of quantum devices suffers from noise or errors, and therefore, it is challenging to implement deep quantum circuits that are relevant for practical applications. Likewise, the experimental implementations of QML and QAML also face this crucial challenge arising from the limitations of the current quantum processors, due to limited numbers of qubits and high levels of noise. Although a proof-of-concept QAML study was experimentally implemented in a recent work [17], sophisticated QAML applications of the future will require error mitigation and correction. Another interesting line of research is to explore if the presence of noise helps in adversarial robustness of QML models [29]. It might be possible that the noise in quantum devices dilutes the presence of adversarial attacks which in itself are based on the carefully crafted noise in the datasets, leading to overall better performance. Significant more research is needed to fully understand both the role of noise in the working of quantum adversarial architectures and their performance when implemented with error correction or mitigation schemes.
4. **Quantum generative adversarial learning.** The interplay of adversarial ML with generative adversarial networks is an interesting line of research. Generative networks have been extensively used in adversarial ML context, both in generating strong attacks and effective defense. Recently, quantum generalizations of generative adversarial networks have been proposed. It consists of a generative network where either the generator or the discriminator (or both) has been implemented by a QML model [30]. The benchmarking of the performance of quantum adversarial generative networks in the context of either generating or detecting

adversarial examples is another interesting line of research concerning hybrid quantum-classical models; for example, it could be that a quantum discriminator may exhibit superior performance in detecting adversarial perturbations which were themselves generated by a quantum network.

5. **Quantum machine learning beyond images.** While the focus of QML and QAML has been primarily on image datasets, it is important to adapt these models for generic datasets such as signals and text to broaden the scope of their applications. A recent work has been reported on the benchmarking of QAML for signals, which has shown similar robustness against adversarial attacks as previously reported for image datasets [31]. More work is needed to adapt QAML framework for a wide range of signal datasets including microwave, radio frequency, and radar signals and perform detailed studies to understand quantum adversarial solutions for signals.

6. **Quantum transfer learning.** An interesting line of research is to combine QML models with classical ML techniques to create new hybrid architectures that may retain unique properties of QML while enabling applications for complex large-sized datasets. In this context, quantum transfer learning has been reported as an effective technique where a quantum variational circuit is concatenated with a classical ML model pretrained on ImageNet dataset [32]. The resulting hybrid architecture demonstrated promising performance when benchmarked on a variety of image datasets such as CIFAR-10, traffic signs, and And and Bees. While this work was based on transfer learning from a classical to a quantum network, future research may also investigate transfer learning between two quantum architectures or from a quantum to a classical architecture.

7. **QML exploiting data symmetries.** Optimizing QML architectures by explicitly exploiting data symmetries has been a fruitful line of research in the past few years. It has been reported that the training and test accuracies can be drastically boosted by developing QML models which take into account reflection [33] and rotation [34] symmetries of datasets. Although these studies have been confined to image datasets, the focus can be expanded to many other datasets as symmetries are key characteristics of many real-world applications.

8. **Quantum attacks.** QML offers robustness against classical adversarial attacks and therefore may lead to quantum advantage for early adopters of quantum technology. However, if an adversary also has access to a quantum computer, it is yet not fully known if QML will be robust against quantum attacks, *i.e.*, attacks natively generated on quantum computers. Recent work indicated that quantum attacks are effective on simple quantum architectures based on variational classifiers [12]; however, a comprehensive analysis is needed to fully determine the scope and extent of attacks and defense in the context of QML.

9. **Quantum machine learning on quantum data.** As the loading of classical data into a quantum state is an expensive step in the QML pipeline, it is considered that QML implemented directly on quantum data such as from a quantum sensing device may provide a robust pathway to achieve quantum advantage [18]. However, it is not clear yet how a QML model would be trained

directly on quantum data in a practical setting, which will require significant research breakthroughs in the future.

8.3 Recommendation for Advancement of QML and QAML

Quantum computing is often regarded as a promising technology with the potential to provide advantages over classical approaches in certain computational tasks. Its integration with machine learning (ML) systems is being explored for possible benefits, such as faster training, novel feature extraction, and enhanced resilience against data spoofing and cyberattacks, which could be relevant in military and defense applications. However, while theoretical studies suggest potential advantages of Quantum Machine Learning (QML) and Quantum-Assisted Machine Learning (QAML), practical implementation is still in its early stages. Current limitations, including noisy hardware and a limited number of qubits, restrict their ability to perform the complex quantum circuits often required for these tasks. Advancing this field will require designing optimized architectures with reduced circuit depths, developing more efficient data encoding strategies, and rigorously benchmarking QML/QAML models with error mitigation and correction techniques.

8.4 Conclusion

Quantum machine learning is a rapidly advancing field of research that has the potential to offer transformational socioeconomic impact by addressing challenging problems such as personalized drugs for complex diseases like cancer, climate science by finding novel materials for decarbonization, congestion control through everyday traffic modeling, or predicting future financial crisis by modeling large banking and stock datasets. The current state of the field is largely at the proof-of-concept level where new quantum machine learning models are being developed and tested on the near-term quantum devices. With remarkable advancements in the scalability and quality of quantum processors, it is anticipated that quantum machine learning will also demonstrate increasingly capable performances in the next few years, and some selective applications could start emerging with possible advantages over classical methods.

The integration of quantum computing in ML and AI systems will have important implications for the robustness of future autonomous military systems, including electronic/cyber warfare and the rapid determination of best countermeasures against unknown or emerging threats. Ultimately, a quantum machine learning-based system will be a self-contained system emulating all aspects of the quantum adversarial ML approach for threat identification and mitigation in state-of-the-art and future command, communication and control, intelligence and surveillance systems, and autonomous robotic systems underpinned by quantum algorithms.

References

1. R. Acharya et al., Quantum error correction below the surface code threshold. Nature **638**, 920–926 (2025)
2. Y. Cao et al., Quantum chemistry in the age of quantum computing. Chem. Rev. **119**(19), 10856–10915 (2019)
3. R. Santagati et al., Drug design on quantum computers. Nat. Phys. **20**, 549–557 (2024)
4. D. Herman et al., Quantum computing for finance. Nat. Rev. Phys. **5**, 450–465 (2023)
5. V.V. Dixit et al., Quantum computing for transport network design problems. Sci. Rep. **13**, 12267 (2023)
6. J. Biamonte et al., Quantum machine learning. Nature **549**, 195–202 (2017)
7. M. Cerezo et al., Challenges and opportunities in quantum machine learning. Nat. Comput. Sci. **2**, 567–576 (2022)
8. M.T. West et al., Towards quantum enhanced adversarial robustness in machine learning. Nat. Mach. Intell. **5**, 581–589 (2023)
9. D. Ristè, M.P. Da Silva, C.A. Ryan, A.W. Cross, A.D. Córcoles, J.A. Smolin, J.M. Gambetta, J.M. Chow, B.R. Johnson, Demonstration of quantum advantage in machine learning. npj Quantum Inf. **3**(1), 1–5 (2017)
10. Y. Liu, S. Arunachalam, K. Temme, A rigorous and robust quantum speed-up in supervised machine learning. Nat. Phys. **17**(9), 1013–1017 (2021)
11. A. Kurakin, I. Goodfellow, S. Bengio, Adversarial machine learning at scale. arXiv preprint arXiv:1611.01236 (2016)
12. M.T. West et al., Benchmarking adversarially robust quantum machine learning at scale. Phys. Rev. Res. **5**, 023186 (2023)
13. S. Lu, L.-M. Duan, D.-L. Deng, Quantum adversarial machine learning. Phys. Rev. Res. **2**(3), 033212 (2020)
14. N. Liu, P. Wittek, Vulnerability of quantum classification to adversarial perturbations. Phys. Rev. A **101**, 062331 (2020)
15. N. Dowling et al., Adversarial robustness guarantees for quantum classifiers. arXiv:2405.10360 (2024)
16. M.T. West et al., Drastic circuit depth reductions with preserved adversarial robustness by approximate encoding for quantum machine learning. Intell. Comput. **3**, 100 (2024)
17. W. Ren, W. Li, S. Xu, K. Wang, W. Jiang, F. Jin, X. Zhu, J. Chen, Z. Song, P. Zhang, et al., Experimental quantum adversarial learning with programmable superconducting qubits. arXiv preprint arXiv:2204.01738 (2022)
18. H.-Y. Huang et al., Quantum advantage in learning from experiments. Science **376**, 1182–1186 (2022)
19. Z. Zhou et al., Humans can decipher adversarial images. Nat. Commun. **10**, 1334 (2019)
20. K. Ren et al., Adversarial attacks and defenses in deep learning. Engineering **6**, 346–360 (2020)
21. R. LaRose, B. Coyle, Robust data encodings for quantum classifiers. Phys. Rev. A **102**(3), 032420 (2020)
22. R. Dilip, Y.-J. Liu, A. Smith, F. Pollmann, Data compression for quantum machine learning. arXiv preprint arXiv:2204.11170 (2022)
23. A. Madry, A. Makelov, L. Schmidt, D. Tsipras, A. Vladu, Towards deep learning models resistant to adversarial attacks. arXiv preprint arXiv:1706.06083 (2017)
24. I.J. Goodfellow, J. Shlens, C. Szegedy, Explaining and harnessing adversarial examples. arXiv preprint arXiv:1412.6572 (2014)
25. F. Croce, M. Hein, Reliable evaluation of adversarial robustness with an ensemble of diverse parameter-free attacks, in *International Conference on Machine Learning*. PMLR (2020), pp. 2206–2216
26. J. Romero, J.P. Olson, A. Aspuru-Guzik, Quantum autoencoders for efficient compression of quantum data. Quantum Sci. Technol. **2**(4), 045001 (2017)

27. M. Henderson, S. Shakya, S. Pradhan, T. Cook, Quanvolutional neural networks: powering image recognition with quantum circuits. Quantum Mach. Intell. **2**(1), 1–9 (2020)
28. J. Heredge et al., Non-unitary quantum machine learning. arXiv:2405.17388 (2024)
29. Y. Du, M.-H. Hsieh, T. Liu, D. Tao, N. Liu, Quantum noise protects quantum classifiers against adversaries. Phys. Rev. Res. **3**(2), 023153 (2021)
30. S. Tsang et al., Hybrid quantum-classical generative adversarial network for high resolution image generation. IEEE Trans. Quantum Eng. **4**, 3102419 (2023)
31. Y. Wu et al., Radio signal classification by adversarially robust quantum machine learning. arXiv:2312.07821 (2023)
32. A. Khatun et al., Quantum transfer learning with adversarial robustness for classification of high-resolution image datasets. Adv. Quant. Technol. **8**, 2400268 (2024)
33. M.T. West, J. Heredge, M. Sevior, M. Usman, Provably trainable rotationally equivariant quantum machine learning. PRX Quantum **5**, 030320 (2024)
34. M.T. West, M. Sevior, M. Usman, Reflection equivariant quantum neural networks for enhanced image classification. Mach. Learn. Sci. Technol. **4**(3), 035027 (2023)

Professor Muhammad Usman is Head of Quantum Systems and Principal Staff Researcher at CSIRO's Data61 which is Australia's National Research Organization. He has over 15 years of research and teaching experience in the field of quantum computing, with research interests in quantum algorithms, quantum software engineering, and quantum security. He is serving on the executive editorial boards of two IOP journals (Nano Futures and MSMSE), is a fellow of the Australian Institute of Physics (AIP), and has honorary associate professor positions at the University of Melbourne and Monash University. Dr. Usman was nominated as Innovative of the Year 2023 Award by Defense Industry, Winner of the Australian Army Quantum Technology Challenge in three years in a row (2021, 2022, and 2023), Rising Stars in Computational Materials Science by Elsevier in 2020, and Dean's Award for Excellence in Research (Early Career) at the University of Melbourne in 2019. He served as the chair of the organizing committee for the 8th International Conference on Quantum Techniques in Machine Learning (QTML 2024) held in Australia.

Open Access This chapter is licensed under the terms of the Creative Commons Attribution 4.0 International License (http://creativecommons.org/licenses/by/4.0/), which permits use, sharing, adaptation, distribution and reproduction in any medium or format, as long as you give appropriate credit to the original author(s) and the source, provide a link to the Creative Commons license and indicate if changes were made.

The images or other third party material in this chapter are included in the chapter's Creative Commons license, unless indicated otherwise in a credit line to the material. If material is not included in the chapter's Creative Commons license and your intended use is not permitted by statutory regulation or exceeds the permitted use, you will need to obtain permission directly from the copyright holder.

Chapter 9
Enabling and Accelerating Quantum Computing with AI Supercomputing

Mark Wolf

Abstract In the last few years, generative AI has become a revolutionary technology impacting every corner of science and industry, including quantum computing. As quantum computers continue to mature, they will integrate with supercomputers to solve some of the hardest problems in the world. Quantum computers are extremely complex, and both their design and operation face numerous physics and engineering challenges. Fortunately, the combination of AI and supercomputing hardware is well suited to address many of these challenges and is already beginning to accelerate progress across the quantum ecosystem. This chapter will survey some key AI for quantum applications being explored and discuss their implications for quantum strategy.

9.1 Introduction

The end of 2022 marked a monumental shift in technology and human capability, as ChatGPT and other large language models led to a "big bang" moment for AI. This transformative moment didn't arise in isolation; it was the culmination of decades of advancements in computing hardware and algorithm development. These breakthroughs have enabled machines to quickly process vast amounts of data to learn, adapt, and make decisions like humans, with impacts in nearly every industry. Yet, there remain fundamentally difficult problems well suited for the unique capabilities of quantum computers.

Despite their apparent differences, an intimate relationship is developing between AI and quantum computing. Realizing the benefits of quantum computers is difficult and requires solutions to a number of physics and engineering challenges. In the near term, the greatest challenge is noise, as quantum devices are susceptible to even the slightest environmental disturbances. Long term, development of quantum

---

M. Wolf (✉)
NVIDIA Corporation, Santa Clara, CA, USA
e-mail: mawolf@nvidia.com

processors becomes even more challenging as factors like speed and scalability also limit the ability to run highly impactful quantum applications.

Just as breakthroughs in AI were enabled by decades of computing development, breakthroughs in quantum computing will stand on the shoulders of AI [1, 2]. The following section highlights a few examples where AI is already demonstrating great promise for addressing three of the most central aspects of quantum computing. For a comprehensive analysis of this topic, we direct readers to a recent review article detailing many more AI for quantum computing use cases [1].

9.2 Analysis

Generally speaking, three of the core aspects of quantum computing are: the processor, quantum error correction, and algorithms. Each faces its own set of challenges. The processor needs to manipulate and measure the qubits with as little noise as possible. Quantum error correction routines then need to quickly and repeatedly help ameliorate residual errors and ensure the computation avoids corruption. Finally, the utility of an algorithm depends on how efficiently it can run given the hardware constraints and error correction capabilities.

To accomplish these goals, fast and reliable execution of many auxiliary tasks must happen in concert to overcome bottlenecks posed by the many physics and engineering limitations. Many of these tasks are themselves extremely complex and span a wide range of scientific disciplines from electrical engineering to applied mathematics. However, they do share the common need for abstract decision-making that is fast and scalable, all quintessential traits of AI.

The next three sections will briefly discuss how AI can benefit these core aspects of quantum computing.

9.2.1 The Processor

The goal of a quantum processor is to protect and manipulate qubits in such a way that quantum information can be processed without being corrupted by external noise sources. Devices with as little noise as possible are crucial for useful quantum computing.

One of the ways device noise is minimized is by carefully ordering and tuning how the device components (e.g., lasers) interact with and control the qubits. These operations are collectively known as a control sequence. Determining the optimal control sequence for a device is challenging and requires consideration of many interconnected engineering systems and their constraints. As devices scale and include more components, determining the optimal control sequence becomes very difficult.

AI is currently being explored as a tool for determining control sequences and maximizing device performance. One example is the work of Ares and coworkers, which demonstrates how the large context windows and scalability of transformer models make them well suited for controlling complex quantum systems over other state-of-the-art approaches [3].

Quantum computing hardware also requires calibration, which involves many iterations of measurements and adjustments before a quantum device can be used. AI can help automate calibration procedures, so they are quicker and more reliable. Recent work has demonstrated how AI techniques like reinforcement learning can be used to reduce the number of costly experimental repetitions to recalibrate a quantum device [4].

AI can also help develop quantum computers and reveal patterns hidden in the complexities of the quantum mechanics governing the qubits. An example of this is work by Saffman and coworkers which realized up to a 56% reduction in single-qubit readout errors on a neutral atom quantum processor by leveraging a convolutional neural network [5].

9.2.2 Quantum Error Correction

Even the best quantum processors will have error rates far too high for running practical quantum applications without any corrective measures. Quantum error correction is a critical step toward ensuring errors can be detected and fixed before a quantum algorithm completes. This is usually accomplished by encoding logical qubits as many noisy physical qubits and repeatedly performing a set of cleverly designed operations that allow errors to be decoded and fixed.

Error correction schemes must be fast. Otherwise, information could be corrupted, and the effort moot, or the procedure works but is too slow for time-sensitive applications. Practical error correction will require tight integration between the quantum device and a supercomputer so communication between the devices does not violate the strict time constraints [6].

Developing good error correction codes is an extremely complex math problem. AI is being used to help discover new error correction techniques [7] and improve the most challenging parts of existing error correction codes like decoding which error occurred and how to fix it [8].

One of the most noteworthy examples of using AI for quantum error correction is Google's AlphaQubit [8]. AlphaQubit is a sophisticated transformer-based AI model for decoding surface code errors. It was trained on advanced noise models and refined using experimental data from Google's superconducting quantum processor and outperformed state-of-the-art decoders. Though AlphaQubit provides great improvements in decoding accuracy, challenges relating to speed and availability of training data remain for larger-scale applications.

9.2.3 Quantum Algorithms

A quantum algorithm prescribes a set of mathematical operations that inform how qubits are physically manipulated to solve problems. Quantum algorithms are represented as circuits that depict the operations occurring on each qubit. The goal of algorithm design is leveraging the power of quantum mechanics within the constrained resources of the hardware.

Qubit count is probably the most colloquially discussed limitation, but there are other more nuanced considerations. Each step of an algorithm corresponds to some physical operations on the device that take time and provide an opportunity for noise to enter into the system. Therefore, algorithms need to be carefully designed to ensure they can fully realize the benefits of a quantum device, a task where AI has already proven helpful in a number of ways.

There are multiple ways AI can be used to generally improve the performance of most algorithms. One example is quantum circuit synthesis [9]. Circuit synthesis involves finding ways to implement algorithms with compact circuits that require as few operations as possible. Recent work has utilized generative pretrained transformer models, the same model behind "ChatGPT," to generate compact quantum circuits [10].

Another example is quantum circuit compilation. The mathematical description of a quantum circuit needs to be translated into a set of physical operations that will manipulate the physical qubits. Each device is different, so AI can help automate compilation [11] to take into consideration factors like the device layout or the time and quality of each type of operation.

One final example that connects quantum algorithms with the processor and error correction sections is scheduling. Accelerated quantum supercomputing will require many tasks running in concert on a multitude of different processors. Automation with AI can help manage how quantum algorithms and their auxiliary operational tasks are distributed [12, 13] across multiple QPUs, CPUs, and GPUs, such that noise, time, and other important requirements are met.

9.2.4 Recommendations for National Investment in AI for Quantum

AI for quantum is fundamental and will likely become a permanent fixture of practical accelerated quantum supercomputing. Different quantum hardware or end applications might change the specifics of how AI is leveraged, but not its necessity in most cases. This fact has consequences for two regimes, one or both nations will likely encounter while building a robust quantum computing strategy: operating a quantum computer and developing quantum applications.

Some nations are opting to host their own quantum devices to ensure "digital sovereignty" [14]. This will require a sufficient HPC and accelerated computing infrastructure to support the AI and other tasks necessary to operate the devices. This can be a de-risking investment as many of the AI for quantum tasks can be executed on processors that also support other AI applications already used in production today. However, certain time-sensitive tasks, such as quantum error correction, might require investment in hardware that is specialized and tightly integrated with the quantum device.

Regardless of where the hardware is hosted, nations will need to develop hybrid applications that are optimized for accelerated quantum supercomputers. This sort of development will naturally be interdisciplinary as quantum experts, AI practitioners, and domain scientists will need to collaborate. Therefore, an open-source development platform that can be programmed with familiar languages and integrates well with other popular scientific computing tools is ideal. It should also allow code to be written once and run on any quantum computer without the developer needing to make changes. Finally, such a platform must also be highly performant with libraries optimized for a heterogeneous supercomputing infrastructure to ensure maximum utility for hybrid applications.

9.3 Conclusion

Quantum computing will be a powerful accelerator for supercomputers and could help solve some of the hardest problems in the world. AI is already proving to be a powerful enabler of quantum computing, addressing many of the barriers to practical quantum computing and serving as an invaluable research tool. As quantum computers evolve, AI will likely become a critical and permanent fixture of scalable accelerated quantum supercomputers.

Given the massive national security risk posed by a potential "big bang" moment for quantum computing, it is crucial for policymakers to be prepared. Fortunately, from a risk management perspective, the research community is making it abundantly clear that investment in AI supercomputing does not come at the expense of quantum investment. Investment in AI supercomputing is an investment in quantum computing.

References

1. Y. Alexeev, M.H. Farag, T.L. Patti, M.E. Wolf, N. Ares, A. Aspuru-Guzik, S.C. Benjamin, Z. Cai, Z. Chandani, F. Fedele, N. Harrigan, J.-S. Kim, E. Kyoseva, J.G. Lietz, T. Lubowe, A. McCaskey, R.G. Melko, K. Nakaji, A. Peruzzo, S. Stanwyck, N.M. Tubman, H. Wang, T. Costa, Artificial intelligence for quantum computing (2024)
2. M. Krenn, J. Landgraf, T. Foesel, F. Marquardt, Artificial intelligence and machine learning for quantum technologies. Phys. Rev. A **107**, 010101 (2023)
3. P. Vaidhyanathan, F. Marquardt, M.T. Mitchison, N. Ares, Quantum feedback control with a transformer neural network architecture (2024)

4. T. Crosta, L. Rebón, F. Vilariño, J.M. Matera, M. Bilkis, Automatic re-calibration of quantum devices by reinforcement learning (2024)
5. L. Phuttitarn, B.M. Becker, R. Chinnarasu, T.M. Graham, M. Saffman, Enhanced measurement of neutral-atom qubits with machine learning. Phys. Rev. Appl. **22**, 024011 (2024)
6. Y. Kurman, L. Ella, R. Szmuk, O. Wertheim, B. Dorschner, S. Stanwyck, Y. Cohen, Control requirements and benchmarks for quantum error correction, (2024)
7. J. Olle, R. Zen, M. Puviani, F. Marquardt, Simultaneous discovery of quantum error correction codes and encoders with a noise-aware reinforcement learning agent. npj Quantum Inf. **10**, 126 (2024)
8. J. Bausch, A.W. Senior, F.J.H. Heras, T. Edlich, A. Davies, M. Newman, C. Jones, K. Satzinger, M.Y. Niu, S. Blackwell, et al., Learning high-accuracy error decoding for quantum processors. Nature **65**, 1–7 (2024)
9. F.J.R. Ruiz, T. Laakkonen, J. Bausch, M. Balog, M. Barekatain, F.J.H. Heras, A. Novikov, N. Fitzpatrick, B. Romera-Paredes, J. van de Wetering, A. Fawzi, K. Meichanetzidis, P. Kohli, Quantum circuit optimization with alphatensor (2024)
10. K. Nakaji, L.B. Kristensen, J.A. Campos-Gonzalez-Angulo, M.G. Vakili, H. Huang, M. Bagherimehrab, C. Gorgulla, F. Wong, A. McCaskey, J.-S. Kim, T. Nguyen, P. Rao, A. Aspuru-Guzik, The generative quantum eigensolver (GQE) and its application for ground state search (2024)
11. N. Quetschlich, L. Burgholzer, R. Wille, Compiler optimization for quantum computing using reinforcement learning, in *2023 60th ACM/IEEE Design Automation Conference (DAC)* (2023), pp. 1–6
12. P. Promponas, A. Mudvari, L.D. Chiesa, P. Polakos, L. Samuel, L. Tassiulas, Compiler for distributed quantum computing: a reinforcement learning approach (2024)
13. P. Seitz, M. Geiger, C. Ufrecht, A. Plinge, C. Mutschler, D.D. Scherer, C.B. Mendl, SCIM MILQ: An HPC quantum scheduler, in *2024 IEEE International Conference on Quantum Computing and Engineering (QCE)* (2024)
14. G. Gordon, Digital sovereignty, digital infrastructures, and quantum horizons. AI Soc. **39**(1), 125–137 (2024)

Mark Wolf is a technical marketing engineer for quantum computing and HPC at NVIDIA. Before that, he was a technical solutions specialist at Quantinuum. Mark holds a PhD from the University of Georgia in physical chemistry, where his research focused on high-accuracy *ab initio* simulation of small molecules.

Open Access This chapter is licensed under the terms of the Creative Commons Attribution 4.0 International License (http://creativecommons.org/licenses/by/4.0/), which permits use, sharing, adaptation, distribution and reproduction in any medium or format, as long as you give appropriate credit to the original author(s) and the source, provide a link to the Creative Commons license and indicate if changes were made.

The images or other third party material in this chapter are included in the chapter's Creative Commons license, unless indicated otherwise in a credit line to the material. If material is not included in the chapter's Creative Commons license and your intended use is not permitted by statutory regulation or exceeds the permitted use, you will need to obtain permission directly from the copyright holder.

Summary Part I

Part I of this book explored the foundational advancements and current state of quantum computing technologies, providing a comprehensive analysis of quantum hardware approaches, error correction strategies, and early applications in optimization and artificial intelligence.

A comparison of leading quantum hardware technologies was presented, highlighting the distinct strengths and limitations of each approach. Superconducting qubits were noted for their fast gate speeds and compatibility with existing semiconductor processes, though they faced challenges in achieving longer coherence times and scalability. Trapped-ion systems offered high-fidelity operations and extended coherence times, but their slower gate speeds posed performance limitations. Neutral atom platforms showed promise due to their potential for natural scalability and room-temperature operation yet required advancements in gate fidelity and error correction. Semiconductor spin qubits benefited from their compatibility with conventional semiconductor fabrication techniques but were limited by noise and gate fidelity issues. The discussion emphasized the importance of addressing key challenges, particularly error correction, as a critical step in advancing quantum hardware and enabling the transition from noisy intermediate-scale quantum (NISQ) devices to fully fault-tolerant systems.

Table 1 summarizes the key advantages and challenges of each hardware technology and the companies leading their development.

Further developments in quantum computing were examined, with a focus on quantum optimization, quantum annealing, and quantum machine learning (QML), highlighting various ways in which quantum mechanisms could help overcome the limitations of traditional optimization and machine learning approaches. Quantum annealing, pioneered by D-Wave, was presented as a specialized quantum hardware approach for addressing specific combinatorial optimization problems.

The integration of quantum computing with artificial intelligence (AI) and high-performance computing (HPC) was identified as a key enabler of accelerated progress in the field. AI techniques were being applied to optimize quantum control protocols and error correction strategies, while HPC systems played a critical role in managing complex, large-scale quantum workloads.

Table 1 Comparison of quantum hardware technologies

Technology	Advantages	Challenges	Key players
Superconducting qubits	Fast gate speeds, compatible with semiconductor processes	Coherence time, scalability, noise reduction	IBM, Google
Trapped-ion qubits	High fidelity, long coherence times	Slow gate speeds, scaling complexity	IonQ, Quantinuum
Neutral atom qubits	Room-temperature operation, natural scalability	Gate fidelity, error correction	QuEra
Semiconductor spin qubits	Compatibility with existing semiconductor processes	Coherence time, gate fidelities, noise	Intel, IMEC

It was noted that although quantum computing had made substantial advances in theoretical foundations and early hardware demonstrations, the realization of fault-tolerant quantum systems capable of outperforming classical machines in practical scenarios remained one of the most pressing and unresolved challenges in the field.

Part II
Quantum Communication

Part II explores the field of quantum communication, focusing on technologies that promise to secure information in an era where quantum computers pose a significant threat to classical encryption. It examines quantum random number generators (QRNG), quantum key distribution (QKD), and post-quantum cryptography (PQC), highlighting their unique contributions to enhancing security. The part emphasizes both the current applications and limitations of these technologies, including practical deployment challenges and scalability concerns. Additionally, it examines the ongoing debate between QKD and PQC and the growing interest in space-based quantum communication as a way to overcome terrestrial limitations. By addressing both the advancements and the barriers in these fields, Part II provides a comprehensive view of the future of quantum-safe communication.

Chapter 10
Quantum Threats

Rajiv Krishnakumar

Abstract With the recent advancements in quantum computing, there is a threat that today's widely used digital encryption schemes will become vulnerable to cryptography-breaking quantum algorithms. In particular, today's most widely used asymmetric encryption schemes will be the most vulnerable. On the other hand, it is likely that symmetric encryption and hashing schemes will remain robust even with the advent of powerful quantum computers of the future. In addition, today's quantum computers are not powerful enough to implement the asymmetric cryptography-breaking algorithms; however, as quantum computers become more powerful and more research is put into these quantum algorithms, it is only a matter of years before the most widely used asymmetric encryption schemes of today are no longer secure. Therefore, a global effort being led by the *National Institute of Standards and Technology* (NIST) is underway to tackle this issue. As long as these efforts continue to progress at the current pace the potential adverse effects of these cryptography-breaking quantum algorithms are likely to be largely mitigated.

10.1 Introduction

This chapter discusses how quantum computers are on the path to breaking many widely used systems of encryption that exist today and the current state of how this threat is being tackled. However, before delving into the various encryption-breaking algorithms, it is important to establish the basics of the different types of encryption schemes as well as the expected evolution of quantum computers in the near term such that one is aware of exactly which kinds of encryption schemes are at risk and the expected timeline for them to be broken.

R. Krishnakumar (✉)
QuantumBasel, Arlesheim, Switzerland

Center for Quantum Computing and Quantum Coherence (QC2), University of Basel, Basel, Switzerland
e-mail: rajiv.krishnakumar@quantumbasel.com

10.2 Common Types of Encryption

Encryption is the act of taking some information, whether it is physical or digital, and encoding it in such a way that if a third party intercepts a message containing this information, it is very difficult or even impossible for them to interpret the information in any meaningful way. The three most common types of encryption schemes in the digital space are symmetric encryption, asymmetric encryption, and hashing schemes [1].

10.2.1 Symmetric Encryption

A symmetric encryption scheme uses a single secret key, shared beforehand by two parties, that is used to both encode and decode any transmitted information between them. A typical example of a symmetric key is a randomly generated string of bits. Today's symmetric keys typically use 128, 192, or 256 bits. Even taking the smallest number of 128 bits, this results in over 3×10^{38} different possible keys, a number of combinations that would take even the most powerful supercomputer many times the age of the universe to go through, making it impossible for a third party to decode any intercepted message. This is what makes this method of encryption very secure. However, this way of encryption requires both parties to first share the key through a secure channel before being able to send each other messages. In addition, individual separate keys need to be generated every time a new pair of entities would like to share information using symmetric encryption. Therefore, although symmetric encryption is secure when properly implemented, it is difficult to implement efficiently on a global scale. Hence, it is usually used in situations where the information is intended solely for personal use, such as encrypting files on one's own computer, or when the secret key generated during the scheme is used to create secure static items that do not change after they have been initialized (e.g., in credit cards). Although there exist quantum algorithms that are more efficient than their classical counterparts at trying to break symmetric encryption schemes, it is explained later in this chapter how symmetric encryption schemes will still remain secure even with the advent of powerful quantum computers in the future.

10.2.2 Asymmetric Encryption

Asymmetric encryption is a form of encryption that uses two types of keys: a public key and a private key. The public key is used to encode messages and, as the name suggests, is made public to everyone. However, a private key that is different from the public key is required to decode these messages, and using the same public key to try to decode them will not work. This means that any party can create a public key to allow people to send them secure messages without worrying about malicious parties using this public key to decrypt these messages. The ability to have separate keys to encrypt and decrypt messages comes from the fact that asymmetric encryption schemes are based on mathematical problems that are easy to solve one way but difficult to solve in reverse. For example, the most common form of asymmetric encryption known as RSA [2], named after its three inventors Rivest, Shamir, and Adleman in 1978,[1] is based on finding prime factors of a large integer. If one were to give you two prime numbers p and q, finding the answer to $p \times q$ is a very simple task for any computer to do. On the other hand, if one were to give you a large integer and ask for its two prime factors p and q, this would take even the most powerful supercomputer many lifetimes of the universe to find, as long as that integer in question is large enough, such as one composed of 2048 bits, which is typical in today's implementations of RSA.

Compared to symmetric keys, asymmetric keys tend to be more complicated to implement and slower to execute due to the large key sizes. However, they are much easier to use at larger scales given that the public key can be shared in an open channel that everyone can have direct access to. This is why most systems on the internet use asymmetric encryption schemes, including website browsing, e-mail systems, mobile text communications, e-banking, and any other online systems that require a wide range of people to be able to transfer digital information securely.

Although there exist asymmetric encryption schemes other than RSA, the vast majority of the ones in use today—including RSA, elliptic-curve cryptography [3, 4] and Diffie–Hellman [5]—are actually different variations of the same abstract mathematical problem known the *hidden subgroup problem* (HSP). Hence, any method that can break the RSA encryption scheme can be easily adapted to break any of the other schemes based on the HSP. Therefore, the rest of the chapter focuses on the RSA encryption scheme when discussing the breaking of asymmetric encryption schemes using a quantum computer since everything discussed in this context can also be applied to other HSP-based encryption schemes.

10.2.3 Hashing

Hashing is a scheme used to transform data into a unique serial number of fixed length, similar to how different books, regardless of their length, can be represented by an ISBN number of 13 digits. However, in the case of hashing, it is not possible to retrieve the original information from the hash value, assuming the hashing function is properly implemented. Thus, this encryption scheme, although extremely powerful, is used only for very specific tasks, e.g., to store users' passwords without

---

[1] An equivalent system was developed secretly four years prior by the mathematician Clifford Cooks at the British Government Communications Headquarters (GCHQ). However, that system was only declassified in 1997, hence why the encryption was not named after Cooks.

revealing them to the system administrator or as a part of digital signatures creation.[2] To date, there is no evidence that any computer (classical or quantum) will be able to undermine the security of today's most up-to-date hashing algorithms assuming their proper implementations.

10.3 The Timeline to Powerful Quantum Computers

Currently, a few different encryption-breaking quantum algorithms exist. However, before discussing them, it is important to have an understanding of the power of the hardware that they will be implemented on, that is, the power of existing and future quantum computers.

In its infancy, the quantum computing industry aimed to demonstrate the ability to build a very basic quantum computer, including creating and controlling a few qubits in a way that allowed for them to interact with each other for a limited amount of time before being measured at the end of those interactions. Having accomplished this task sometime in the late 1990s [6, 7], another big step was to create more robust versions of these small-qubit quantum computers that could be accessed through the cloud. The first instance of such a machine was made in 2016 [8]. Since then, the quantum hardware industry has been focusing on scaling up quantum computers in terms of computing power (i.e., increasing the number of qubits and decreasing noise) and in terms of accessibility through the cloud. This current era is known as the *noisy intermediate scale quantum* (NISQ) era [9], where we now have a handful of quantum computers accessible through the cloud, each with anywhere between 20 and 200 noisy qubits. This applies primarily to universal gate-based quantum computers, whereas quantum annealers, though they may contain thousands of qubits, represent a more specialized form of quantum computing designed specifically for optimization problems. These computers can perform advanced calculations but are limited in two ways: (1) the size of the input data that can be fed into them is limited due to the limited number of qubits and (2) the number of operations that can be performed sequentially is minimal due to the noise or *decoherence rate* of the qubits. Currently, it is still unknown whether we will find quantum algorithms, whether encryption-breaking or otherwise, that are able to run on NISQ computers that can give us an advantage in speed, accuracy, or energy efficiency over today's classical algorithms that run on CPUs and GPUs in solving practical problems.

However, the NISQ era is only temporary, and the quantum computing community is now working toward the *fault-tolerant* (FT) era, where quantum computers

---

[2] It is important to note here that in digital signature schemes, the hashing is only used to verify the integrity of the data, whereas asymmetric encryption is used to verify the authenticity of it, which makes most current digital signature schemes also vulnerable to cryptographic-breaking quantum algorithms.

will have over a million qubits and can perform many consecutive operations thanks to the implementation of *quantum error correction* protocols. These protocols propose a way to use many additional redundant physical qubits to continuously correct any errors occurring during the computation. Quantum error correction protocols are different from those in classical error correction as the no-cloning theorem prohibits the cloning of an unknown quantum state. The FT era should allow us to run many more complicated quantum algorithms on real hardware, including the famous Shor's algorithm [10] that can break RSA encryption. The timeline of when FT quantum computers will be readily available is a topic of debate, but there is a general agreement that it will occur sometime within the next 5–25 years.

10.4 Quantum Algorithms to Break Encryption

Many quantum algorithms, similar to classical algorithms, work in an iterative way. For example, if one had to create a program to search through a list of N colors and find the row which had the color "orange," the classical algorithm would have to iteratively go through roughly N elements and check if each one matched the word "orange." However, if we were told in advance that the list was ordered alphabetically, we could create a much faster binary search algorithm that would only have to look through roughly $\log_2(N)$ items before finding the word "orange." In a similar sense, many quantum algorithms have an iterative structure. They start by putting all their input states into an equal superposition such that each answer, including all the incorrect ones, has an equal probability of being measured. Then, they use a specific set of quantum operations in an iterative way until the probability of measuring the correct answer is very high (e.g., more than two-third) and the probability of measuring one of the wrong answers is heavily suppressed. The specific set of quantum operations to be implemented iteratively and the number of iterations required to get a sufficiently accurate solution depend on the structure of the problem. Therefore, the way quantum algorithms scale with the size of a problem is use case specific. So, for a given use case, if a quantum algorithm requires many fewer iterations to solve a problem than its most optimal classical counterpart, then it may be said to have achieved a quantum advantage for that problem.

Currently there are several encryption-breaking quantum algorithms that exist that have an advantage over their classical counterparts, leading to a weakening or breaking of different symmetric and asymmetric encryption schemes.

10.4.1 The Robustness of Symmetric Encryption

As discussed earlier, symmetric keys are often produced by randomly generating bit-strings. That means that to break a symmetrically encrypted message, the best way is to randomly try different keys until applying one of them happens to make the encrypted information intelligible. Quantum computing can offer an algorithm that technically can reduce the complexity of this combinatorial task. However, since there is no structure to how the key is generated—as long as the implementation faithfully picks it at random—the best speedup that a quantum computer can offer is a quadratic speedup [11]. This would mean that even if we take keys of only 128 bits, a quantum computer would still have to perform roughly 2×10^{19} iterations of the appropriate set of quantum operations (i.e., roughly the square root of 3×10^{38} iterations mentioned earlier), which although technically weakens the symmetric encryption scheme, still requires far too many iterations to run in any practical time frame, even with future quantum computers from the FT era. And even so, one can just double the key size if one really wants to counteract this slight weakening. Therefore, it is unlikely that quantum computers will ever be a real threat to symmetric encryption schemes.

10.4.2 Established Algorithms to Break Asymmetric Encryption

For asymmetric encryption schemes, the situation is different. Focusing on RSA, the task of an encryption-breaking algorithm is to find the prime factors of a large N-bit (i.e., typically 2048-bit) integer. The state-of-the-art classical algorithm to solve this problem [12] grows exponentially[3] with N, which makes it unusable to solve this problem in any reasonable time frame. However, the famous Shor's algorithm, discovered in 1994 by Peter Shor [10], is a quantum algorithm that only grows as roughly N^2. This algorithm starts by mapping the prime factors problem onto a corresponding period finding problem before solving the latter with the help of a quantum computer. Still, to fully implement this algorithm to factor a 2048-bit integer, we will need an FT quantum computer. Current estimates suggest that a quantum computer with roughly 6000 error-corrected qubits would be enough to run a version of Shor's algorithm that can break RSA-2048 in several hours [13]. It should be noted that to have 6000 error-corrected qubits, one would require orders of magnitude more redundant qubits to perform the error correction during the running of the algorithm, which leads to a little under a million required physical qubits in total. Therefore, we cannot implement this algorithm on today's NISQ computers for meaningful key sizes.

A more recent quantum algorithm to break RSA was discovered by Oded Regev in 2023 [14]. In this algorithm, the prime factors problem is mapped onto a lattice finding problem, which is then solved efficiently with the help of a quantum computer. This algorithm slightly decreases the required number of qubits and

---

[3] Technically it is slightly sub-exponential, but regardless it is not practically usable for large integers.

operations by a small polynomial factor. It is estimated that, in practice, this translates to a reduction in the number of required qubits and operations by a factor of 2–3 when compared to Shor's algorithm, although this is yet to be confirmed with more rigorous resource estimate calculations. However, even if this were confirmed, Regev's algorithm would still require too many resources to be implementable on today's NISQ computers and will likely only have a small effect on the timeline to when an FT quantum computer could implement an RSA-2048-breaking quantum algorithm. In any case, it is useful to keep an eye on the progress of such algorithms due to their potential to shorten the timeline of when quantum computers will be able to break RSA-2048.

10.4.3 Candidate Algorithms to Break Asymmetric Encryption

In addition to the two algorithms mentioned in the previous section, there is a variety of other candidate algorithms that attempt to break RSA-2048 efficiently using near-term NISQ computers that range from unlikely to succeed to almost certainly failing. Still, it is useful to discuss these algorithms to be aware of them just in case progress on one of them renders it successful, but also to understand how some of them fail.

These algorithms can be split up into a few groups. The first one is the set of algorithms that are able to find prime factors of integers, but do not do it more efficiently than the most efficient classical algorithm, and therefore will not be able to break RSA-2048 in any reasonable time frame. These include the quantum version of Schnorr's algorithm [15], the distributed hybrid Shor's algorithm [16], and algorithms based on today's annealing methodologies [17] which are all shown to scale exponentially with the size of the integer being factored. The second category of these algorithms is when the algorithm attempts to use a variational quantum circuit, where, similar to machine learning algorithms, a parametrized quantum circuit is proposed and iteratively optimized via a cost function until it can factor integers [18]. Although there is no proof of the way these algorithms scale, there is strong evidence to suggest that as you increase the size of the integer that you want to factor, the number of quantum operations required increases exponentially. Finally, for the last category, there are some quantum algorithms that can be used to compute prime factors of large integers efficiently using NISQ devices, with the caveat that the solution is encoded in quantum states that require an exponential number of read-out measurements to extract to a sufficiently high precision [19]. This read-out roadblock is likely to be insurmountable given that it is a well-known roadblock that has been studied extensively in many cases. However, if it were circumvented, it would greatly decrease the timeline for when quantum computers could break RSA-2048 encryption.

In addition, the exploration of quantum algorithms could maybe even inadvertently lead to the discovery of efficient classical cryptography-breaking algorithms. Although this is very speculative given the long history of failed attempts at finding such classical algorithms, there may be new ideas arising from the field of quantum algorithms that could be applied to classical algorithms, which slightly increases the chances of the community to find an efficient cryptography-breaking classical algorithm.

10.5 Recommendations for Further Actions

Although today's quantum computers do not have the ability to break asymmetric encryption, it is still imperative that nations, organizations, and individuals around the world start to take appropriate action to defend against this eventuality. For starters, one cannot predict the exact timeline for when this eventuality will occur, so it is recommended to be prepared for it sooner rather than later. In addition, there are likely already initiatives around the world to "harvest now, decrypt later." This is when one intercepts encrypted messages, but instead of immediately trying to decrypt them, one stores them while waiting for quantum computers to become powerful enough to decrypt the messages in the future.

It is always a futile endeavor to try and propose blanket solutions or roadmaps given the diversity of situations in which different countries, organizations, and private citizens find themselves in. Therefore, in this section, we will describe the current efforts of the global cybersecurity community to tackle the threat to cybersecurity by quantum computers and then lay out some potential directions that some of the aforementioned entities can take to integrate the threat of quantum computers into their cybersecurity strategies. Our only recommendation is that each entity consider the extent to which they would like to pursue each of these proposed directions based on their individual circumstances.

Currently, there is an ongoing global initiative led by the United States agency of the *National Institute of Standards and Technology* (NIST) to tackle the cybersecurity risks posed by quantum computers. Although this is an evolving process, the overall effort consists of finding new (classical) asymmetric encoding schemes that are also based on mathematical problems that are easy to solve one way and difficult to solve in reverse. However, unlike mathematical problems based on the HSP, these new problems should still be difficult to solve in reverse, even with advanced quantum computers. Encryption schemes based on these mathematical problems are known as *post-quantum cryptographic* (PQC) schemes. A global competition to find the best new PQC approaches was launched by NIST in 2016, and in 2024, they selected the final encryption standards that are to be used to replace the current ones [20]. The main efforts have now shifted to create guidelines around how to implement these new schemes and disseminate these guidelines, although continuous testing of these new methods and the search for backup schemes are still underway. In addition to PQC schemes, which leverage classical computing to counter the quantum threat, there exists another category of techniques based on quantum communication devices, known as *quantum key distribution* (QKD) schemes. These methods are symmetric encryption schemes, i.e., a scheme in which messages are encoded and decoded with the same key. However, unlike the classical symmetric schemes mentioned in previous sections, QKD methods do not require a secure channel to share the key. This is because the key is generated *and shared* using a quantum protocol that is in theory, mathematically provably secured against any eavesdroppers, unlike PQC schemes where, although there is strong evidence to suggest that they are resistant to known quantum threats, we have no formal mathematical proof of their security for current or future cryptography-breaking quantum algorithms. Nevertheless, QKD requires longer time scales, since it needs a novel hardware infrastructure, and is still very much a field under development. The debate on whether PQC schemes represent the final solution or whether we will eventually need to move to QKD schemes is out of scope for this chapter. In either case, due to the "harvest now, decrypt later" threat, there is a clear need to move to new standards sooner rather than later.

10.5.1 Directions for Governments

One of the directions governments can take is to keep up-to-date with the global initiative led by NIST to tackle this problem and continually evaluate the recommendations and guidelines that come out of this initiative. They can also choose to participate in shaping the solutions and guidelines to the extent desired based proactively to set the standards for PQC or reactively if they find any issues with any of the solutions or recommendations coming out of this initiative. In addition, another possible action of the government is to ensure that the guidelines are being followed and implemented across entities within the country, which includes government offices, private organizations, and private individuals. This involves four main pillars:

1. Ensuring that the encryption standards set by the national standards entity are continuously updated in line with the NIST guidelines
2. Ensuring that sections of the guidelines that are appropriate to the different entities are being disseminated to them as when there are major updates
3. Monitoring that these entities are performing their recommended actions based on the guidelines
4. Providing assistance in this capacity when required

10.5.2 Directions for Private and Public Technology Providers

Technology providers, whether they work at a fundamental level like developing internet infrastructure or at a more customer-facing level like providing software services to end users, are the entities that are affected most by this change in encryption guidelines. In addition to considering the directions for organizational end users described in the next section, they can also consider constantly monitoring and evaluating the new guidelines when they come out and bring up any issues they find with the relevant governmental authorities. In parallel, they can already be working on transitioning the encryption schemes present in their products and services to the new PQC ones and be aware of the evolution of these algorithms and their implementations so that they can keep their implementations up-to-date.

10.5.3 Directions for Organizational End Users

There are two main potential actions for organizational end users. The first one is to ensure that their technology providers are indeed keeping their services up-to-date based on the recommended guidelines as mentioned in the previous section. The second is to perform an inventory of their in-house data encryption to understand which parts of it will be affected by the transition to PQC encryption schemes. For example, a change of encryption scheme in the software that they use can affect the speed of their digital operations. In addition, organizations may be required to update any encryption schemes that affect their local data, either by updating third-party software or by upgrading any in-house software with the new PQC schemes in accordance with the latest implementation guidelines.

10.5.4 Directions for Private Individuals

For private individuals, assuming that they are not heavily involved in the cryptography world, the only potential action is to be aware of the ongoing changes and occasionally read up on its progress at a high level. Although there are no technical actions to take, it is always important for the general public to be aware of changes that affect the privacy of their information, especially if they feel that public and private organizations are not acting in their best interest.

10.6 Conclusion

Cryptography-breaking quantum algorithms already exist, but the hardware to implement them is not yet available. However, it is only a matter of years before quantum computers become powerful enough to be able to implement these algorithms. A global effort being led by NIST is underway to tackle this issue, with a focus on upgrading the asymmetric encryption schemes used around the world today. This focus comes from the fact that asymmetric schemes are the most vulnerable to quantum algorithms, as opposed to symmetric encryption and hashing schemes, which will remain robust even with the advent of advanced quantum computers in the future. As long as the ongoing efforts to tackle this issue continue to progress at the current pace, with the different entities playing their part in the effort, the potential adverse effects of these cryptography-breaking quantum algorithms are likely to be largely mitigated.

References

1. J.A. González, 3 Types of Encryption - Detailed Guide with Pros & Cons (2024)
2. R.L. Rivest, A. Shamir, L. Adleman, A method for obtaining digital signatures and public-key cryptosystems. Commun. ACM **21**(2), 120–126 (1978)
3. V.S. Miller, *Use of Elliptic Curves in Cryptography* (Springer, Berlin, 1986), pp. 417–426
4. N. Koblitz, Elliptic curve cryptosystems. Math. Comput. **48**(177), 203–209 (1987)
5. W. Diffie, M. Hellman, New directions in cryptography. IEEE Trans. Inf. Theory **22**(6), 644–654 (1976)
6. C. Monroe, D.M. Meekhof, B.E. King, W.M. Itano, D.J. Wineland, Demonstration of a fundamental quantum logic gate. Phys. Rev. Lett. **75**(25), 4714–4717 (1995)
7. I.L. Chuang, L.M.K. Vandersypen, X. Zhou, D.W. Leung, S. Lloyd, Experimental realization of a quantum algorithm. Nature **393**(6681), 143–146 (1998)
8. IBM Makes Quantum Computing Available on IBM Cloud to Accelerate Innovation — https://uk.newsroom.ibm.com (2016)
9. J. Preskill, Quantum computing in the NISQ era and beyond. Quantum **2**, 79 (2018)
10. P.W. Shor, Polynomial-time algorithms for prime factorization and discrete logarithms, in *Proceedings of the 35th Annual Symposium on Foundations of Computer Science*, vol. 124 (1994), pp. 124–134
11. C.H. Bennett, E. Bernstein, G. Brassard, U. Vazirani, Strengths and weaknesses of quantum computing. SIAM J. Comput. **26**(5), 1510–1523 (1997)
12. C. Pomerance, A tale of two sieves. Not. Am. Math. Soc. **43**(12), 1473–1485 (1996)
13. C. Gidney, How to factor 2048 bit RSA integers with less than a million noisy qubits (2025)
14. O. Regev, *An Efficient Quantum Factoring Algorithm*, vol. 72(1) (Association for Computing Machinery, New York, NY, 2025). https://dl.acm.org/doi/full/10.1145/3708471. ISSN:0004-5411
15. B. Yan, Z. Tan, S. Wei, H. Jiang, W. Wang, H. Wang, L. Luo, Q. Duan, Y. Liu, W. Shi, Y. Fei, X. Meng, Y. Han, Z. Shan, J. Chen, X. Zhu, C. Zhang, F. Jin, H. Li, C. Song, Z. Wang, Z. Ma, H. Wang, G.-L. Long, Factoring integers with sublinear resources on a superconducting quantum processor (2022)
16. L. Xiao, D. Qiu, L. Luo, P. Mateus, Distributed quantum-classical hybrid Shor's algorithm (2023)
17. C. Wang, Q.-D. Wang, C.-L. Hong, Q.-Y. Hu, Z. Pei, Quantum annealing public key cryptographic attack algorithm based on D-wave advantage. Chinese J. Comput. **47**(5), 1030-1044 (2024)
18. E.R. Anschuetz, J.P. Olson, A. Aspuru-Guzik, Y. Cao, *Variational Quantum Factoring*, in *Quantum Technology and Optimization Problems* (Springer International Publishing, Cham, 2019), pp. 74–85. ISBN: 978-3-030-14082-3
19. D. Biswas, S. Dutta, S. Utagi, P. Mandayam, A modified order-finding algorithm for NISQ devices, in *2024 16th International Conference on COMmunication Systems & NETworkS (COMSNETS)* IEEE (2024)
20. C. Boutin, NIST Releases First 3 Finalized Post-Quantum Encryption Standards. *NIST* (2024). Last Modified: 2024-08-13T11:20-04:00

Rajiv Krishnakumar is a quantum algorithms researcher working at QuantumBasel. He has been in the quantum algorithms space for the past 5 years. His current interests are in understanding how quantum computing can help enhance current AI algorithms, in particular investigating quantum enhancements to reservoir computing to solve time series and classification problems. Previously, Rajiv was at Goldman Sachs, where he first worked as a data scientist on the trading floor, before transitioning to the R&D team, where he worked as a quantum algorithms researcher on applications of quantum computing for finance use cases. Prior to his career in the private sector, Rajiv obtained his PhD in applied physics from Stanford University, where he worked on quantum sensors, after which he pursued a brief postdoctoral fellowship on Quantum Technologies joint with Caltech and AT&T.

Open Access This chapter is licensed under the terms of the Creative Commons Attribution 4.0 International License (http://creativecommons.org/licenses/by/4.0/), which permits use, sharing, adaptation, distribution and reproduction in any medium or format, as long as you give appropriate credit to the original author(s) and the source, provide a link to the Creative Commons license and indicate if changes were made.

The images or other third party material in this chapter are included in the chapter's Creative Commons license, unless indicated otherwise in a credit line to the material. If material is not included in the chapter's Creative Commons license and your intended use is not permitted by statutory regulation or exceeds the permitted use, you will need to obtain permission directly from the copyright holder.

Chapter 11
Quantum Random Number Generators (QRNG)

Bruno Huttner and Gilles Trachsel

Abstract Cryptographic processes rely on randomness to ensure secure encryption by generating unpredictable keys and patterns, thereby preventing attackers from guessing them. This chapter explores various methods for generating randomness, with a focus on Quantum Random Number Generators (QRNGs), which are considered the most secure option for cryptographic implementations. QRNGs leverage the inherent unpredictability of quantum phenomena and are being explored for a variety of use cases, from small devices to large-scale servers, with the potential to enhance security in diverse systems. However, their broader adoption faces limitations, such as cost, scalability, and integration challenges, which must be addressed for widespread practical implementation.

11.1 The Importance of Randomness in Data Security

Random numbers are the building blocks of cryptography and data security. Cybersecurity starts with strong encryption keys. Being secure today and quantum-safe tomorrow means protecting data with keys that are as strong as possible. Given the extent to which random numbers are used to secure our data, it will come as no surprise that the performance and characteristics of random number generators have a strong impact on security. To put it simply, attackers don't crack encryption; they steal or guess keys. Therefore, the strength of random numbers has an immense impact on overall security. Poor quality or insufficient quantity of random numbers can increase the risk of a breach and data loss and reduce security to well below its designed level, making the overall system vulnerable.

B. Huttner (✉)
ID Quantique, Geneva, Switzerland
e-mail: bruno.huttner@idquantique.com

G. Trachsel
QuintessenceLabs, Geneva, Switzerland
e-mail: gilles.trachsel@bluewin.ch

Indeed, many real-world security issues have resulted from poor random number generators. Some examples are given below:

- In Taiwan, weak random numbers used for the nation's digital ID system enabled attackers to carry out identity theft [1].
- Public keys generated in the RSA security protocol were based on improperly generated random numbers, allowing simple factoring of keys, and therefore, access to the protected data [2].
- In 2013, the RSA crypto library was discovered to have a backdoor in its PRNG, believed to allow the NSA to access those numbers to aid in decrypting protected data [3].
- The Java platform still relies on a linear congruential generator (LCG) for its PRNG, long known to be of low quality [4].
- Weak random numbers, along with a weakness in the authentication protocol, allowed any key in a cryptographic RFID system to be found in a matter of seconds [5].

This list is not exhaustive—there are many more similar examples—but it shows that poor quality random numbers present issues ranging from obvious and known to unnoticed and unknown.

Unfortunately, generating good randomness is not so easy. This stems from the fact that our classical world is deterministic. The evolution of a physical system with known initial conditions can, in principle, be entirely determined. Quantum systems are different. Measurement of a quantum system gives random results. This is the basis for *Quantum Random Number Generators* (QRNGs). Today, QRNGs based on different quantum systems are available for practical applications. QRNG chips offer low cost and small form factors and can be integrated into most computing devices. High-end QRNGs with faster rates can be integrated as appliances into data centers, for example, to enhance the security of cloud applications. Thanks to QRNGs, good randomness can now be implemented.

11.2 Analysis

11.2.1 Entropy and Randomness

Although often used interchangeably, the two notions of entropy and randomness are not identical. These concepts can be made more precise by using the NIST Special Publication (SP) 800-90 series of Recommendations [6–8]. A *random number generator* (RNG) or *random bit generator* (RBG)[1] is usually made of two

---

[1] An RBG generates a string of bits, zeros and ones only, while an RNG generates a string of numbers. However, since the transition from RBG to RNG is a well-defined mathematical process, both will be used interchangeably in this chapter.

parts, an entropy source and a *deterministic random bit generator* (DRBG), which processes the entropy and provides random numbers. In some specific instances, where full entropy is required, the DRBG may be omitted and replaced by an entropy extraction scheme. This will be discussed in Sect. 11.2.2.4. In all cases, the entropy source is a physical system, which either generates entropy itself or collects it from external noise. Since physical systems cannot be perfect, the entropy generated by such systems cannot be perfect either. This is measured by the value of the entropy per bit of the generator. A perfect system should produce one bit of entropy per bit. An imperfect one will produce less than one bit of entropy per bit. Fortunately, if the entropy per bit is known, it can still be used as the input of the DRBG. The requirement is that the total entropy of the string exceeds the amount of input entropy required by the DRBG. Therefore, if the entropy source does not have perfect entropy, but still has a known entropy per bit, it is sufficient to use a longer string as the input of the DRBG. The requirements for the entropy source are described in the NIST SP 800-90B recommendation [7].

11.2.2 Methods for Entropy Generation

11.2.2.1 External Noise

One method to generate entropy is to rely on external noise. The entropy source captures a signal, which is deemed to be random. For example, one can extract randomness from small movements of the mouse of a computer, from timing of user-generated processes, or even from a signal coming from faraway stars. This method is quite limited in the entropy rate and relies on the availability and quality of this noise, which cannot be guaranteed. It cannot be used in isolated locations, where no external connection is available. Evaluating the entropy per bit of the source, as required by the DRBG, is usually difficult to assess. In addition, if the same noise is available to others, it cannot be used for cryptographic purposes, which require secrecy of the source. For example, the NIST broadcasts an entropy beacon with guaranteed perfect entropy [9]. It is clearly specified that this source should not be used for cryptographic purposes. As a result of the above, an external entropy source should only be used in special circumstances.

11.2.2.2 Chaotic Processes

A second method is to use a classical chaotic process. A chaotic system is a deterministic system, which is very sensitive to initial conditions, so that, even when the initial state is known well, the systems will quickly evolve into a state, which is impossible to predict. Many such systems have been used as entropy sources, from so-called lava lamps [10] to electronic oscillators. There are two limitations to these chaotic systems. One, the state of the system at time $t+1$ results from the evolution of the same system at time t, so there is always a logical link between two successive outputs. They cannot be truly independent as required for genuine entropy generation. Two, new mathematical methods such as machine learning and possibly the quantum computer will improve the previsions on the evolution of a chaotic system. For example, improved models enable better precision in weather forecasts, which is a chaotic system. The same may apply to the different chaotic systems used to provide entropy. The evolution of a chaotic system may not look so random after these improvements. All the above make the evaluation of the entropy per bit difficult. The quality of the entropy will also diminish with time, as technology evolves.

11.2.2.3 Quantum Systems

The third method, based on quantum systems, is the easiest to analyze theoretically. This comes from the fact that quantum mechanics is a nondeterministic theory. A quantum system can be prepared in a perfectly well-characterized state, with no uncertainty. However, under suitably chosen conditions, measuring this state produces a random result. At least theoretically, there is absolutely no link between the result of a measurement on one quantum system and the result of the measurement of the consecutive one. This verifies the independence requirement on successive measurements by design. In addition, the theory provides a good estimate of the entropy per bit for each system. Imperfections in the system and in the design can be analyzed in detail and taken into account in the estimation of the value of the entropy per bit. The physical processes at play in the underlying physical model are simpler compared to classical entropy sources based on complicated processes believed to be too difficult to model and predict. The simpler design may also lead to increased resistance to tampering and higher quality of initial entropy before extraction.

Although quantum entropy sources were initially considered as more complex and harder to implement than other types of entropy sources, this is now changing. Complete QRNG chips, which include the entropy source and the DRBG, are available commercially. They have a small enough form factor to be integrated into most IoT devices. Their power consumption can even be lower than for RNGs based on classical entropy sources.

11.2.2.4 Full Entropy

In some instances, such as the generation of the keys in quantum key distribution, or when the RNG is used by many users, as in large data centers, it is necessary to have a full entropy source. This means that the entropy has to be perfect: one bit of entropy per bit of the string. In this case, one has to implement an entropy extraction scheme. This is a computation which receives the bit strings generated by the entropy source with known entropy per bit and processes them to get shorter but almost perfect entropy strings. The cost is that the final rate of the entropy source is lower than the initial rate. The source generates fewer bits, but they are of higher quality. This type of source can be built from chaotic processes, but is best obtained from quantum systems.

11.2.3 *From Entropy Source to Random Number Generators*

The combination of an entropy source, which is a physical system, and of a DRBG, which is a deterministic algorithm, is necessary to create an RBG. The requirements for the construction of the DRBG are described by the NIST SP 800-90A recommendation [6]. The entropy source provides the necessary entropy input for the DRBG. The DRBG generates the strings of random bits, which can then be processed to provide random numbers. The way to build the complete random number generator from these two components is described in the NIST SP 800-90C recommendation [8].

The different types of RNGs are described in Table 11.1. The most widely used random number generators are pseudo-random number generators (PRNGs), which rely on mathematical algorithms and the presence of a secure seed. Carefully designed PRNGs pass statistical randomness tests and, therefore, provide good randomness. However, they are fundamentally predictable and deterministic once the seed is known. The security of a PRNG used for cryptographic applications depends entirely on the quality and the security of the seed. Therefore, it is very

Table 11.1 The different types of random number generators

Method	Description	Pros and cons	Entropy
Pseudo-random number generator (PRNG)	Uses algorithms to generate random numbers from a short random seed or entropy source	+ Capable of high throughputs	Based on the seed or entropy source renewal
		− Attacker can derive random number from knowledge of the seed	
Hardware/true random number generator (TRNG)	Measures a physical phenomenon expected to be random	+ Can deliver high-quality random	Dependant on physical source
		− Rate-limited until enough entropy is sampled to meet the demand	
Quantum random number generator (QRNG)	Provides randomness from quantum effects	+ Full entropy, throughput depending on form factor; instant delivery of high-quality random for all crypto keys	Full entropy
		− Specialized hardware	

important to combine the PRNG with a solid seeding mechanism based on a good entropy source, which renews the seed regularly. The possible entropy sources have been discussed in Sect. 11.2.2. A limitation of such RNGs is that the random numbers are derived from a single seed at a time. For security reasons, they cannot be shared by different users but should be restricted to single-user applications, such as a PC, smartphone, or IoT device.

A second type of random number generator is capable of producing random numbers directly from an entropy source. This is known as a true random number generator (TRNG). The random processes in TRNGs usually refer to classical physical processes like thermal noise, atmospheric turbulence, or internally generated chaotic processes [11]. Even though these TRNGs can generate large amounts of entropy, the fundamental physics behind these classical processes is still deterministic. The unpredictability comes from the complexity of the physical system, whose evolution is hard to predict or simulate.

Thanks to the inherent random nature of quantum mechanics, quantum random number generators (QRNGs) can, in principle, yield true random numbers which are mathematically unpredictable and nondeterministic. Compared to other quantum technologies, QRNGs are usually simpler and more mature and are ready to be implemented to solve real-life challenges.

The main features that set QRNGs apart from traditional TRNGs are the following:

- They rely on quantum features to generate new, physically fundamental randomness. This is in stark contrast to traditional TRNGs, which are based on unknown, but, in principle, knowable information implicitly preexistent in a physical device, a kind of information that could even be potentially implanted.
- Certification and validation are helped by the relatively simple physics and simple randomness-generation processes that are at the basis of QRNGs.
- The entropy source can be high-quality, meaning that the entropy generated requires a minimum amount of post-processing to produce perfect random numbers.

11.2.4 Standards and Testing

Perfect random number generators must produce "unlikely" sequences of random numbers at exactly the right average rate. Since these events may happen very infrequently, a large amount of data is necessary before any test can be run. Therefore, detecting flaws in RNGs based on their output is complex. Statistical tests, such as Diehard, ENT, and Rabbit, have been the dominant method of validating the randomness of RNGs. The NIST has standardized a series of statistical tests in a document [12]: "A Statistical Test Suite for Random and Pseudorandom Number Generators for Cryptographic Applications," known as SP800-22.

Unfortunately, although this testing suite was designed to push weak generators to an unambiguous failure, passing these statistical tests is not sufficient for cryptographic applications. Some RNGs can easily pass these tests but offer no security at all. There are two main components required to build trust in the output of an RNG:

- Testing the randomness of the sequences that it produces through these statistical tests
- Knowing and validating the process through which those sequences are produced

Both components are essential. As explained above, the first deals with the quality of the random sequences that can be ascertained by checking output sequences through a suite of tests and handling the RNG as a black box, that is, without caring about the inner workings of the RNG. The second ensures that the inner workings of the RNG are designed to provide security. The construction of RNGs is described in the NIST series of Special Publications, 800-90A (Deterministic Random Bit Generators), 800-90B (Entropy Sources Used for Random Bit Generators), and 800-90C (Recommendation for Random Bit Generator Constructions).

Furthermore, NIST has also developed the so-called Cryptographic Module Validation Program (CMVP). Random number generation being so central to cryptography, the CMVP makes use of an entropy source that has been evaluated according to the NIST Entropy Source Validation (ESV) program requirement (SP 800-90B) [7]. The CMVP requires that all FIPS 140-2 and FIPS 140-3 module validation submissions include documentation justifying conformance to SP 800-90B, if applicable. Parties developing cryptographic solutions used by the US government will have to be certified according to the CMVP program of NIST and therefore use an ESV-certified RNG.

11.2.5 Trends

The development of quantum computers has brought new threats to cryptography and on cybersecurity. As far as randomness is concerned, there are two different aspects. One, the need for randomness is quantitatively higher with the newly developed *post-quantum cryptography* (PQC) algorithms than with current public-key cryptosystems. For example, while current cryptosystems, such as RSA, which are based on factorization, need two large random primes, lattice-based PQC requires generating large random matrices. In addition, with most PQC algorithms, the keys are longer, which, in turn, rely on more randomness. Faster, good quality RNGs are a must. Two, the quantum computer and new machine learning techniques may improve the predictions of the trajectories of chaotic systems, thus reducing the security of chaos-based RNGs. Since QRNGs are not based on mathematical analysis, they will remain immune to this issue. Today, RNGs, which are used in devices with long lifetimes, such as automotive, critical infrastructures, or satellites should be based on quantum sources.

One interesting aspect of randomness is that mixing different sources can only improve the randomness. One example suffices. Adding a random string to a completely deterministic string, say a string built from ones only, still gives a random string where all zeros become ones. Therefore, one should not rely on a single entropy source, which may become compromised. Instead, it is preferable to mix entropy from different sources, if possible based on different technologies. Many computing devices include an entropy source in the processor. Adding a quantum entropy source ensures improved randomness, which will remain valid in the long run. Replacing an entropy source does not make much sense. Adding an extra entropy source improves the security.

Today, QRNGs rely on a precise characterization of the device in order to know the quality of the entropy generated and to be able to apply the correct processing. A unique aspect of quantum is that it is possible to reduce this need for characterization. A *measurement device independent* (MDI) QRNG is a QRNG where the user controls the source, but can give the measurement part to an adversary, while being assured of the quality of the entropy [13]. This is achieved by switching between different inputs. Any attempt by the adversary to deviate from the agreed protocol or any imperfection in the measurement devices will be discovered by the user. As long as these attempts or these imperfections are suitably small, the user can still extract good random numbers. The ultimate security, where the users can give the whole QRNG device to an adversary is the *device independent* (DI) QRNG [14]. In DI-QRNG, two independent users provide some classical input, typically bits, to a potential adversary, who is in charge of generating pure random numbers, according to an agreed-upon process. The two users only need to examine and process the data provided by the adversary to check whether they followed the protocol, or if there were deviations, which could be due to imperfect devices or true cheating attempts. An added bonus of this scheme is that the freshness of the random numbers can be assured. The adversary could not pretend to perform the measurements while only giving prerecorded data. Technically, to assess the scheme, the users will calculate if a Bell inequality is verified. As for MDI-QRNG, small enough deviations can be corrected and good random numbers can be extracted. The situation is similar to the case of *quantum key distribution* (QKD). In MDI-QRNG, DI-QRNG, or QKD, it is not possible to prevent an adversary from attacking the systems. However, attacks can either be corrected, if they are weak enough—this covers mostly imperfections in the devices—or discovered, to allow the protocol to abort before causing damage to the crypto function. Both MDI-QRNG and DI-QRNG have been implemented experimentally [13, 15], but still at an academic level. In addition, the higher the security, the lower the QRNG rate. Both systems are unsuitable for practical applications yet. They will become so once the technology evolves and will provide the highest level of security.

Implementing QRNGs in practical applications still faces some challenges. The main hurdle is that they require specialized quantum hardware, such as photodetectors and optical components, which can be expensive and difficult to integrate into existing systems. This has been mostly solved for QRNG chips, which may soon be integrated directly into computer chips. For high-throughput systems, which are required for large-scale data centers and high-speed environments, distributed systems or larger appliances are available. In addition, although there are a growing number of QRNG companies and solutions available, they are still relatively limited in comparison to traditional random number generators. A solid ecosystem must be developed. Finally, integration with existing software, hardware, and cryptographic protocols may require a significant development effort, and the initiative toward universal standards and certification processes is still ongoing.

11.3 Implementations and Use Cases

QRNGs have two major implementations. Small form-factor, low-power QRNG chips are integrated inside small information-processing devices with single users. Larger QRNG appliances, with high rates, are preferred for datacenter applications, with large number of different users.

The small chips have found applications in Samsung smartphones [16], Thales hardware security modules [17], Hitachi encryption cards [18], and many others. Within the Eagle program of the *European Space Agency* (ESA), a customized chip has been tested for space applications [19]. Satellites will soon be able to use QRNGs to improve the security of data transmissions. Indeed, any information processing system would benefit from adding a QRNG to its existing entropy generation devices.

In data centers and for Entropy-as-a-Service (EaaS) infrastructure, there is a need for much higher rates of randomness. A server can have to deal with thousands of processes in parallel, each requiring randomness. Today, QRNG appliances with bandwidth in the GHz regions are available, which will be enough for this type of application [20, 21].

QRNGs are the ideal solution in many scenarios or circumstances because of their fundamental properties. This is particularly true in those cases where any potential practical downsides related to speed, size, or cost can be overlooked because of substantial gains. What kinds of threat scenarios and use cases might already seriously benefit from the properties of QRNGs? Experts' opinions indicate the following ones as best fit for QRNGs:

- Those protecting high-value assets and critical systems. This may include confidential information to be shared in encrypted form or authentication for access to strategic applications and databases, at the military, governmental, or enterprise level, particularly in the financial sector.
- In terms of security, integrated QRNG could help to overcome faulty private key generation in smartcards or cryptographic modules, which need to generate the keys internally. Secure device keying during manufacturing (e.g., IoT, automotive, consumer electronics), especially for products expected to be in use for a long time.

- In cryptography, high-value keying material for cryptographic functions (e.g., military applications, certifying authority key generation using HSMs). Keying for health-related data to be stored for decades.
- The security claim of QKD devices requires information-theoretically secure random numbers. There is no way to validate this assumption without physical, certifiable randomness.
- Those where the ability to ensure the random nature of the numbers generated is paramount to guarantee fairness and to establish or maintain trust.

11.4 Final Recommendations for End-Users

1. Carefully consider where your random numbers are coming from. Random numbers are critically important to cybersecurity systems; simply put, if someone can discover the random numbers, then they will be able to compute the security keys protecting your data. Random numbers are most likely coming from your operating system, unless you are specifically asking for them from something else. While the operating system may be good at collecting randomness from various hardware components and system events around it, all of the places from which the OS would source randomness are virtualized when you move to the cloud, and security assumptions made by the OS designers may no longer hold true.
2. Consider RNG exhaustion. Some implementations of traditional RNGs can temporarily run out of entropy and, depending on the implementation, may tell the requesting application using an error message. If the error is ignored by the application, then the application may mistakenly use nonrandom numbers for critical operations.
3. Consider upgrading to a QRNG for instantly improving your current security posture and also when upgrading to post-quantum cryptography. For better quantum-computing resistance, QRNGs offer higher-quality random numbers than PRNGs; they also offer improved ease of verification or certification and real-time health checks with respect to traditional TRNGs. Given the effort to be spent in moving to a quantum-safe solution, it is reasonable to strengthen the source of randomness used at the same time, choosing one of the highest possible quality and reliability. There is the expectation that the QRNG take-up will increase considerably in the next 10 years. Quantum random number generators, although relatively new emerging tools, are mature and proven. They are now commercially available from various vendors, in different form factors, from system-on-chip (SoC), to high-end appliances and Cloud-based services. They should be given proper consideration for the added value and unique properties they offer, particularly for products and services that are required to protect high-value critical assets for a long time. Despite some limitations, QRNGs offer unparalleled security and represent a significant step forward in the quest for enhanced data security solutions, today and tomorrow.

11.5 Conclusion

QRNGs are increasingly being explored as practical commercial systems, with potential applications ranging from integration into information processing devices to use in appliances within large data centers. With advancements in technology and computing, such as machine learning, the security of traditional RNGs is being reevaluated, raising concerns about their robustness. QRNGs, leveraging the inherent unpredictability of quantum phenomena, are designed to address these vulnerabilities. While adding a QRNG to existing cybersecurity infrastructures may enhance security, its feasibility and cost-effectiveness depend on the specific application and system requirements. However, barriers such as the cost of specialized hardware, scalability challenges, and integration complexities still limit their broader adoption.

References

1. D. Goodin, Fatal Crypto Flaw in Some Government-Certified Smartcards Makes Forgery a Snap. Ars Technica, 2013-09-16
2. A.K. Lenstra et al., Ron was Wrong, Whit is Right. International Association for Cryptologic Research (2012)
3. N. Perlroth, N.S.A. Able to Foil Basic Safeguards of Privacy on Web. The New York Times, 2013-09-05
4. M. Tibouchi, P.-A. Fouque, J.C. Zapalowicz, Recovering private keys generated with weak PRNGs, in *4th IMA International Conference on Cryptography and Coding, 2013-12-17*
5. K. Nohl et al., Reverse-engineering a cryptographic RFID Tag, in *SS'08 Proceedings of the 17th Conference on Security Symposium, 2008-07-28*
6. Recommendation for Random Number Generation Using Deterministic Random Bit Generators. https://csrc.nist.gov/pubs/sp/800/90/a/r1/final
7. Recommendation for the Entropy Sources Used for Random Bit Generation. https://csrc.nist.gov/pubs/sp/800/90/b/final
8. Recommendation for Random Bit Generator (RBG) Constructions. https://csrc.nist.gov/pubs/sp/800/90/c/4pd
9. Interoperable Randomness Beacons. https://csrc.nist.gov/projects/interoperable-randomness-beacons
10. J. Liebow-Feeser, LavaRand in Production: The Nitty-Gritty Technical Details. https://blog.cloudflare.com/lavarand-in-production-the-nitty-gritty-technical-details
11. X. Ma, X. Yuan, Z. Cao, B. Qi, Z. Zhang, Quantum random number generation. npj Quantum Inf. **2**, 1601 (2016)
12. A Statistical Test Suite for Random and Pseudorandom Number Generators for Cryptographic Applications. https://csrc.nist.gov/pubs/sp/800/22/r1/upd1/final
13. N. You-Qi et al., Experimental measurement-device-independent quantum random-number generation. Phys. Rev. A **94**, 060301 (2016)
14. R. Colbeck, R. Renner, Free randomness can be amplified. Nat. Phys. **8**, 450–453 (2012)
15. Y. Liu et al., Device independent quantum random number generation. Nature **562**, 548–451 (2018)
16. B. Baker, Samsung Launches Smartphone with Quantum Chip for Security. https://www.iotworldtoday.com/quantum/samsung-launches-smartphone-with-quantum-chip-for-security
17. Quantum Enhanced Keys. https://www.thalestct.com/quantum-enhanced-keys/

18. H. Yoshida, Hitachi ABB Provides Quantum Safe encryption. https://community.hitachivantara.com/blogs/hubert-yoshida/2021/08/11/hitachi-abb-provides-quantum-safe-encryption
19. ID Quantique joins EAGLE-1, Europe's pioneering quantum key distribution initiative. https://www.idquantique.com/id-quantique-joins-eagle-1-europes-pioneering-quantum-key-distribution-initiative/
20. qStream™ 200 Plus. https://info.quintessencelabs.com/hubfs/PDFs/QuintessenceLabs-qStream-200-Plus-Product-Sheet.pdf
21. API3 Integrates QuintessenceLabs to Provide QRNG Service. https://www.prnewswire.com/news-releases/api3-integrates-quintessencelabs-to-provide-qrng-service-301782474.html

Bruno Huttner is the Director of Strategic Quantum Initiatives, and a quantum key distribution expert at ID Quantique. He is also the co-chairman of the Quantum-Safe Security Working Group (QSS WG) organized by the Cloud Security Alliance. Bruno joined ID Quantique in 2014, participating in business development and product management in the Quantum Security division. He then started the space programs, aiming at developing quantum key distribution globally, using satellites. Bruno is an engineer (Ecole Centrale Paris) and a physicist (PhD from the Technion, Israel Institute of Technology).

Gilles Trachsel As Vice President at QuintessenceLabs, Gilles Trachsel is responsible for managing all business development activities for the company across the EMEA theatre and India, working with governments and commercial organizations worldwide to secure the post-quantum computing future. Before joining QuintessenceLabs, Gilles worked at ID Quantique for 6 years, holding various functions and responsibilities and gaining a solid expertise in quantum cryptography and QRNG, with major successful worldwide market introductions for both technologies. Previously, Gilles spent more than 10 years at Juniper Networks Ltd., being responsible for the product and solutions marketing for the whole enterprise portfolio throughout the EMEA region and being also in charge of the Advanced Technologies division, covering Eastern and Southeastern Europe. Prior to this, Gilles held several EMEA and Asia Pacific positions with Peribit Networks (successful US startup), U.S. Robotics, and 3Com. Gilles is an engineer, holding a master's degree in telecommunication.

Open Access This chapter is licensed under the terms of the Creative Commons Attribution 4.0 International License (http://creativecommons.org/licenses/by/4.0/), which permits use, sharing, adaptation, distribution and reproduction in any medium or format, as long as you give appropriate credit to the original author(s) and the source, provide a link to the Creative Commons license and indicate if changes were made.

The images or other third party material in this chapter are included in the chapter's Creative Commons license, unless indicated otherwise in a credit line to the material. If material is not included in the chapter's Creative Commons license and your intended use is not permitted by statutory regulation or exceeds the permitted use, you will need to obtain permission directly from the copyright holder.

Chapter 12
Trends in Quantum Key Distribution (QKD)

Sebastian Kish, Josef Pieprzyk, and Seyit Camtepe

Abstract Quantum key distribution (QKD) is a technology designed to enhance secure communication by utilizing principles of quantum mechanics, such as quantum uncertainty and the no-cloning theorem. This chapter provides an overview of the current state and trends in QKD, highlighting advancements in single-photon sources and detection technologies that are gradually moving QKD toward broader adoption, including early deployments in practical settings. It also addresses challenges such as cost, integration into existing systems, standardization efforts, and the development of quantum repeaters needed for long-distance communication. While still facing hurdles, QKD's potential to achieve information-theoretic security positions it as a promising approach for protecting mission-critical communications against future quantum threats and complementing quantum-safe cryptographic algorithms and protocols.

12.1 Introduction

Recent advancements have led to the development of quantum computers, which pose a potential threat to many of the encryption algorithms currently in use. In response, quantum key distribution (QKD) has emerged as a promising technology for secure communication, leveraging the principles of quantum mechanics rather than relying on assumptions about an adversary's computational power. Global efforts are underway to connect individual QKD links into larger testbed networks, paving the way toward practical and commercially viable solutions. Countries such

---

S. Kish (✉) · S. Camtepe
CSIRO, Canberra, ACT, Australia
e-mail: Sebastian.Kish@data61.csiro.au; Seyit.Camtepe@data61.csiro.au

J. Pieprzyk
Institute of Computer Science, Polish Academy of Sciences, Warsaw, Poland

CSIRO, Canberra, ACT, Australia
e-mail: Josef.Pieprzyk@data61.csiro.au

as China and Japan are making significant progress in advancing QKD technology through large-scale research and development initiatives, while Switzerland has distinguished itself in commercializing QKD. However, its implementations remain limited by scalability, as it is suitable for relatively short distances, and cost-effectiveness, as it requires dedicated point-to-point links. Overcoming these challenges presents an opportunity for international collaboration between industry and governments to shape the future of secure communications.

12.1.1 Challenges and Opportunities

Quantum computers will soon threaten secure data traffic, necessitating new cryptographic methods. Current cryptography relies on symmetric encryption (e.g., AES) and public-key encryption, with the latter often used to distribute symmetric keys. While symmetric encryption is less vulnerable, Grover's algorithm weakens AES-256 to a 128-bit security level. However, public-key methods like RSA are significantly more at risk due to Shor's algorithm, which provides an exponential speedup for breaking these systems. This highlights the need for quantum-safe solutions, such as quantum key distribution (QKD), which leverages quantum mechanics to securely exchange symmetric keys and detect eavesdropping, making it immune to quantum and classical computational advances. Unlike post-quantum cryptography (PQC), which relies on unproven assumptions about mathematical problem hardness, QKD provides a future-proof solution, mitigating the risk of "store now, decrypt later" attacks and ensuring long-term data confidentiality without dependency on computational assumptions.

12.1.2 Definition of QKD

All QKD protocols are executed by two parties, Alice and Bob, as depicted in Fig. 12.1. Their goal is to establish a common and secret key K. An adversary, Eve, is assumed to have access to the communication channels they use. Alice and Bob are connected by both unidirectional quantum and bidirectional classical channels. The *quantum channel* can be optical fiber or alternatively free space, which is able to transmit photons. The *classical channel* is assumed to be authenticated, i.e., a receiver is able to verify if a message comes from an alleged sender. It can be implemented by appending a digital signature or message authentication code (MAC) to the message. A key management system (KMS) is used to manage keys that can also function as a standard-based key scheduler for shared randomness. QKD's security is rooted in two fundamental principles of quantum mechanics: the *no-cloning* theorem and the quantum *uncertainty* principle.

The no-cloning theorem states that it is impossible to create an exact copy of an arbitrary unknown quantum state. This principle underpins the security of QKD

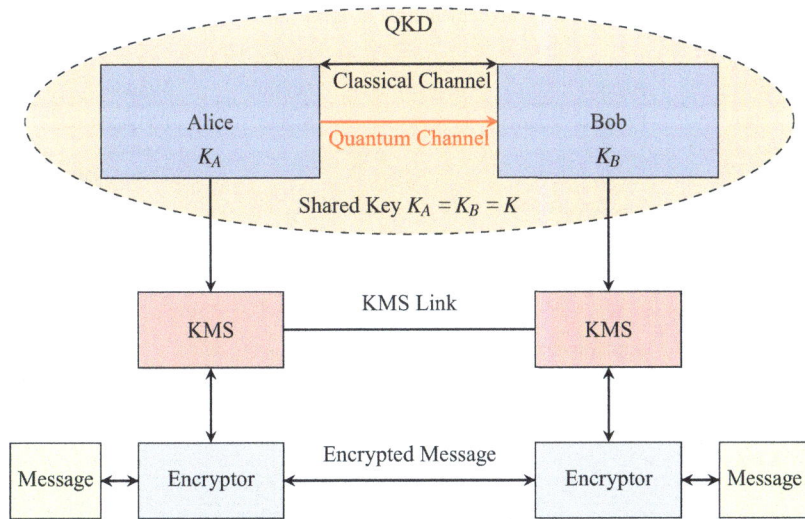

Fig. 12.1 Quantum key distribution (QKD) system

because it prevents an eavesdropper like Eve from intercepting photons sent by Alice to Bob and duplicating them to avoid detection. Any attempt by Eve to measure or clone the quantum states will inevitably disturb them, introducing detectable anomalies.

Additionally, the quantum uncertainty principle ensures that certain pairs of properties (e.g., position and momentum, or orthogonal polarization states) cannot be simultaneously measured with perfect accuracy. In the context of QKD, if Eve attempts to intercept and measure the quantum states sent by Alice, her actions will disturb the states in a way that introduces errors in the key generation process. Bob can detect these disturbances by comparing a subset of their measurement results with Alice's through an authenticated public channel. If the error rate exceeds a predefined threshold, Alice and Bob know the communication has been compromised and can discard the affected key.

Through this process, Alice and Bob can ensure that their key is secure, even in the presence of a potential eavesdropper, provided they have an authenticated communication channel for exchanging classical information.

12.2 Maturity of QKD Technology

12.2.1 QKD Systems

The development of QKD systems has reached a level of technical maturity, with multiple vendors producing commercially available products tailored for

Table 12.1 QKD protocol security, implementation maturity, and vendors

Protocol	Aspect	Current	Future outlook	Vendors
Decoy-state (includes BB84)	Protocol security	Proven[a]	Stable[a]	ID Quantique, Toshiba, ThinkQuantum
	Implementation maturity	Promising[a]	Mature[a]	
Gaussian-modulated CV-QKD	Protocol security	Proven[a]	Stable[a]	QuintessenceLabs, LuxQuanta
	Implementation maturity	Improving[a]	Mature[a]	
Discrete-modulated CV-QKD (e.g., QPSK)	Protocol security	Developing[b]	Promising[a]	Huawei, AIT
	Implementation maturity	Moderate[b]	Improving[a]	
Coherent one-way	Protocol security	Developing[b]	Promising[a]	ID Quantique, QNu Labs
	Implementation maturity	Moderate[b]	Improving[a]	
Entanglement-based protocols (e.g., E91)	Protocol security	Proven[a]	Stable[a]	S-Fifteen, Toshiba, ID Quantique
	Implementation maturity	Challenging[c]	Developing[b]	
Twin-field QKD	Protocol security	Promising[a]	Advancing[a]	Toshiba demo (not yet available)
	Implementation maturity	Challenging[c]	Developing[b]	

[a] Technology is developed
[b] Technology is not yet fully developed but is progressing
[c] Technology is considered fundamentally or practically difficult to develop

various applications. Companies like ID Quantique, Toshiba, QuintessenceLabs, and LuxQuanta are leading efforts to commercialize QKD, offering solutions that integrate seamlessly into existing communication infrastructures. These vendors provide systems based on diverse protocols, such as decoy-state BB84, Gaussian-modulated CV-QKD, and Coherent One-Way QKD, each optimized for different use cases, as summarized in Table 12.1.

Over the past two decades, advancements in single-photon sources and detection technologies have significantly reduced costs, making QKD more accessible. In particular, the development and widespread adoption of avalanche photodiodes (APDs) for the decoy-state QKD protocol have eliminated the reliance on costly superconducting nanowire single-photon detectors (SNSPDs), which require cryogenic cooling. For example, Toshiba's proprietary T12 protocol leverages APDs and other cost-effective single-photon technologies to achieve key distribution over distances of up to 150 km [1]. These innovations are crucial in reducing the cost barriers associated with QKD systems, enabling their deployment in more affordable and scalable configurations.

Other approaches to reduce costs and enhance compatibility with existing optical communication systems include Continuous-Variable QKD (CV-QKD). QuintessenceLabs Inc., an Australian company, has released a product based on the GG02 protocol and heterodyne detection. These protocols, while less expensive compared to discrete-variable QKD systems, are limited in range due to phase-locking noise. Similarly, LuxQuanta has introduced a CV-QKD system available through the AWS Marketplace, demonstrating growing commercial interest in this cost-effective approach to quantum-secure communication.

To further reduce production costs, ID Quantique has developed a product based on the coherent one-way QKD protocol. Although this protocol currently lacks a fully proven information-theoretic security proof, it leverages off-the-shelf components to provide a more practical and scalable solution. Such advancements make quantum communication systems increasingly accessible to a broader range of users, particularly for enterprise applications.

These QKD protocol developments, as summarized in Table 12.1, illustrate the ongoing progress in making QKD systems more affordable, scalable, and adaptable to existing communication infrastructure, driving broader adoption across industries.

12.2.2 QKD Activities and Testbeds

QKD activities have advanced significantly, transitioning from purely experimental setups to more sophisticated testbeds and early-stage deployments. Some of the most notable QKD initiatives demonstrating significant progress are shown in Table 12.2. A notable example is the SwissQuantum testbed in Geneva, launched in 2008. Spanning approximately 20 km, it connected multiple nodes, including corporate offices and data centers, serving as a robust platform for evaluating QKD technology [2]. Such projects highlight the potential for integrating QKD into modern communication systems and pave the way for broader adoption.

The Madrid Quantum Communication Infrastructure (MadQCI) demonstrates significant progress in QKD by integrating quantum communication channels with classical channels for data transmission and network control, managed dynamically through software-defined networking (SDN) [3]. Its architecture includes a local key management system (LKMS) that collects, stores, and manages keys from QKD modules, enabling real-time network monitoring and dynamic reconfiguration. By addressing challenges in hybrid network management, MadQCI highlights the feasibility of scalable QKD systems for real-world applications.

Table 12.2 QKD activities and testbeds worldwide

QKD activity	Region	Year commissioned	Key features	Maturity	Number of nodes	Covered distance	Use
SwissQuantum QKD Network	Switzerland	2008	A notable testbed in Geneva deployed by ID Quantique, a pioneer of commercializing QKD and quantum encryption. Network included 2 Gbps channel fiber and IPSec encryptors	High	3	20	Research
MadQCI	Spain	2021	Integrated with commercial telecom networks; compatible with IPsec encryption devices; utilizes ID Quantique, Toshiba, AIT & Huawei QKD systems [3] SDN architecture implemented	High	10	200 km	Commercial
SK Telecom	South Korea	2019	Nationwide deployment for government organizations; subscription-based QKD service for enterprises; employs ID Quantique's QKD systems [4] SDN-based control of heterogeneous QKD networks	High	15	150 km	Commercial
Singapore QKD	Singapore	2020	Integrated into national infrastructure for secure communication; positioned as a regional hub for quantum security; collaborates with ID Quantique	High	8	100 km	Commercial
EuroQCI	EU	2023	Developing a quantum network across 27 member states; focuses on security for critical infrastructures; involves multiple vendors including Toshiba and ID Quantique, cross-border space links, intra-city and inter-city fiber links	High	2 – –10	10–1000 km	Research

Name	Country	Year	Description	Security	Nodes	Distance	Type
PSNC QKD Link	Poland	2022	380 km intercity QKD link within PIONIER network; includes international QKD links with the Czech Republic; utilizes ID Quantique's systems	High	5	380 km	Research
Cambridge QKD	UK	2023	Operates on dense wavelength division multiplexing (DWDM) networks; demonstrates high-bandwidth quantum communication; vendor information not specified	High	3	25 km	Research
DARPA Quantum Network	USA	2004	Integrated with Internet technologies; used QKD-derived keys for IPsec; one of the first QKD networks deployed; utilized proprietary QKD systems	High	3	50 km	Research
Bristol Quantum Network	UK	2020	QKD provided over 5GUK test network using specially developed Open Source software, also trusted-node free quantum network; University of Bristol	High	4–8	13 km	Research
Tokyo QKD Network	Japan	2010	Multi-node testbed on NICT's JGN-X open fiber network; collaborative research platform for universities and industry; involved multiple vendors	Medium	7	300 km	Research
CSIRO Testbed	Australia	2024	Laboratory-based QKD research environment; focuses on experimental validation and development; employs QuintessenceLabs' QKD system	Low	2	20 km	Research

In South Korea, SK Telecom, in partnership with ID Quantique, has developed one of the most advanced QKD testbeds globally, deploying QKD systems over the past five years to connect 48 government organizations [4]. This testbed secures critical communications for government, financial institutions, and enterprises, showcasing the scalability of quantum-safe solutions. Additionally, QKD services have been successfully deployed at Equinix's SL1 data center, offering enterprise clients a subscription-based model that reduces upfront costs, demonstrating the practicality of large-scale QKD implementations.

Singapore has also made significant strides in quantum communication by building a comprehensive QKD testbed in collaboration with ID Quantique. As part of its nationwide quantum security initiative, Singapore has deployed QKD technology to secure its sensitive government and enterprise communications, positioning itself as a leader in quantum-safe communication in Asia. This effort integrates QKD into the broader national infrastructure, demonstrating its commitment to securing critical communications against future quantum threats. With these developments, Singapore is poised to be a hub for quantum innovation in the region.

The European Union's EuroQCI initiative is building a secure quantum communication infrastructure across all 27 EU Member States to enhance security for critical infrastructures and government institutions. As part of this effort, Poland has been advancing its QKD activities through the Poznań Supercomputing and Networking Center (PSNC) in collaboration with ID Quantique, establishing a 380 km intercity QKD link between Poznań and Warsaw within the PIONIER network, and creating the first international QKD link with Czech institutions between Cieszyn and Ostrava. These efforts position Poland as a key contributor to EuroQCI, integrating quantum technologies into secure communication testbeds.

These efforts in South Korea and Singapore, alongside initiatives in Europe with EuroQCI and MadQCI, underscore the global momentum toward quantum-safe communication. They highlight the potential of QKD to transition from isolated demonstrations to integral components of national and enterprise-level cybersecurity strategies.

12.3 Trends and Innovations of QKD

QKD is rapidly advancing through theoretical and practical innovations, offering information-theoretic security based on quantum mechanics. While foundational protocols like BB84 and decoy-state QKD have established security proofs, newer protocols often lack complete analyses, particularly under real-world conditions with finite datasets. Research is focused on addressing these gaps to ensure practical security.

There are additional challenges, as outlined in the following bullet points, that continue to hinder the large-scale deployment of QKD technology. For each challenge, we provide an overview, assess its severity in impacting the advancement of QKD, and offer a time estimate for its potential resolution.

- **Implementation Security**
  QKD's theoretical promise of "unconditional security" can be compromised in real-world implementations due to hardware imperfections. These vulnerabilities have been exploited in various *side-channel attacks* and/or quantum hacking, such as photon-number-splitting (PNS) attacks, detector blinding, and time-shift attacks [5].
  Severity: Medium. While vulnerabilities exist, countermeasures like measurement-device-independent QKD (MDI-QKD) and (semi-) device independent QKD are advancing rapidly and already offer solutions for mitigating these risks.
  Timeline for Resolution: Short to medium term (3–7 years). Many countermeasures are being standardized and are expected to integrate seamlessly into commercial systems soon.
- **Limited Role as a Cryptographic Solution**
  QKD is often criticized for being a partial solution, as it generates keying material but does not inherently provide source authentication. The authentication of the QKD transmission source typically relies on pre-placed symmetric keys or asymmetric cryptography [6], which limits its standalone utility.
  Emerging quantum technologies, such as Quantum Digital Signatures (QDS) and Quantum-Secure Identifiers (QSIs), leverage quantum principles to address this limitation. Hybrid solutions combining QKD with post-quantum cryptography (PQC), such as lattice-based cryptographic algorithms, are also gaining traction as a practical approach for robust security.
  Severity: Medium. Current cryptographic tools and emerging technologies provide adequate solutions, making this a manageable challenge.
  Timeline for Resolution: Short term (1–3 years) for hybrid solutions; longer term (5–10 years) for full reliance on quantum-based authentication technologies like QDS and QSIs.
- **Key Extraction Efficiency**
  Efficiently extracting secret keys from raw quantum measurement data is critical for real-time operation. The bottleneck in error reconciliation, especially under noisy conditions or high-loss scenarios, has been a challenge. However, modern low-leakage error correction codes and advanced reconciliation techniques already perform well, with minimal delays in key generation.
  Severity: Low. While not ideal in all scenarios, backlogged keys can be stored and processed without compromising security.
  Timeline for Resolution: Very short term (1–2 years). Existing solutions are already effective and are continuously improving with incremental advancements in algorithms and hardware acceleration.
- **Cost and Scalability**
  The cost of deploying QKD infrastructure, particularly for discrete-variable (DV-QKD) systems, remains a barrier due to the specialized hardware required. Continuous-variable (CV-QKD) systems, which are more cost-effective and compatible with standard telecom components, face limitations in range and noise tolerance.

Severity: Medium. Cost and scalability are challenges, but innovative approaches such as Quantum Safe-as-a-Service (QaaS) models and hybrid networks are helping reduce deployment costs.

Timeline for Resolution: Medium term (3–5 years). Market competition and advancements in off-the-shelf components are expected to make QKD increasingly affordable and scalable.

- **Standardization and Interoperability**

  The lack of standardized protocols and evaluation criteria poses a barrier to widespread adoption. However, organizations like ETSI, ISO, and ITU are actively developing global standards.

  Severity: Medium. Progress is steady, with global collaboration ensuring cross-vendor compatibility.

  Timeline for Resolution: Short to medium term (3–5 years). Certification frameworks are maturing rapidly and will soon establish clear interoperability guidelines.

- **Integration with Classical Systems**

  Integrating QKD with existing cryptographic frameworks and networks introduces complexity. However, hybrid systems combining QKD with classical encryption methods are showing promise.

  Severity: Low. Integration challenges are manageable with existing technology and ongoing developments in hybrid systems.

  Timeline for Resolution: Short term (2–3 years). Active development and testing are already underway.

- **Quantum Repeaters and Long-Distance Communication**

  Transmission losses and the absence of practical quantum repeaters limit the achievable distance of QKD without trusted nodes. However, significant advancements in quantum memory and entanglement distribution are being made.

  Severity: Medium. While a challenge for global-scale QKD networks, near-term applications can rely on trusted nodes.

  Timeline for Resolution: Medium to long term (5–10 years). Progress in quantum repeaters and satellite-based QKD is accelerating, making this a solvable issue within the next decade.

- **Comparison with Post-Quantum Cryptography (PQC)**

  While PQC provides an alternative to QKD for quantum-safe communication, it relies on computational assumptions. QKD offers the advantage of information-theoretic security based on physical principles.

  Severity: Low. PQC and QKD are complementary rather than competing technologies.

  Timeline for Resolution: Short term (1–2 years). Hybrid systems integrating QKD and PQC already provide practical and robust solutions.

Due to these trends, many countries and defense organizations prefer to monitor QKD's development and adopt it selectively or incrementally as the technology matures and its cost-effectiveness improves.

12.3.1 Vision and Future Outlook

Current QKD developments reflect the dual narrative of QKD's transformative potential and the challenges limiting its scalability. Technological advancements in integrated photonics, cost-effective avalanche photodiodes, and continuous-variable QKD systems are driving down costs, making scalable implementations more feasible [7]. Distance limitations are being addressed through satellite-based QKD, exemplified by China's *Micius* satellite enabling intercontinental secure communication, and the development of quantum repeaters to extend transmission ranges further [8, 9]. Integration with classical cryptographic systems combines QKD's information-theoretic security with traditional authentication and session management, ensuring compatibility with existing infrastructures. Government agencies, such as the UK's NCSC and the USA's NSA, emphasize the need for cost-benefit analyses given QKD's high costs and scalability constraints, advocating for a cautious approach. In parallel, initiatives like NIST's PQC standardization focus on scalable cryptographic alternatives. Despite this, private sectors, including finance, telecommunications, and technology, increasingly recognize QKD's value. For instance, JPMorgan Chase has secured financial networks using QKD, BT has deployed quantum-secure industrial networks, and Toshiba has implemented QKD for healthcare data protection. These examples underscore QKD's growing adoption in mission-critical applications as a complementary strategy to PQC.

12.4 Recommendations

Advancing QKD as a potential technology for quantum-secure communication requires addressing key challenges such as implementation security, scalability, and interoperability. Establishing national and regional QKD testbeds could help integrate advanced protocols with existing systems, enabling real-world testing and contributing to standardization efforts. Research into quantum repeaters and satellite-based QKD is needed to address distance limitations, and international collaborations could play a role in accelerating progress. Public-private partnerships may help reduce costs, making QKD more accessible for broader use in enterprise and government applications. Additionally, workforce development through education and training programs will be important for building expertise in quantum technologies. Active engagement in global standardization efforts, such as those by ETSI and ISO, can further support interoperability and promote adoption. These combined efforts could help position QKD as a promising tool for addressing evolving cybersecurity challenges.

12.5 Conclusion

Quantum Key Distribution (QKD) has the potential to become a foundational technology for securing communications in the quantum era, offering strong information-theoretic security. While challenges remain in scalability, cost, and integration with classical systems, ongoing global investments highlight its strategic significance. Through targeted research, innovation, and collaboration between industry and academia, countries and organizations can advance the adoption of QKD. By addressing these key challenges and promoting international cooperation, QKD could play a significant role in the future cybersecurity landscape, providing robust protection against emerging quantum threats.

References

1. M. Lucamarini, K.A. Patel, J.F. Dynes, B. Fröhlich, A.W. Sharpe, A.R. Dixon, Z.L. Yuan, R.V. Penty, A.J. Shields, Efficient decoy-state quantum key distribution with quantified security. Opt. Express **21**(21), 24550–24565 (2013)
2. D. Stucki, M. Legré, F. Buntschu, B. Clausen, N. Felber, N. Gisin, L. Henzen, P. Junod, G. Litzistorf, P. Monbaron, L. Monat, J.-B. Page, D. Perroud, G. Ribordy, A. Rochas, S. Robyr, J. Tavares, R. Thew, P. Trinkler, S. Ventura, R. Voirol, N. Walenta, H. Zbinden, Long-term performance of the SwissQuantum quantum key distribution network in a field environment. New J. Phys. **13**(12), 123001 (2011)
3. V. Martin, J.P. Brito, L. Ortíz, R.B. Méndez, J.S. Buruaga, R.J. Vicente, A. Sebastián-Lombraña, D. Rincón, F. Pérez, C. Sánchez, M. Peev, H.H. Brunner, F. Fung, A. Poppe, F. Fröwis, A.J. Shields, R.I. Woodward, H. Griesser, S. Roehrich, F. de la Iglesia, C. Abellán, M. Hentschel, J.M. Rivas-Moscoso, A. Pastor-Perales, J. Folgueira, D. López, MadQCI: a heterogeneous and scalable SDN-QKD network deployed in production facilities. npj Quant. Inf. **10**(1), 80 (2024)
4. T. Kim, S.-B. Cho, J.S. Cho, J.W. Choi, S.H. Kwak, Development of quantum communication technologies in SK telecom, in *2012 17th Opto-Electronics and Communications Conference* (2012), pp. 105–106
5. V. Makarov, A. Anisimov, J. Skaar, Effects of detector efficiency mismatch on security of quantum cryptosystems. Phys. Rev. A **74**, 022313 (2006)
6. National Security Agency, Quantum key distribution (QKD) and quantum cryptography (QC) (2024). Accessed: 09 Dec 2024.
7. F. Grünenfelder, A. Boaron, G.V. Resta, M. Perrenoud, D. Rusca, C. Barreiro, R. Houlmann, R. Sax, L. Stasi, S. El-Khoury, E. Hänggi, N. Bosshard, F. Bussières, H. Zbinden, Fast single-photon detectors and real-time key distillation enable high secret-key-rate quantum key distribution systems. Nat. Photon. **17**(5), 422–426 (2023)
8. Y.-A. Chen, Q. Zhang, T.-Y. Chen, W.-Q. Cai, S.-K. Liao, J. Zhang, K. Chen, J. Yin, J.-G. Ren, Z. Chen, S.-L. Han, Q. Yu, K. Liang, F. Zhou, X. Yuan, M.-S. Zhao, T.-Y. Wang, X. Jiang, L. Zhang, W.-Y. Liu, Y. Li, Q. Shen, Y. Cao, C.-Y. Lu, R. Shu, J.-Y. Wang, L. Li, N.-L. Liu, F. Xu, X.-B. Wang, C.-Z. Peng, J.-W. Pan, An integrated space-to-ground quantum communication network over 4,600 kilometres. Nature **589**(7841), 214–219 (2021)
9. K. Azuma, S.E. Economou, D. Elkouss, P. Hilaire, L. Jiang, H.-K. Lo, I. Tzitrin, Quantum repeaters: From quantum networks to the quantum internet. Rev. Mod. Phys. **95**, 045006 (2023)

Dr. Seyit Camtepe is a principal research scientist at CSIRO's Data61, leading the Autonomous and Software Security team. He focuses on innovative solutions to cybersecurity challenges, including Android malware and encryption. Seyit holds a PhD from Rensselaer Polytechnic Institute and has worked as a senior researcher at TU-Berlin and as an ECARD lecturer at QUT, Australia.

Dr. Sebastian Kish is a research scientist at CSIRO's Data61, leading projects on Quantum Key Distribution since 2023. He specializes in developing and implementing QKD protocols for a quantum-encrypted network in Sydney. He holds a BSc (Hons) and PhD in physics from The University of Queensland, with postdoctoral experience at UNSW and ANU in quantum communication and information. Sebastian has an extensive background in quantum physics and has published in top quantum journals.

Dr. Josef Pieprzyk (IACR Fellow, 2021) is a professor at the Institute of Computer Science, Polish Academy of Sciences, and a senior principal research scientist at CSIRO's Data61, focusing on cryptology and information security. His research includes cryptographic algorithms, secure protocols, and cybercrime prevention. He has authored 5 books, edited 10 conference proceedings, and published over 250 papers. He serves on editorial boards for journals like the *International Journal of Information Security*.

Open Access This chapter is licensed under the terms of the Creative Commons Attribution 4.0 International License (http://creativecommons.org/licenses/by/4.0/), which permits use, sharing, adaptation, distribution and reproduction in any medium or format, as long as you give appropriate credit to the original author(s) and the source, provide a link to the Creative Commons license and indicate if changes were made.

The images or other third party material in this chapter are included in the chapter's Creative Commons license, unless indicated otherwise in a credit line to the material. If material is not included in the chapter's Creative Commons license and your intended use is not permitted by statutory regulation or exceeds the permitted use, you will need to obtain permission directly from the copyright holder.

Chapter 13
Migrating to Quantum Key Distribution

Bruno Huttner

Abstract The potential future development of quantum computers, which could threaten the security of current networks, underscores the importance of planning for the transition to quantum-safe solutions. One approach under consideration, and the focus of this chapter, is the development of *quantum key distribution* (QKD) networks, which enable the secure distribution of secret keys between pairs of users within the network. At the foundation of a QKD network is a QKD link, which consists of a single optical connection between two QKD devices. This chapter explores the technology behind QKD links, introduces various models of QKD networks, and highlights real-world implementations being pursued by several countries worldwide.

13.1 Introduction: The Largest Crypto Migration Ever

It is now well understood that quantum computers will break existing asymmetric cryptography and require a complete upgrade of the security framework of all our communication infrastructure. In the existing cybersecurity infrastructure, most solutions are built with the same underlying algorithms. In the quantum era, cybersecurity will require different types of solutions for different applications. There exist two types of solutions. One, which will keep the same infrastructure, based on hard mathematical problems, is known as *post-quantum cryptography* (PQC). The new quantum-resistant algorithms will replace the current ones, which are not quantum-safe. This is the approach pioneered by NIST, which has recently standardized a set of algorithms and is pursuing work on several others [1]. These algorithms should upgrade the Internet and networks with low to medium security requirements. The main drawback of this approach is that long-term security is not fully assured. Both classical and quantum resistance are still under study.

B. Huttner (✉)
ID Quantique, Geneva, Switzerland
e-mail: bruno.huttner@idquantique.com

Suffice it to recall that two algorithms under consideration were broken on a classical computer [2, 3]. Resistance against a quantum computer, which has not been studied so thoroughly, is even more uncertain. This is why, in addition to PQC, security should be improved by applying the same quantum principles, which render the quantum computer so powerful. Quantum cryptography, or QKD, offers a completely different type of solution, based on the properties of quantum mechanics. QKD provides provably secure key distribution between two nodes, connected by a quantum channel [4]. The keys are then used in symmetric encryption and possibly other cryptographic functions. QKD does not address identification and authentication issues, which must be performed with either a pre-shared key, which will then be renewed by QKD, or with quantum-resistant authentication algorithms, such as a stateful *hash-based signature* (HBS) scheme [5] recommended by NIST or one of the newly standardized schemes, SLH-DSA [6] or ML-DSA [7]. In order to provide security over complex networks, QKD links should be combined into QKD networks. These networks rely on secure relay nodes to distribute secure keys from any point to any point. Hybrid systems, which combine QKD and PQC, offer defense-in-depth capabilities by combining different technologies.

13.2 Analysis

This chapter presents the quantum and hybrid answers to the quantum computer attacks. Purely algorithmic solutions, such as PQC, are presented in other chapters.

13.2.1 QKD Links

The core of a QKD link is a quantum channel, which connects two nodes, with an optical link, typically an optical fiber or a free-space connection. Since a quantum channel cannot be amplified without losing its quantum properties, the distance between the two nodes is limited. For fiber-based channels, commercial systems reach about 150 km. Experimental systems achieved much longer distances, above 800 km [8]. With proper telescopes, free space systems can link satellites to optical ground stations (OGS) and provide global QKD links [9]. The quantum channel transfers qubits, which are measured by the users. The basic property of quantum mechanics, which provides provable security, is the fact that an attempt at eavesdropping represents a quantum measurement, which perturbs the state of the qubit and results in transmission errors. This disturbance will be discovered during the key processing.

The establishment of the key consists of several steps.
Step 1: preparation, exchange, and measurement of the qubits
In the so-called prepare and measure protocols, the transmitter, Alice, prepares qubits and forwards them to the receiver, Bob, who measures them. The idea behind

QKD is that any attempt at eavesdropping on the exchange represents a quantum measurement of the qubit. This measurement modifies the qubits and will be later discovered by Alice and Bob.

Alternatively, in entanglement-based protocols, a third party, say Charly, prepares entangled pairs and forwards one element of each pair to Alice and to Bob. If Charly performs his duties as planned, he should obtain no information about the states measured by Alice and Bob. However, thanks to entanglement, Charly does not have to be trusted. If he tries to cheat and to gather information on the qubits, he cannot send fully entangled states. This will be discovered by Alice and Bob, in the same way as they will discover an eavesdropper. Therefore, the remaining will be restricted to the "prepare and measure" protocol.

A quantum channel is a physical channel, which has loss. In addition, detection of qubits is not perfectly efficient. This means that many of the qubits sent by Alice are not detected by Bob. In practice, the detection rate may be as low as one out of several hundreds. The following step is therefore a public discussion over a classical channel, to discard all the lost qubits and perform key sifting.

Step 2: public discussion over a classical channel

The second step for Alice and Bob is to exchange, over a classical channel, which of the qubits are detected. There is also a sifting process, whereby they identify and discard all the qubits, which were measured in incompatible bases and are not correlated. After this stage, Alice and Bob both possess a long string of bits, which, in the absence of an eavesdropper, should be identical.

Step 3: error estimation and reconciliation

If an eavesdropper is prying into the communication, errors will be introduced. In practice, due to errors in the transmission and the possible presence of an eavesdropper, the two strings of bits are never identical. Alice and Bob select some of their bits at random and disclose them in order to estimate the error rate. All the disclosed bits are obviously discarded. Alice and Bob now use an error correction code, which corrects the errors, at the expense of shortening the strings. At the end of this step, they share a string of perfectly correlated bits.

Step 4: privacy amplification

In order to ensure the highest possible security, Alice and Bob must assume that all the errors before error correction were potentially generated by an eavesdropper. They have to estimate the amount of information, which may have leaked to the eavesdropper, as a function of the error rate. Intuitively, it is clear that a zero error rate (no disturbance) means that no information was leaked. The higher the error rate, the more information that may have leaked. Transforming this intuition into a quantitative value is the domain of quantum security proofs. This is a highly complex and protocol-dependent calculation. Complete security proofs, even encompassing the statistical analysis needed for finite samples, have been derived for several protocols, including the *prepare and measure BB84* protocol [4], the *entanglement-based E91* protocol [4], and the *Gaussian-modulated coherent state* (GMCS) CV-QKD protocol [4]. For certain protocols, some assumptions restricting the technology available to the eavesdropper must be accepted.

Once the link between the error rate and the information leaked is obtained, the last step is to reduce the information available to Eve by a classical mathematical procedure known as privacy amplification. Alice and Bob lower the final amount of information available to Eve to an arbitrarily low value, at the expense of reducing the length of the string they have. Typically, the so-called security factor is chosen to be 10^{-9} bits or less known by Eve per bit of the secret key.

If the error rate is too high, the error correction and privacy amplification procedures consume all the bits. In this case, no secure key can be extracted, and the procedure aborts. This limit depends on the protocol.

At the end of the process, Alice and Bob either possess a secret key string or know that the error rate was too high and could not generate a secret key. This is the main advantage of QKD: the key string is known to be secret, without relying on computational assumptions.

However, as single optical span is limited in length, QKD links have restricted applications. For example, QKD can be applied to secure the link between two data centers, separated by up to 150 km. Linking many users and achieving longer distances require QKD networks, which are presented in the next section.

13.2.2 Design of a QKD Network

Combining several links at secure relay nodes enables to build long-distance networks and large networks with complex topologies. An example of a QKD network is presented in Fig. 13.1.

Detailed analysis of a QKD network is similar to the *open systems interconnection* (OSI) model of computer networks [10] and is organized in a number of abstraction layers, each with a specific role. This is presented in Fig. 13.2.

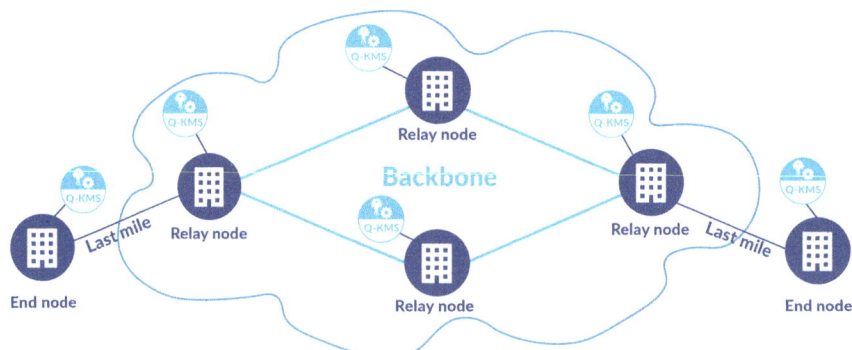

Fig. 13.1 A QKD network. The QKD backbone connects the major relay nodes and the last-mile links connect to end users. In addition to a standard equipment management system, the Quantum-Key Management System (Q-KMS) is responsible for managing the QKD-keys and computing the end-to-end keys

13 Migrating to Quantum Key Distribution   137

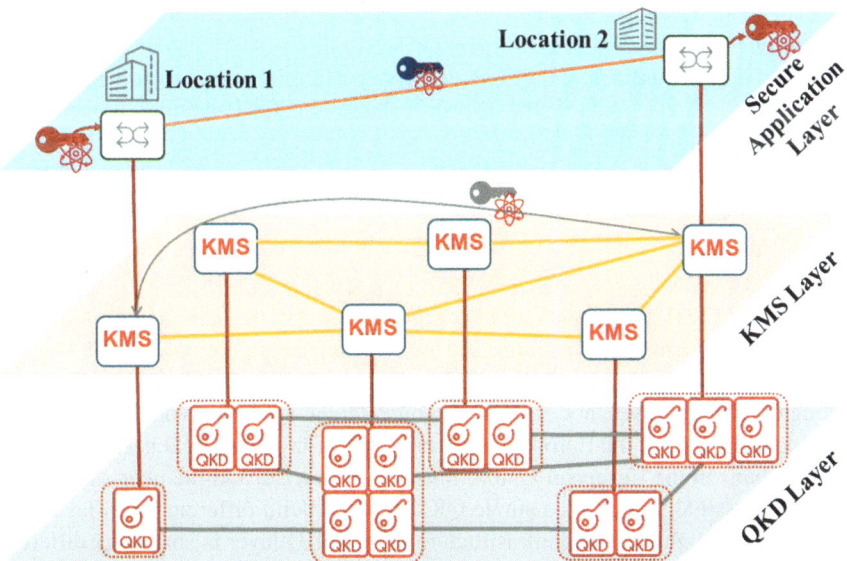

Fig. 13.2 The different abstraction layers of a QKD network. The gray layer is the QKD layer, which represents the physical layer with QKD devices and links. The QKD-keys are generated in this layer. The orange layer is the key management system layer, which manages the QKD-keys and computes the end-to-end keys in gray. The end-to-end keys are transmitted to the secure application layer (blue layer) for utilization. In this example, the end-to-end keys are used to encrypt secret keys (in dark red) generated by a quantum random number generator (QRNG) in Location 1. The encrypted key (in dark blue) is forwarded to Location 2 and decoded with the same end-to-end key

The QKD layer (in gray) is the physical layer, with pairs of QKD devices connected by optical links. Today, QKD devices always come in pairs, with proprietary interfaces for the quantum channel. However, the connections to the *key management system* (KMS) layer are now following a standard interface (red lines), the ETSI GS QKD 014 Application Programming Interface (API) [11]. This means that the integration of QKD devices from different manufacturers into a single KMS is easily achieved. The KMS layer is responsible for key routing, end-to-end key distribution and key buffering, to ensure uninterrupted availability of keys. In the case of a disruption of a QKD link, the KMS will first use the buffered keys and then re-route the distribution path to offer seamless redundancy. This redundancy is a major requirement for real-world implementation of QKD networks.

The connection between the KMS layer and the secure application layer mostly follows the same ETSI GS QKD 014 API [11], although some classical network equipment and encryption manufacturers still prefer to implement their own proprietary interface. The QKD-keys generated by the network can be used in a variety of ways.

- As described in Fig. 13.2 they can be used to encrypt keys generated locally by a *quantum random number generator* (QRNG).
- Today, many manufacturers of link encryptors offer the option to add an external key to their device. Adding the keys provided by the QKD network immediately assures quantum-safe security, with no need to upgrade existing devices.
- It is also possible to improve security by generating a secret key with the QRNG, encrypting it with a NIST-standardized PQC algorithm and re-encrypting with a QKD-key. This combines the strengths of QKD and PQC to build a hybrid system.

Although Fig. 13.2 presents a rather simple network, the same layer model can be applied to various applications and more complex topologies. Thanks to the standardization efforts, independent QKD networks can be combined at gateways through common KMS nodes, thus building larger QKD networks. This is the approach adopted for the Euro-QCI network, a pan-European QKD network, which is being built in the European Union, financed by the EU and member states [12]. It is also possible to harness a single QKD layer to build different KMS layers. In this case, although the basic infrastructure at the QKD layer is shared by different users, each of them keeps complete control over their KMS layer, which means that each user manages its own keys without relying on external management. This is the approach which has been implemented in the Korean government network [13]. Different government entities have different KMS layers on a single underlying QKD backbone.

13.2.3 Building a QKD Infrastructure

The initial investment to build a national or transnational QKD infrastructure can be significant. For emerging technologies, Asian governments often initiate the development of new infrastructures, which can then be used by the whole community. A QKD backbone, which can be initially used by government agencies and later linked to many end-users, is a long-term asset, which can be used to provide enhanced security for high-value users around the country. This is the model adopted, for example, in China [14] and more recently in South Korea [13]. This QKD backbone should not replace the PQC transition but will add a different layer of security, in case some of the chosen PQC algorithms are attacked and broken. The QKD backbone will be provided by the government or a public entity. Private enterprises will connect to the backbone with a short QKD link. In such networks, where the secure relay nodes are controlled by a single entity, which may not be fully trusted by all users, security at the relay node has to be addressed. This includes both physical security, such as physical protection and access control, and digital security, which means restricting access to the keys. This can be achieved through regulation and technical solutions, for example, splitting keys and sending the key elements through different independent channels, or adding a layer of end-to-end encryption.

A different model has been adopted in Singapore. Two leading telecom operators, including Singtel, the main telecom operator in Singapore, are building QKD networks and plans to offer Keys-as-a-Service (KaaS) to enterprises [15]. Several customers, especially in the fields of critical infrastructure and banking, have expressed interest and plan for register to the service. In terms of hardware, a QKD network built by a telco is very similar to the above and consists of a QKD backbone with core nodes, linked to edge nodes at the customer premises. However, the ownership and management of the whole network, including the edge nodes, are with the telco, which offers KaaS to the end customer. Technically, it is possible today to build 1-to-N QKD links from a core node to many edge nodes, which will lower the cost for the end user. The emphasis for this last mile is on low cost and not performance.

In addition to governments or telecom operators, large enterprises, such as banks, utilities, high tech, pharmaceutical, and other IP-intensive companies, have very strong security requirements. For example, if IP documents are exchanged within the company, confidentiality should be assured for more than ten years. Due to the "harvest now, decrypt later" attack, these companies should therefore move to quantum-safe now and provide long-term confidentiality. The options are either to harness an existing QKD backbone and share infrastructure, as described above, or to build their own private network. The second option represents a major investment but would provide complete control over the network. This is in contrast to a government or telco network described above where organization and management of the network are outsourced. Therefore, a private QKD network could be used in conjunction with PQC to offer the highest confidentiality.

All three models described above have already been implemented or are in the process of being implemented in various countries. The hardware part, the QKD layer, is very similar for all. The difference lies in the management of the network and of the keys. In the enterprise model, there is one single user who has complete control. This model is useful for large entities who can afford the investment in their own QKD backbone. In the government model, the backbone is a shared investment. Single users can either manage their end-points, or, if they have multiple end-points, build their own KMS layer. Finally, in the telco model, the end users outsource the whole process. The telco provides all the equipment and the keys. This should enable small to medium businesses to have access to QKD security.

13.2.4 QKD for Defense

Secure communication is paramount for defense applications. For key exchange, combining different security layers, like PQC, out-of-band key exchange, and QKD, ensures a more resilient structure. PQC is a more flexible solution, which does not require a new infrastructure and should be relatively cheap to implement. However, due to the uncertainty regarding long-term security, the military may be reluctant to trust PQC entirely, especially for strategic networks, where the information exchanged may have a significant long-term value. In fact, even in the pre-quantum era, asymmetric cryptography has not always been well-accepted for military applications. The use of symmetric keys, either pre-shared or exchanged out-of-band, is seen as more secure. This is well-adapted to QKD, which offers an added method for the key exchange. A QKD network is primarily a hardware solution and is potentially more costly. However, it may be needed for use cases with large amounts of keys that need to be exchanged over many sites.

A QKD network for military applications would be similar to the enterprise network described in Sect. 13.2.3 and would be fully controlled. An important aspect of military communication is the existence of many mobile assets which cannot be linked to a fixed network. A military QKD network should, therefore, encompass specific edge nodes, better described as key distribution stations. Upon suitable authentication, mobile assets should download keys at these stations (like an ATM for cash), use them in the field, and recharge at any station when the keys are depleted. Key recharging could also be performed via short free-space QKD links. This model separates key distribution, which can be done in advance with less speed requirements, and key usage, which has to be very quick. Two major advantages of this symmetric key approach are the low computing power requirement at the mobile edge and low latency with respect to public key systems.

13.3 Conclusion: Recommendations

In today's interconnected world, network security is increasingly important. The potential emergence of quantum computers poses a significant challenge to existing cybersecurity systems, requiring a careful assessment of their impact and a gradual overhaul of current infrastructures. This process should begin with evaluating how quantum threats might affect specific cybersecurity systems, followed by selecting appropriate solutions, such as post-quantum cryptography (PQC) and quantum key distribution (QKD), tailored to individual needs.

Since no single solution fits all scenarios, security frameworks must integrate multiple approaches, combining flexibility with a mix of technologies. These hybrid systems should be designed to ensure that the failure of one security function does not compromise the entire system. PQC can replace algorithms vulnerable to quantum attacks, while QKD can provide an additional layer of security wherever feasible.

References

1. The NIST post-quantum cryptography project. https://csrc.nist.gov/projects/post-quantum-cryptography
2. W. Beullens, Breaking rainbow takes a weekend on a laptop. Cryptology ePrint Archive, Paper 2022/214 (2022)

3. The SIKE Consortium, The SIKE website, with statement that it is insecure. https://sike.org/
4. R. Wolf, *Quantum Key Distribution* (Springer, Cham, 2021)
5. NIST SP 800-208 - Recommendation for Stateful Hash-Based Signature Schemes. https://csrc.nist.gov/pubs/sp/800/208/final
6. FIPS 205 - Stateless Hash-Based Digital Signature Standard. https://csrc.nist.gov/pubs/fips/205/final.
7. FIPS 204 - Module-Lattice-Based Digital Signature Standard. https://csrc.nist.gov/pubs/fips/204/final
8. S. Wang, Z.Q. Yin, D.Y. He, W. Chen, R.Q. Wang, P. Ye, et al., Twin-field quantum key distribution over 830-km fibre. Nat. Photon. **16**, 154–161 (2022)
9. Y. Li, W.-Q. Cai, J. Wang, C.-Z. Wang, M. Yang, L. Zhang, H.-Y. Wu, L. Chang, J.-C. Wu, B. Jin, H.-J. Xue, X.-J. Li, H. Liu, G.-W. Yu, X.-Y. Tao, T. Chen, C.-F. Liu, W.-B. Luo, J. Zhou, J.-W. Pan, Microsatellite-based real-time quantum key distribution. Nature **640**, 47–54 (2025). https://doi.org/10.1038/s41586-025-08739-z
10. The OSI Model. https://en.wikipedia.org/wiki/OSI_model
11. ETSI, Quantum Key Distribution (QKD); Protocol and data format of REST-based key delivery API. https://www.etsi.org/deliver/etsi_gs/QKD/001_099/014/01.01.01_60/gs_QKD014v010101p.pdf
12. The European Quantum Communication Infrastructure (EuroQCI) Initiative. https://digital-strategy.ec.europa.eu/en/policies/european-quantum-communication-infrastructure-euroqci.
13. M. Park, Quantum Security Arrives in South Korea Thanks to SK Broadband. *Korea Tech Today* (2023)
14. Y.A. Chen, Q. Zhang, T.Y. Chen, W.Q. Cai, S.K. Liao, J. Zhang, et al., An integrated space-to-ground quantum communication network over 4,600 kilometres. Nature **589**, 214–219 (2021)
15. Singtel Quantum-Safe Network. https://www.singtel.com/business/campaign/quantumsafenetwork

Bruno Huttner is the Director of Strategic Quantum Initiatives and a quantum key distribution expert at ID Quantique. He is also the co-chairman of the Quantum-Safe Security Working Group (QSS WG) organized by the Cloud Security Alliance. Bruno joined ID Quantique in 2014, participating in business development and product management in the Quantum Security division. He then started the space programs, aiming at developing quantum key distribution globally using satellites. Bruno is an engineer (Ecole Centrale Paris) and a physicist (PhD from the Technion, Israel Institute of Technology).

Open Access This chapter is licensed under the terms of the Creative Commons Attribution 4.0 International License (http://creativecommons.org/licenses/by/4.0/), which permits use, sharing, adaptation, distribution and reproduction in any medium or format, as long as you give appropriate credit to the original author(s) and the source, provide a link to the Creative Commons license and indicate if changes were made.

The images or other third party material in this chapter are included in the chapter's Creative Commons license, unless indicated otherwise in a credit line to the material. If material is not included in the chapter's Creative Commons license and your intended use is not permitted by statutory regulation or exceeds the permitted use, you will need to obtain permission directly from the copyright holder.

Chapter 14
Post-Quantum Cryptography

Steven Galbraith

Abstract Large-scale and error-tolerant quantum computers will break the currently used tools for enabling confidentiality and integrity on the internet and elsewhere. It has been recognized for the last 10 years that there is an urgent need to develop cryptosystems that can withstand an attacker in the future with a quantum computer. Post-quantum cryptography (PQC), also sometimes known as quantum-resistant cryptography or quantum safe cryptography, means cryptographic algorithms that can run on today's computers and networks and yet be secure against attackers in the future who have large-scale and error-tolerant quantum computers. This chapter will argue that post-quantum cryptography is more practical and trusted for most real-world systems than quantum key distribution (QKD). The purpose of this chapter is to put cryptography into the broader context of cybersecurity, to briefly explain the threats and risks associated with quantum computing, and to give a nontechnical overview of the post-quantum cryptosystems that are available now.

14.1 Introduction

14.1.1 Cybersecurity and Cryptography

Cybersecurity is a broad topic that covers a wide range of attacks by a wide range of attackers. Major cybersecurity issues nowadays include ransomware, scams, and fraud. These topics are out of scope of this chapter.

The field of cryptography is central to cybersecurity. Cryptography provides tools for privacy and authentication in digital systems. It enables many of the systems and services that we take for granted in modern life, such as online shopping. Many of these systems rely on public key cryptosystems, which are based

---

S. Galbraith (✉)
University of Auckland, Auckland, New Zealand
e-mail: s.galbraith@auckland.ac.nz

on hard computational problems in mathematics. Some widely used examples of systems enabled by cryptography include TLS, secure email, private messaging, e-commerce, cloud storage and computing, VPN, software and firmware updates, e-voting, Internet of Things (IoT), blockchain, etc.

There are two main forms of cryptography. Symmetric key systems require both sender and receiver to hold the same secret key. Asymmetric algorithms, also known as public-key algorithms, allow a user to make their encryption key public while keeping their decryption key secret. Public key systems enable digital signatures, which have major applications such as software updates, digital currencies, and smart contracts. Another important application of public key cryptography is to set up shared keys using a key exchange or key encapsulation protocol. Each type of cryptography has its strengths and weaknesses, and so large-scale systems usually use a combination of both approaches.

The leading symmetric key cryptosystem for most applications is AES. This is used to encrypt large volumes of data to ensure data integrity. For example, secure internet sessions protect all data sent between client and server by encrypting it using AES. The shared key for the secure internet session is set up in a handshake protocol, which is built using public-key cryptography.

The RSA cryptosystem was proposed in the 1970s, almost immediately after the invention of public key cryptography. It provides public key encryption and digital signatures. It has been very widely used in practice since the 1980s, and especially with the rapid growth in the internet through the 1990s and early 2000s. The hardness of the integer factoring problem is the basis for RSA encryption and signatures.

Elliptic curve cryptography (ECC) was proposed in 1985. It fits into the discrete logarithm paradigm proposed by Diffie and Hellman and developed further by Elgamal and others. It provides key exchange, public key encryption, and digital signatures. For the last 20 years, ECC has been the most popular choice for newly built systems. The security of ECC comes from the difficulty of the elliptic curve discrete logarithm problem (ECDLP).

RSA and ECC are used in almost all key exchange, public key encryption, and digital signature algorithms today and, hence, are the basis of sessions protected by internet protocols such as TLS. Hence, our security depends on the difficulty of just two computational problems: integer factoring and elliptic curve discrete logarithms. These problems have been studied intensively for at least the last 30 years and have survived sustained public scrutiny and mathematical analysis.

14.1.2 Quantum Threat Revisited

Shor's algorithm, which requires an appropriately general-purpose quantum computer, efficiently solves the two problems underlying almost all currently used public key crypto, namely integer factoring and elliptic curve discrete logarithms. Hence, if large-scale general quantum computers can be built, then we immediately lose all security for the current public key cryptosystems that are used to secure a wide range of systems.

For a number of technical reasons, current quantum computers are not powerful enough to run Shor's algorithm on the large numbers needed to break the security systems being used today. In short, they cannot process enough data (i.e., they do not have enough qubits to store large enough numbers), and they cannot yet accurately perform the operations required due to issues of decoherence and error-tolerance that need to be solved using error-correction. The challenge for quantum computing, at least in the context of breaking cryptography, is to construct a large-scale and error-tolerant quantum computer on which Shor's algorithm can be performed to break the public keys currently in use on the internet.

If a large-scale quantum computer becomes available in 10–30 years, what will an attacker be able to do? They will be able to read messages sent using secure end-to-end encrypted messaging systems. They will be able to spoof webpages and hence steal user data without resorting to phishing. They will be able to bypass the security checks on software updates, and, hence, install malware on systems without having to trick users into clicking a link.

Most critically, for some government agencies and institutions, an attacker with a large-scale and error-tolerant quantum computer will be able to decrypt private communications from decades in the past. Suppose an attacker, either today or already in the past, intercepts files from your organization that are encrypted using public key cryptography, or with secret keys from an RSA or elliptic curve key exchange protocol. Are there consequences if those files are decrypted in 20 years time? This is known as a "store now and decrypt later" attack.

A survey and report were conducted in 2019 by Mosca and Piani for the Global Risk Institute [1] and were updated in 2023 [2]. In particular, they surveyed a wide range of experts to determine estimates for when quantum computers will be a "significant threat" to public key cryptography—defined as the ability to factor a 2048-bit RSA integer in less than one day of computation. In 2019 the majority of experts believed the risk to be low (i.e., less than 5%) before 2029, though this still does not exclude the possibility of a breakthrough. About half of the respondents in 2019 considered the risk by 2034 to be at least 50% of a significant threat. In the 2023 update the majority considered there to be less than 1% chance of a threat before 2028, but almost half considered it more than 5% likely by 2033.

By this measure, a reasonable recommendation would be to migrate to post-quantum crypto within the next 10 years (i.e., to be fully migrated by 2035). Given the standardization and development cycle for security products, it means we need to be acting with urgency now.

14.1.3 Post-Quantum Cryptography

It has been recognized for the last 10 years that there is an urgent need to develop cryptosystems that can be used today on current computing devices and be incorporated into existing internet protocols while at the same time withstand an attacker in the future with a quantum computer. Using post-quantum cryptography, we can use today's computers to protect our information against a quantum attacker in the future. However, post-quantum cryptography can be less practical and efficient than current systems, and the process of migration to using new technology is slow, typically 5–10 years.

Post-quantum cryptography is based on mathematical problems that are believed to be intractable even for quantum computers. There are five general areas of mathematics that seem to provide plausible candidates for practical post-quantum cryptosystems.

1. **Lattices**

   This refers to Euclidean lattices (i.e., grids of points in high dimension space). Lattices have been a major topic in algorithmic number theory since the 1980s and were suggested for cryptography in the 1990s. In the last 20 years, they have received a huge amount of research attention from cryptographers, partly due to post-quantum crypto and partly due to other applications in cryptography, such as homomorphic encryption. Lattices are a very versatile tool and can be used for key exchange, public key encryption, digital signatures, and more.

   Overall, lattices seem to be the most mature and trusted of the five branches of post-quantum public key cryptography, and NIST has standardized lattice schemes both for key exchange/public key encryption and signatures.

2. **Codes**

   Error-correcting codes are widely used to enable reliable electronic communications, since physical systems are prone to noise and faults. However, it was proposed by McEliece in the late 1970s that one could build cryptosystems from error-correcting codes. This concept was not seriously developed for a long time due to the large key sizes, until the relevance to post-quantum cryptography became understood. Code-based cryptography has become very highly studied in the last 10–15 years and is generally thought to be a mature area. There are several well-known code-based schemes, but they are often perceived as less efficient or less practical than lattice-based systems.

3. **Hashing**

   This refers to a particular method to build digital signatures from cryptographic hash functions. It is a mature field that is well trusted. The main drawback is that it is only suitable for specific applications and is not a general solution to all the challenges of post-quantum security.

4. **Multivariate**

   This refers to problems related to solving systems of polynomial equations in a very large number of variables and over a small finite field. While such computational problems are definitely believed to be hard in general, multivariate cryptography is not fully trusted as there is a long history of broken schemes. However, recently there are some digital signature proposals that are gaining greater interest.

5. **Isogeny**
   This is the most recent of the five branches of post-quantum public key cryptography, and it experienced a major setback in 2022. Currently, isogeny-based cryptography is being developed by a number of researchers, but it is not clear if it will have major practical applications in the near future.

It is worth noting that post-quantum cryptosystems are typically less efficient than current systems, either in terms of bandwidth/storage or in terms of execution time/computing power required or both. Hence, the migration to post-quantum cryptography may cause some inconvenience to some businesses and users [3–5].

14.2 Trends

14.2.1 Standardization

The US National Institute of Standards and Technology (NIST) launched the Post-Quantum Cryptography Standardization process [6] in 2016 with an open call for algorithms to be submitted and reviewed in a public competitive process. The goal was to standardize and recommend one or more public-key encryption and key-establishment algorithms, and one or more digital signature algorithms, for future use. The initial round attracted 69 submissions. Similar standardization processes are being conducted by other standards bodies internationally.

After multiple rounds of evaluations, on July 5, 2022, NIST announced the first PQC algorithms selected for standardization. CRYSTALS-Kyber was selected as a type of public key encryption or key exchange scheme called a Key Encapsulation Mechanism (KEM), and CRYSTALS-Dilithium, FALCON, and SPHINCS+ were selected as digital signature algorithms. SPHINCS+ is a hash-based signature, and the other three are lattice-based cryptosystems. On August 13, 2024, the standards were published as Federal Information Processing Standards (FIPS):

- FIPS 203: This is intended as the primary standard for general encryption. The standard is based on the CRYSTALS-Kyber algorithm and has been renamed ML-KEM short for Module-Lattice-Based Key-Encapsulation Mechanism.
- FIPS 204: This is intended as the primary standard for protecting digital signatures. The standard uses the CRYSTALS-Dilithium algorithm, which has been renamed ML-DSA, short for Module-Lattice-Based Digital Signature Algorithm.
- FIPS 205: This is also a digital signature scheme. The standard employs the SPHINCS+ algorithm, which has been renamed SLH-DSA, short for Stateless Hash-Based Digital Signature Algorithm.

The process of standardizing FALCON (or a variant of it) is ongoing at the time of writing this chapter.

Many government and industry groups are required or expected to migrate to the new protocols as soon as practicable. The schemes are already implemented and usable. Indeed, starting from August 2023 the Chrome browser has supported the X25519Kyber768 hybrid post-quantum key exchange for TLS.

While NIST is a US government agency connected to the NSA, it has a huge influence on other international standards. As with previous NIST standards like AES and SHA-3, most Western governments are expected to approve the NIST standards for their own use. Bodies such as IETF will adopt the NIST standards [5]. A report by the European Union Agency for Cybersecurity (ENISA) [7] only lists algorithms that advanced through the NIST evaluation process. It is also worth noting that the design and development teams for the winning systems CRYSTALS-Kyber, CRYSTALS-Dilithium, and SPHINCS+ all comprise a majority of European researchers. The use of PQC in hybrid mode with trusted classical systems also helps to reduce any sovereignty or trust issues.

By *hybrid mode* we mean combining two schemes in such a way that the security holds even if one of the two schemes is broken. To take one example, the X25519Kyber768 hybrid post-quantum key exchange for TLS combines both classical elliptic curve cryptography and lattice-based post-quantum cryptography. A public key for such a hybrid scheme is a pair of public keys: an elliptic curve public key and a lattice public key. At a high level, the protocol performs in parallel an elliptic curve key exchange protocol and a lattice-based key exchange protocol. At the end of the protocol, the shared key is derived from (e.g., by hashing) both the shared key produced by the elliptic curve protocol and the shared key produced by the lattice-based protocol. Even if one of the schemes is broken, the attacker only knows one of the two keys and so cannot deduce the shared key of the hybrid scheme.

14.3 Analysis

14.3.1 Comparison Between Post-Quantum Cryptography (PQC) and Quantum Key Distribution (QKD)

Quantum key distribution (QKD) is another approach to secure communication. It differs from post-quantum cryptography in a number of important ways. Most importantly, it requires new hardware, while PQC can be used with current computing and networking systems. Further, QKD needs an authenticated classical channel of communication, and the only practical way we know to implement this is using cryptography. To be secure against a quantum computer, the authenticated classical channel will have to be protected using post-quantum cryptography. So QKD is not an alternative to PQC, rather PQC is needed to build quantum-secure QKD.

Post-quantum cryptography is a much more mature and thoroughly tested technology than QKD. As noted in [8], there are no published standards for QKD and nor is there a widely accepted evaluation methodology for physical attacks against QKD systems. In contrast, standards for post-quantum cryptography are published and implementations are already being used daily to protect internet communications [3].

In January 2024, the French Cybersecurity Agency (ANSSI), the German Federal Office for Information Security (BSI), the Netherlands National Communications Security Agency (NLNCSA), and the Swedish National Communications Security Authority issued a Position Paper [8] on Quantum Key Distribution. Their findings are clear: *"Due to current and inherent limitations, QKD can however currently only be used in practice in some niche use cases. For the vast majority of use cases where classical key agreement schemes are currently used it is not possible to use QKD in practice. Furthermore, QKD is not yet sufficiently mature from a security perspective. In light of the urgent need to stop relying only on quantum-vulnerable public-key cryptography for key establishment, the clear priorities should therefore be the migration to post-quantum cryptography and/or the adoption of symmetric keying."*

The NSA has published [9] an opinion on QKD for real-world systems. To quote from this document: *"NSA does not recommend the usage of quantum key distribution and quantum cryptography for securing the transmission of data in National Security Systems (NSS) unless the limitations ... are overcome"* and *"NSA views quantum-resistant (or post-quantum) cryptography as a more cost-effective and easily maintained solution than quantum key distribution. For all of these reasons, NSA does not support the usage of QKD or QC to protect communications in National Security Systems."*

14.3.2 Post-Quantum Symmetric Key Cryptography

Symmetric key cryptography means ciphers designed for encryption and message authentication (MAC) where both sender and receiver share a secret key. Typically, the shared secret key is the outcome of a previous key exchange or key transfer protocol, based on public key tools. The most widely used symmetric encryption scheme is AES, which is a block cipher. Symmetric ciphers are used together with a mode of operation to provide appropriate security; the most usual situation is to use a mode of operation that provides authenticated encryption with associated data (AEAD).

Symmetric cryptosystems have an n-bit key; for AES, typical values for n are 128, 192, and 256. The best classical attacks to determine the secret key used in a given session take essentially 2^n executions of the encryption algorithm.

The impact of quantum computers on symmetric key cryptography is a topic of debate. In theory, Grover's algorithm reduces the cost of computing the key from 2^n operations on a classical computer to $2^{n/2}$ operations on a quantum computer. Such an attack usually assumes the attacker is provided with a number of message-ciphertext pairs $(m, E_K(m))$ where m is a message and $E_K(m)$ denotes the encryption function with secret key K. To prevent such attacks, a natural strategy would be to double the key lengths, for example, to use AES with 256-bit keys as a minimum. However, this is an oversimplified analysis since the real-world costs of Grover's algorithm do not achieve the full square-root speedup. For example, Table 13 of [10] states that Grover's algorithm reduces the cost to compute an AES-256 key from 2^{256} executions of AES to 2^{192} executions of quantum gates, which is much greater than $2^{n/2} = 2^{128}$.

There are also several different attack models to be considered. One can consider a quantum attacker who is given a set of message-ciphertext pairs $(m, E_K(m))$. Alternatively, one can consider a quantum attacker in a much stronger model (e.g., the superposition model or quantum chosen-plaintext attack) where the attacker is provided with access to a quantum circuit that computes $E_K(m)$ and so can execute this circuit on a quantum state that is a superposition of messages. In reality, this latter model seems unnecessarily strong and is not usually considered when evaluating the security of current real-world systems. For more discussion see [11].

The paper [12] gives a quantum security analysis of AES. The paper concludes that *"AES seems a resistant primitive in the post-quantum world as well as in the classical one."*

The NIST document [13] gives further discussion. It says *"Grover's algorithm requires a long-running serial computation, which is difficult to implement in practice. In a realistic attack, one has to run many smaller instances of the algorithm in parallel, which makes the quantum speedup less dramatic."* This is modeled by NIST using the "MAXDEPTH" value. The document claims that a quantum attack on AES 128/192/256 requires, respectively, at least 2^{93}, 2^{157}, 2^{221} operations (this is taking MAXDEPTH = 2^{64}.) In other words, the quantum attacks are not as good as the naive 2^{64}, 2^{96}, 2^{128} that would be expected from a square-root speedup.

14.3.3 NIST Security Levels

As part of the NIST post-quantum standardization process, submitters were requested to propose specific schemes and parameters to reach certain security levels. The security levels were defined in terms of existing standardized and widely used symmetric encryption and hashing primitives. Specifically, the NIST security levels were defined as follows [14].

1. The cost of key search on a block cipher with a 128-bit key (e.g., AES128)
2. The cost of collision search on a 256-bit hash function (e.g., SHA256/SHA3-256)
3. The cost of key search on a block cipher with a 192-bit key (e.g., AES192)
4. The cost of collision search on a 384-bit hash function (e.g., SHA384/SHA3-384)
5. The cost of key search on a block cipher with a 256-bit key (e.g., AES 256)

In addition, the documents state *"Here, computational resources may be measured using a variety of different metrics (e.g., number of classical elementary operations, quantum circuit size, etc.). In order for a cryptosystem to satisfy one of the above security requirements, any attack must require computational resources comparable to or greater than the stated threshold, with respect to all metrics that NIST deems to be potentially relevant to practical security."*

There are a number of challenges in deciding whether a claimed set of parameters for a post-quantum public-key scheme meets one of these levels.

The first challenge is actually to understand precisely the quantum costs to perform any of the five tasks listed above. For example, with level 1 as we have seen it is a nontrivial problem to estimate precisely the cost to break AES128 on a quantum computer. Indeed, in [10] the authors' assessment of the quantum security of AES showed it was a little easier than originally thought, hence *"making it easier for submitters to claim a certain quantum security category."*

14.3.4 Timeline and Challenges for PQC Migration

The PQC schemes under standardization provide the same interfaces for cryptographic operations as the current public-key schemes. However, the deployment of new PQC schemes is challenging. Regarding performance, PQC schemes often have larger ciphertext/signature size, key size, processing time, and/or memory usage than ECC [3–5]. For example, a CRYSTALS-Dilithium signature can be more than one or two thousand bytes, compared with tens of bytes for ECC signatures.

There is also a challenge with the wide variety of PQC schemes being standardized. For example, should one use lattice schemes, or a code-based scheme and a hash-based signature?

As already mentioned, if one has a system that requires data to remain private for a long time, then one should consider urgently migrating to post-quantum encryption schemes. This is because the development time to bring new tools to market is long. As an intermediate step one should use hybrid schemes, which combine both pre-quantum and post-quantum crypto.

The situation with authentication systems is a little different. For many, though not all, applications of digital signatures, it is acceptable to continue using elliptic curve public key signatures until such time as there is a realistic threat that the ECDLP can be solved using a quantum computer. An exception to this might be the use of digital signatures for firmware updates.

Government and commercial organizations should be thinking about their security needs and risk management and planning for when they may need to move to post-quantum crypto. Organizations need to invest in reviewing their systems. As stated in [4] it is *"difficult to determine where and with what priority post-quantum algorithms will need to replace the current public-key systems. Tools are urgently needed to facilitate the discovery of where and how public-key cryptography is being used in existing technology infrastructures."*

PQC is already supported in a number of products. In 2023 Chrome announced support for a hybrid ECC-lattice encryption scheme, and the Signal end-to-end-encrypted messenger app was upgraded to support PQC. In early 2024, the iMessage app was upgraded to support PQC.

14.4 Recommendations

New cryptanalysis, either using quantum computers or classical computers, can happen at any time. Hence, it is necessary for major nation states to maintain expertise and capability in cybersecurity. They can do this by supporting fundamental research into the mathematics and engineering behind PQC.

It is also necessary to aim to be agile with cryptography deployed in real-world systems, though this is extremely challenging in practice, as current systems rely on RSA and ECC and are not very agile.

Post-quantum schemes should be used in a hybrid mode together with ECC, so that as long as at least one cryptosystem is unbroken, then the whole scheme remains secure.

The biggest immediate risk is public key encryption and key-agreement schemes. An attacker can harvest internet traffic today and then try to break the systems when a quantum computer is built in the future. Hence, depending on the nature of the information being protected, it may be necessary to migrate to post-quantum cryptography as soon as possible.

It is recommended that companies and government agencies comply with the NIST and/or European standardized systems and start migrating to post-quantum cryptography for data related to national security, health, and for securing critical infrastructure. While QKD is an active area of research, it is not suitable for securing real-world systems, and its use is discouraged for most government and industry systems.

14.5 Conclusion

Post-quantum cryptography is a mature and standardized technology for protecting internet traffic and other online information from an attacker in the future with a quantum computer. NIST has published standards for post-quantum key agreements and digital signatures. Organizations can start migrating to post-quantum cryptography now, using existing hardware and networks, by combining the NIST schemes in hybrid mode with classical schemes such as elliptic curve cryptography.

References

1. M. Mosca, M. Piani, Quantum threat timeline (2019). https://globalriskinstitute.org/publications/quantum-threat-timeline/
2. M. Mosca, M. Piani, 2023 quantum threat timeline report (2023). https://globalriskinstitute.org/publication/2023-quantum-threat-timeline-report/
3. B. Westerbaan, The state of the post-quantum internet. The Cloudflare Blog (2024)

4. W. Barker, W. Polk, M. Souppaya, Getting ready for post-quantum cryptography: Explore challenges associated with adoption and use of post-quantum cryptographic algorithms (2020). https://csrc.nist.gov/publications/detail/white-paper/2020/05/26/getting-ready-for-post-quantum-cryptography/draft
5. D. Stebila, Standardizing post-quantum cryptography at the IETF. Talk at Real World Post-Quantum Cryptography, 2023-03-26 (2023)
6. NIST, Post-quantum cryptography (2024). https://csrc.nist.gov/projects/post-quantum-cryptography
7. European Union Agency for Cybersecurity (ENISA), Post-quantum cryptography: Current state and quantum mitigation, (2021)
8. ANSSI, BSI, NLNCSA, and Swedish National Communications Security Authority, Position paper on quantum key distribution (2024). https://www.bsi.bund.de/SharedDocs/Downloads/EN/BSI/Crypto/Quantum_Positionspapier.html
9. NSA, Quantum key distribution (QKD) and quantum cryptography (QC) (2017). https://www.nsa.gov/Cybersecurity/Quantum-Key-Distribution-QKD-and-Quantum-Cryptography-QC/
10. S. Jaques, M. Naehrig, M. Roetteler, F. Virdia, Implementing Grover oracles for quantum key search on AES and LowMC, in *EUROCRYPT 2020* ed. by A. Canteaut, Y. Ishai. Lecture Notes in Computer Science, vol. 12106 (Springer, Berlin, 2020), pp. 280–310 .
11. M. Naya-Plasencia, Post-quantum symmetric cryptography, in *Symmetric Cryptography 2*. ISTE Editions (2022)
12. X. Bonnetain, M. Naya-Plasencia, A. Schrottenloher, Quantum security analysis of AES. IACR Trans. Symmetric Cryptol. **2019**(2), 55–93 (2019)
13. NIST, Call for additional digital signature schemes for the post-quantum cryptography standardization process (2022). https://csrc.nist.gov/csrc/media/Projects/pqc-dig-sig/documents/call-for-proposals-dig-sig-sept-2022.pdf
14. NIST, Security (evaluation criteria) (2025). https://csrc.nist.gov/projects/post-quantum-cryptography/post-quantum-cryptography-standardization/evaluation-criteria/security-(evaluation-criteria)

Steven Galbraith received an MSc in mathematics from the Georgia Institute of Technology in 1991 followed by a PhD in mathematics from the University of Oxford in 1996. He has worked as a professor at the University of London and is currently the Head of the Mathematics Department at the University of Auckland. His research is about the mathematics of public key cryptography, and for the last 15 years, he has specialized in post-quantum public key cryptography, especially lattices and isogenies.

Open Access This chapter is licensed under the terms of the Creative Commons Attribution 4.0 International License (http://creativecommons.org/licenses/by/4.0/), which permits use, sharing, adaptation, distribution and reproduction in any medium or format, as long as you give appropriate credit to the original author(s) and the source, provide a link to the Creative Commons license and indicate if changes were made.

The images or other third party material in this chapter are included in the chapter's Creative Commons license, unless indicated otherwise in a credit line to the material. If material is not included in the chapter's Creative Commons license and your intended use is not permitted by statutory regulation or exceeds the permitted use, you will need to obtain permission directly from the copyright holder.

Chapter 15
Quantum Readiness: Recommendations for Enterprises

Martin Burkhart and Bernhard Tellenbach

Abstract With the rise of cryptographically relevant quantum computers on the horizon, companies need to start planning for quantum readiness. The relevant threats and a rough timeline of when they become real must be known. Notably, even encrypted data transmitted today may be at risk if it is stored and decrypted later, once a quantum computer becomes available. A first step on the journey toward quantum-safety is to build a cryptographic inventory and rate data assets according to risks imposed by quantum computers. Among other measures, companies must aim at cryptographic agility—in their networks, their software, and their supply chain.

15.1 Introduction

Recently, several government agencies and technology companies have published guidelines for establishing quantum readiness in enterprises. For example, the US Cybersecurity and Infrastructure Security Agency (CISA), the National Security Agency (NSA), and the National Institute of Standards and Technology (NIST) published a joint report [1] in August 2023. Also, the Netherland's National Communications Security Agency published a comprehensive handbook for migration to post-quantum cryptography [2] and the German Federal Office for Information Security (BSI) published an overview on quantum-safe cryptography [3]. Microsoft published blog articles [4], pointing companies to a questionnaire and tools that support them in assessing their state with regard to quantum-safe technology. The goal of these publications is to inform organizations about the impact of possible future quantum capabilities and to encourage them—especially those operating critical infrastructure—to start planning for migration to post-quantum cryptographic standards.

M. Burkhart (✉) · B. Tellenbach
Cyber-Defence Campus - armasuisse, Zurich, Switzerland
e-mail: martin.burkhart@ar.admin.ch; bernhard.tellenbach@ar.admin.ch

© The Author(s) 2026
J. Jang-Jaccard et al. (eds.), *Quantum Technologies*,
https://doi.org/10.1007/978-3-031-90727-2_15

15.2 Threats and Timelines

When planning for quantum-safe technologies, companies must be familiar with the general threats posed by quantum computers and a rough timeline for when these threats could become real.

In general, mainly asymmetric encryption is affected by quantum computers. Symmetric encryption with long enough keys is still considered safe. Depending on the use case, symmetric encryption may therefore be an alternative. For broken encryption algorithms, confidentiality cannot be reassured later on. Hence, a migration to quantum-safe encryption algorithms requires early planning.

For legally binding digital signatures, frequent re-signing is typically required anyway, as several non-quantum risks persist in any case. These include the discovery of insecurities in hash functions (cf. SHA1) or the revocation of certificates used by certificate authorities (CAs). Re-signing documents with quantum-safe algorithms, once they become standardized, provides continuous integrity.

15.2.1 Breaking RSA

The day when cryptographically relevant quantum computers (CRQC) will be available as common-off-the-shelf products or services is still many years in the future. How far exactly—that's a difficult question to answer. In the 2023 edition of its quantum threat timeline report [5], the Global Risk Institute has surveyed the opinions of 37 international leaders from academia and industry working on several aspects of quantum computing. Particularly interesting is the percentage of experts thinking that it was 50% or more likely that "RSA-2048 can be broken in 24 hours using a quantum computer" within a certain time period:

- Within 10 years: Slightly more than a quarter (10/37)
- Within 15 years: More than half of the respondents (20/37)
- Within 20 years: More than 80% of respondents (31/37)

Hence, the majority of quantum experts believe that within 10–20 years there will be a tipping point, when the likelihood of breaking RSA becomes large. However, the specific question asked was when a quantum computer would be able to "factorize a 2048-bit number in less than 24 hours" (page 18 in [5]). That is, the question refers to breaking a single instance of an RSA private key, not breaking RSA on a global scale. Organizations capable of breaking RSA in this manner would have to focus their costly quantum computing powers on a few selected connections. Breaking RSA on a large scale, e.g., reading all encrypted connections routed through an Internet service provider, will still require quantum computation power to increase by several orders of magnitude, which may require years or even decades of further research.

15.2.2 Standardization of Post-Quantum Cryptography and Migration

So even if it takes another 10–20 years until RSA is broken, we should keep in mind that migrating an IT infrastructure away from classical cryptographic algorithms to use post-quantum cryptography (PQC) requires a long lead time. Moreover, standardization of the first PQC algorithms by NIST has only just ended in August 2024 [6] after a period of eight years. CRYSTALS-Kyber was selected for encryption and key exchange. CRYSTALS-Dilithium, Sphincs+, and FALCON were selected for digital signatures.

Even though the winners have been announced, these algorithms will continue to be examined. It is quite possible that some will prove to be unsafe upon further scrutiny. Security statements about the new algorithms will become more reliable the longer they are assessed and no weaknesses are found. Thus, the risk of adopting bleeding edge technology early must be carefully balanced against data protection requirements. Until the quantum-safe algorithms have passed the test of time, an interim solution could be to use them in combination with classical methods, e.g., by deploying hybrid (multi-key) encryption and signature schemes. As long as there are no CRQC on the market, such a combination offers safety in the event of failure of the PQC algorithms in the conventional sense.

15.2.3 Store Now, Decrypt Later

When developing a roadmap for quantum readiness, there is another key consideration to be made: the "shelf-life time" [5]. The shelf-life time of data covers the time when data needs to be preserved, e.g., to meet regulatory compliance. For example, if a business document is encrypted today and put on the digital shelf for 10 years, as may be required by legislation, it will still sit there in 10 years, being encrypted with today's technology. But what if CRQC emerge in 8 years? That would give attackers the opportunity to break encryption and digital signatures on documents issued today. With signatures, confidentiality is not at stake. Thus, documents can be re-signed with secure algorithms to guarantee integrity. However, adversaries trying to manipulate content will leverage old document versions with legacy signatures. For encryption of a central archive with controlled key management, symmetric algorithms with long enough keys could be used from the beginning, as mainly asymmetric algorithms are impacted by quantum computers.

However, the threat of breaking cryptography in the future applies to all types of data, not just regulated information companies keep on the shelf. Think of e-mails or application traffic sent over corporate networks and the Internet. Powerful adversaries may store encrypted data today, waiting for the day when they will be able to decrypt it using a quantum computer. Hence, if RSA is broken in 15 years and migration to PQC takes 10 years in a company, confidentiality of encrypted data is only guaranteed for 5 years. If that's not acceptable, migration time must be shortened.

As a consequence, companies need to start planning their quantum readiness roadmap today. In the next section, we will discuss elements of such a roadmap.

15.3 Recommendations

The journey toward quantum readiness involves several steps and considerations. In this section, we summarize recommendations from industry [4, 7] and government institutes [1–3] and discuss connections to the zero-trust architecture paradigm. First and foremost, an inventory of cryptographic technology has to be established. Based on the criticality of data, the vendor landscape, and the use of custom systems, actions for mitigating risks must be planned.

15.3.1 Build a Cryptographic Inventory

An inventory of quantum-vulnerable cryptographic technology used across a company serves as a map to navigate the quantum readiness journey. This inventory must cover various assets, such as network protocols, IT infrastructure, and OT (operational technology) infrastructure. On-premise deployments and cloud services must be included likewise.

Encryption technology is often encapsulated in software libraries. Third-party libraries cause dependencies on external companies or an open-source community. For every piece of software, e.g., third-party libraries used in custom-built applications, a commercial off-the-shelf software, or an operating system component, the underlying algorithms should be included in the inventory along with the maintainer of the software. Note that encryption technology is often hidden in the firmware of hardware devices such as IoT (Internet of Things) equipment or industrial control systems.

Tools may support the discovery process of cryptographic assets. Established IT asset management and discovery practices provide a good starting point. Assets may be enriched with information about cryptographic protocols. Make sure to distinguish between symmetric and asymmetric algorithms, because quantum threats mainly target asymmetric encryption. Tools like CodeQL [8] are useful for discovering cryptographic vulnerabilities and legacy algorithms in source code. However, tools typically fail to detect everything and must be complemented by other means.

For systems covered by the inventory, the criticality of associated data must be assessed. This should include critical infrastructure protected by access control systems. The criticality of data usually depends on the business value of the data, e.g., determined by the worst case scenario of leaking it to competitors or criminals.

Also, the data lifecycle plays an important role: does data require long-term secrecy or will it be obsolete in a month?

Finally, the inventory should be integrated into established security risk management processes. Risks should be rated with regard to the severity of incidents and the likelihood of these incidents. For instance, the transfer of business-critical data over a public network should be treated with high priority, due to the severity of a corresponding data breach and a relatively high likelihood of an adversary storing the encrypted data today for later decryption. Depending on their rating, risks may be treated by actions, avoided, transferred, or simply accepted if the costs for addressing them are higher than the potential damage.

15.3.2 Engage with Technology Vendors

Companies are likely to have external dependencies regarding quantum-vulnerable cryptography throughout their entire supply chain. This includes third-party or open-source software libraries used in applications developed in-house, cloud services, purchased software solutions, hardware appliances, or industrial control systems. For software maintained by external parties and vendors, it may prove difficult to gather detailed information about employed encryption algorithms. Hence, it is important to engage with the corresponding maintainers and vendors to get the required information. SBOMs (Software Bill of Materials), and if available, CBOMs (Cryptography Bill of Materials) should be requested by vendors for their products and services.

Ask vendors for a post-quantum roadmap and possible migration plans. This communicates a sense of urgency to them and raises the awareness for quantum vulnerabilities in their software. They might need to ask their suppliers to inform them about cryptographic sub-components themselves. Anyhow, solutions to post-quantum threats will need time to find their way through software supply chains. Hence, software inventories must be monitored for an extended period of time, continuously updated with the latest vendor information.

Actions taken toward quantum-safety need to be aligned with the roadmap of key vendors and, at least partly, depend on what the vendors are planning. In the best case, vendors eliminate vulnerable algorithms from their services, and all that's required is a software update. In the worst case, vendors fail to provide convincing post-quantum roadmaps, requiring the replacement of solutions. For future procurements, criteria and questions addressing post-quantum cryptography should be added to RFPs (Request for Proposals).

15.3.3 Update Custom Systems

For custom software systems developed in-house, responsibilities of software maintainers reside within the company. That is, source code needs to be analyzed and searched for cryptographic algorithms. Software engineers and project managers require awareness of quantum technology and its impact on security. Depending on the vulnerability, legacy components could be removed, components could be replaced, code may be refactored, or workarounds might be devised. If applicable, symmetric instead of asymmetric encryption could be considered for certain use cases. Product owners must integrate high-priority issues related to quantum-safety in product roadmaps. Last but not least, endorsement by managers and the executive board is of prime importance to justify costs incurred by mitigation actions.

Some PQC algorithms are more demanding regarding computational resources [2]. Hence, it is important to assess whether the current IT infrastructure, especially if it is comprised of older hardware, is capable of running the new PQC components. In case the company's business is based on selling software products and services, clients' questions must be answered and roadmaps must be published.

15.3.4 Cryptographic Agility

When migrating from classical to post-quantum cryptography, the concept of crypto-agility becomes very important. Crypto-agility means to be agile with regard to cryptographic primitives, schemes, algorithms, or parameters used [7]. In crypto-agile systems, changing cryptographic elements is easy and allows for smooth transitions.

Achieving crypto-agility is not trivial, because changing the cryptographic stack can be a complex and costly endeavor. Moreover, the roles of people and processes interacting with the system might change as well. As an example, think of switching from using a public key infrastructure (PKI) to symmetric encryption. This will have wide-ranging implications regarding key management and trust setups. Components currently only using an insensitive public key may need to handle secret keys in the future, requiring a completely revised system architecture and risk assessments. A powerful way of achieving crypto-agility is the adaption of hybrid (multi-key) encryption and signature schemes. However, this again requires careful system design.

Even though crypto-agility is hard, companies should start investing in it today. Currently, there is still time before CRQCs become available. Adopting crypto-agility now means to be prepared when CRQCs emerge. The unprepared might have to hastily change cryptographic stacks under pressure of looming real-world attacks and public attention. Time pressure will likely cause mistakes, glitches in service availability, and data breaches. Furthermore, investing in crypto-agility pays off even today. Classical cryptographic algorithms are frequently broken by improving classical attacks. In crypto-agile systems, exchanging vulnerable components is easy and safe—before or after the age of quantum computers.

When planning for the procurement of new systems or replacing legacy systems, companies should bring up crypto-agility in vendor RFPs.

15.3.5 Zero Trust Architecture

As discussed above when pondering the shelf-life time of data, exposure of data encrypted with classical algorithms puts it at risk of being decrypted or stored now and being decrypted later by an adversary controlling a CRQC. The availability of CRQCs and the capabilities of adversaries are typically out of our control. However, data exposure can be controlled, at least to some degree.

Even though that might not be a problem today, it is worthwhile to think about the visibility of encrypted data in a company. How much encrypted data is sent over public networks? How critical is that data? Is there an easy alternative to exposing it to the public? The less encrypted data is accessible, the less it can be stored for future decryption. Adopting a zero trust architecture with separated network fragments could further reduce the visibility of encrypted data. Along the same line of reasoning, rethinking access control to encrypted data may prove beneficial. The less data people see, the less potential to store it.

15.4 Conclusion

Quantum computers pose the theoretical threat of breaking encryption schemes widely used throughout the Internet. Most experts think that within 10–20 years, these threats will become relevant to everyday systems, e.g., by being able to break RSA-2048 within 24 hours. Although this event is still a long way off, enterprises should start thinking about a migration to post-quantum cryptography today. This applies in particular to companies that must guarantee the confidentiality of data for long time frames, because attackers can simply store encrypted data today and wait until quantum computers become available to break encryption.

Companies should start out by building a cryptographic inventory to identify systems with quantum-vulnerable components. From there, external dependencies throughout their supply chain should be addressed with technology vendors, including requirements in the procurement process and developing migration roadmaps for products and services. At the same time, custom systems developed in-house should be screened for vulnerable algorithms. Establishing cryptographic agility will not only ease migration to post-quantum cryptography but also benefit the current security architecture in case of emerging attacks against classic cryptographic schemes. In general, limiting exposure of encrypted data through network fragmentation and zero-trust architectures may lower the risk of store now, decrypt later attacks.

Quantum computers and post-quantum cryptography are highly dynamic fields in their early stages. Consequently, the journey to post-quantum readiness is not a one-off project but requires long-term threat monitoring, risk assessment, and evolution of IT systems.

References

1. Cybersecurity and Infrastructure Security Agency (CISA), Quantum-readiness: Migration to post-quantum cryptography. Technical report, CISA, NSA, NIST (2023)
2. Dutch General Intelligence and Security Service (AIVD), The PQC migration handbook. Technical report, Netherlands National Communications Security Agency (2023)
3. Federal Office for Information Security (BSI), Quantum-safe cryptography — fundamentals, current developments and recommendations. Technical report, Federal Office for Information Security (BSI) (2022)
4. M. Braverman-Blumenstyk, Starting your journey to become quantum-safe (2023). https://www.microsoft.com/en-us/security/blog/2023/11/01/starting-your-journey-to-become-quantum-safe/
5. M. Mosca, M. Piani, Quantum threat timeline report 2023. *Global Risk Insitute* (2023)
6. NIST releases first 3 finalized post-quantum encryption standards (2024). https://www.nist.gov/news-events/news/2024/08/nist-releases-first-3-finalized-post-quantum-encryption-standards
7. How agile is your cryptographic strategy? https://safecode.org/blog/how-agile-is-your-cryptographic-strategy/
8. CodeQL. https://codeql.github.com/

Dr. Martin Burkhart obtained an MSc in computer science in 2003 and completed a PhD in network security at ETH Zurich in 2011. He has held the position of Head of Product Management for Airlock at Ergon Informatik AG. Currently, he works as a scientific project manager at the Cyber-Defence Campus.

Dr. Bernhard Tellenbach earned an MSc in electrical engineering and information technology from ETH Zurich in 2005 and completed his PhD in 2012, also at ETH Zurich. He previously worked as a senior IT security consultant at Consecom AG and as a professor for IT security at ZHAW (Zurich University of Applied Sciences). Currently, he is the President of Swiss Cyber Storm and Head of Cybersecurity at the Cyber-Defence Campus.

Open Access This chapter is licensed under the terms of the Creative Commons Attribution 4.0 International License (http://creativecommons.org/licenses/by/4.0/), which permits use, sharing, adaptation, distribution and reproduction in any medium or format, as long as you give appropriate credit to the original author(s) and the source, provide a link to the Creative Commons license and indicate if changes were made.

The images or other third party material in this chapter are included in the chapter's Creative Commons license, unless indicated otherwise in a credit line to the material. If material is not included in the chapter's Creative Commons license and your intended use is not permitted by statutory regulation or exceeds the permitted use, you will need to obtain permission directly from the copyright holder.

Chapter 16
Perspective on the QKD Versus PQC Debate

Renato Renner and Ramona Wolf

Abstract The rise of quantum computing introduces risks to classical encryption systems, emphasizing the need for more resilient alternatives. Post-quantum cryptography (PQC) offers a practical short- to medium-term solution but still relies on classical cryptographic principles, which may have inherent limitations. Quantum key distribution (QKD), on the other hand, aims to provide a fundamentally higher level of security—information-theoretic security—that classical methods cannot achieve. However, QKD faces several challenges, including scalability and cost, which require further technological progress to address. This chapter critically examines the key challenges associated with QKD and explores the potential for overcoming its current limitations through ongoing research and future advancements.

16.1 Challenges and Opportunities for Quantum Key Distribution

Recent publications have discussed the usability and current technical limitations of quantum cryptography, particularly quantum key distribution (QKD) [1–3]. These analyses identify several challenges with QKD in its current state and recommend addressing these issues before broader adoption. In this chapter, we review these challenges identified and explore possible ways to overcome the limitations. Further insights are available in [4], with additional perspectives provided in earlier works (see, for example, [5–8]).

R. Renner
Institute for Theoretical Physics—ETH Zurich, Zurich, Switzerland
e-mail: renner@ethz.ch

R. Wolf (✉)
Department of Physics, University of Siegen, Siegen, Germany
e-mail: ramona.wolf@uni-siegen.de

© The Author(s) 2026
J. Jang-Jaccard et al. (eds.), *Quantum Technologies*,
https://doi.org/10.1007/978-3-031-90727-2_16

Table 16.1 Summary of our assessment of whether Challenges 1–7 are problematic now, in the medium-term, and long-term future. By "medium-term future" we mean the epoch when cheaper optical equipment and quantum repeaters are widely available, whereas "long-term future" refers to the era when universal quantum computers connected by a quantum network are realized

	Problematic now	Problematic medium-term	Problematic long-term
Challenge 1	Not within scope of QKD		
Challenge 2	See Table 16.2	No	No
Challenge 3	Yes	To some extent	To some extent
Challenge 4	Yes	No	No
Challenge 5	Yes	Yes	No
Challenge 6	Yes	No	No
Challenge 7	Yes	Yes	No

In the following, we summarize seven frequently cited challenges associated with QKD. Our assessment of whether these limitations are problematic now, in the medium-term and long-term future, is summarized in Table 16.1. To avoid providing specific time frames for the terms "medium-term" and "long-term," we have chosen to define them based on technological milestones: the realization of quantum repeaters and a universal quantum computer, respectively. This approach is favorable because of the inherent challenge in predicting when these milestones in hardware development will be achieved. By adopting this strategy, we aim to offer an assessment that remains independent of the pace of this development.

Challenge 1: Quantum Key Distribution Does Not Solve the Authentication Problem

Authentication, whether in classical or quantum systems, always requires either a pre-shared secret or a trusted third party (TTP), and addressing this need is generally outside the primary scope of QKD.

That said, the need for authentication does not necessarily compromise the information-theoretic security QKD provides. It has been shown that a small initial secret (e.g., a password) shared by the two parties is sufficient to establish information-theoretically secure authentication [9, 10]. Alternatively, if the two parties can individually establish authentication to a TTP, then the resulting connection between them will also be information-theoretically secure.

Even if the authentication method used in QKD is not information-theoretically secure but instead relies on (computationally secure) asymmetric cryptography, QKD remains future-proof in the sense that "store now, decrypt later" attacks do not work. An attacker would have to hack the authentication procedure in real time to gain access to the generated key. Merely storing the messages exchanged and waiting for more powerful computers to decrypt them would not be sufficient to obtain the key. Once the key generation process is finished, even a complete breach of the authentication procedure does not reveal any information on the generated key.

Table 16.2 Comparison of how well protocol security and implementation security of post-quantum cryptography (PQC) and quantum key distribution (QKD) are understood. Protocol security refers to the abstract protocol. For classical protocols, it usually relies on the conjectured hardness of certain mathematical problems, such as factoring, which is difficult to quantify. Conversely, in quantum cryptography, protocol security relies on physical laws. Implementation security depends on the safety of the hardware and software on which the abstract protocols are run, such as their robustness against side-channel attacks. Here, classical cryptography currently has an advantage compared to quantum cryptography due to the experience acquired over many decades, whereas quantum hardware and software engineering is still in the early stages

		Now	Medium term	Long term
PQC	Protocol security	Bad	Bad	Bad
	Implementation security	Fair	Fair	Fair
QKD	Protocol security	Good	Good	Good
	Implementation security	Bad	Increasing	Good

Challenge 2: Post-Quantum Cryptography Provides a Cheaper and Better-Understood Alternative to QKD

To compare the security of QKD and PQC, one has to distinguish between "protocol security" and "implementation security" (see Table 16.2). Protocol security describes the theoretical security of the abstract protocol: QKD protocols come with a mathematical proof that they are information-theoretically secure [11]. Conversely, the security of PQC protocols is only as well understood as that of classical computationally secure schemes. It relies on the assumption that a given mathematical problem is "hard" to solve for classical and quantum computers. The crux is that evidence for such an assumption is sparse. It depends on how many mathematicians or computer scientists have already tried to solve the problem and for how long. The list of problems considered "hard" is thus generally shrinking over time (see Fig. 16.1). Furthermore, while researchers have decade-long experience regarding hard problems for classical computers, quantum computing is relatively young, and it is conceivable that novel quantum algorithms for solving problems that were initially considered hard will be discovered (as was already the case for the factoring problem).

Conversely, the protocol security of QKD is provable based on the laws of physics. It is thus unaffected by algorithmic discoveries or hardware developments. In addition, the protocol security can be quantified in terms of a bound on the probability that the protocol is broken. The risk profile of QKD protocols is more manageable (see Fig. 16.1).

The situation is a bit different if one considers the security of the actual implementation of a protocol. Implementations of PQC can draw on decades of experience with classical computers, which has led to a good understanding of potential side-channel attacks. On the other hand, the implementation security of QKD is still in the exploratory stage. As QKD is a relatively young technology, researchers have only a little experience with possible side-channel attacks and countermeasures [12]. Still, this understanding will increase in the coming years.

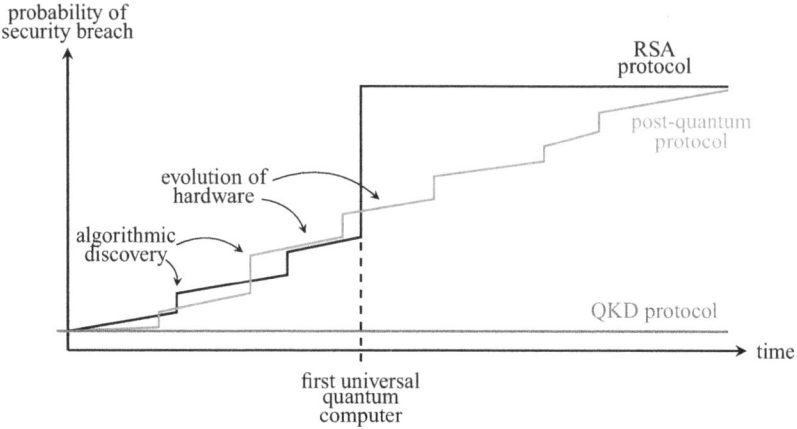

Fig. 16.1 Protocol security of cryptographic protocols over time. The diagram shows schematically the development of the probability that an encryption protocol is broken if the adversary has all the computational power in the world as a function of time. Classical protocols, including post-quantum ones, which aim to provide computational security, are becoming increasingly insecure due to the evolution of hardware and algorithmic discoveries. If an efficient quantum algorithm is found to break it, which is the case for RSA, the scheme will become insecure once the first universal quantum computer is available. On the other hand, the failure probability of quantum key distribution always remains the same because it only relies on the laws of quantum physics, which don't change over time

Furthermore, in the medium- and long-term future, the issue can be resolved with semi-device-independent and fully device-independent QKD, respectively [13, 14].

Challenge 3: QKD Requires Special Purpose Equipment
The requirement of dedicated and, thus, expensive hardware is indeed one of the main reasons why QKD is not widely usable today. Such hardware is anticipated to become more accessible as optical communication technology continues to advance. However, although the cost of QKD hardware is expected to decrease over time, it is likely to remain higher than that of classical communication infrastructure.

Any cryptographic scheme, classical or quantum, ultimately runs on hardware, which may be prone to side-channel attacks. The difficulty of patching flawed hardware is thus not a problem specific to quantum cryptography. However, since QKD comes with a mathematical proof of security, the protocol parameters do not require any updates. This is different in computational cryptography, where algorithmic or hardware breakthroughs may imply that security parameters, such as the key length of RSA [15], need to be adapted.

Challenge 4: Trusted Nodes are Needed to Overcome Signal Loss Over Long Distances
At the current state, QKD protocols indeed require trusted intermediate stations to achieve longer distances. However, the need for trusted relays is not fundamental—

quantum repeaters [16–18] will replace them in the medium-term future. Quantum repeaters work coherently on the quantum level and are thus secured by the laws of quantum theory in the same way as QKD is secured by these laws. Hence, even if they are hacked and controlled by a quantum adversary, security is still guaranteed. While this method is well-established in theory, it has yet to be experimentally realized. The main obstacle is that a quantum repeater requires quantum memory. The storage time of state-of-the-art quantum memories is insufficient to outperform direct optical links, despite considerable progress in recent years [19–21]. However, since quantum memories are a crucial part of quantum computers, they are being intensively researched on various technology platforms.

Challenge 5: Securing and Validating Implementations of QKD Protocols

The gap between theoretical and implementation security is a common challenge in cryptography, including classical systems where side-channel attacks remain an active area of research. In the relatively young field of quantum communication, research into these implementation challenges is still developing, with efforts to address such vulnerabilities already underway [12]. One potential approach is (semi-)device-independent QKD, which relies on minimal assumptions about the behavior of quantum devices, making it more resilient to side-channel attacks. While still in its early stages, this technology shows promise as a potential solution to these challenges in the long-term future [13, 14].

Challenge 6: QKD Lacks Official Standards

To ensure a fair comparison between the security proofs of QKD and PQC, it is important to recognize the different types of security guarantees they provide. PQC algorithms typically offer asymptotic guarantees, which describe security within the limits of large computational resources but do not provide precise quantitative measures. This is why parameters such as key sizes in classical cryptography often require periodic adjustment. In contrast, QKD provides a quantitative security guarantee, specifying the probability of a scheme being compromised, as illustrated in Fig. 16.1. Additionally, QKD security proofs incorporate finite-size effects, considering the actual number of protocol rounds rather than relying solely on asymptotic assumptions. Both approaches have their strengths and limitations, reflecting the differing nature of their security models.

Given these high security standards set for QKD, it is unsurprising that providing security proofs—especially for practical protocols—is particularly challenging. Developing PQC-level (nonquantitative, asymptotic) security proofs for QKD is easier and can already be found in the literature [22]. However, there is no fundamental obstacle that prevents formulating a quantitative finite-size security proof for practically relevant protocols, and the information-theoretic ingredients to such proofs are already available.

Moreover, the need for standards in QKD has been recognized by standardization authorities, and there are already attempts to lay the groundwork for such a standard, for example, by classifying side-channel attacks [12].

Challenge 7: QKD Increases the Risk of Denial-of-Service Attacks
Current implementations of QKD are usually individual point-to-point links. An adversary with access to the link may successfully run a denial-of-service attack. However, future quantum cryptographic solutions are expected to run on a network of quantum connections. Like in classical communication networks, information can be rerouted if one of the links fails to function. Once this stage is reached, there will be no fundamental difference between classical and quantum cryptography regarding their vulnerability to denial-of-service attacks.

16.2 Conclusion and Recommendations

The issues highlighted around the use of QKD are significant and impose severe limitations on the current usability of quantum cryptography. However, it is important to note that these limitations are not inherent to quantum cryptography but rather due to the early stage of the novel hardware required. Some of these limitations can be resolved in the medium-term future with the availability of cheaper and improved quantum technology (see Table 16.1). Overcoming the remaining limitations, though, will require a long-term investment in developing quantum communication technology.

This effort, however, may be justified: Quantum cryptography has the potential to offer advantages over classical cryptography. Unlike traditional encryption schemes, which require periodic updates to address evolving technological threats, quantum cryptography provably provides a higher level of protocol security, including resilience against potential future threats such as quantum computers. Not only do quantum cryptographic protocols guarantee secure communication during their execution, but they also offer everlasting security: Information communicated using quantum cryptography today will remain secure forever, regardless of future developments in software and hardware.

As quantum cryptography is not yet widely available, developing a strategy for securing sensitive data in the interim is essential. While standard encryption schemes such as RSA can still be used for data with a short shelf life (since universal quantum computers are not yet realized), data with a longer lifespan requires protection against "store now, decrypt later" attacks. Therefore, a combination of QKD and PQC in hybrid schemes currently offers an alternative approach to data encryption (this approach was, for example, explored in [8, 23, 24]). A concrete scheme may look as follows: A message is first encrypted using a PQC scheme, which may rely on public-key infrastructure. In addition, the resulting ciphertext is encrypted using a one-time pad, with cryptographic keys generated via QKD. This combination of PQC and QKD provides future-proof encryption resistant to attacks from both quantum and classical computers. The one-time pad ensures that the encryption remains secure even if the PQC scheme is broken in the long-term future. At the same time, the PQC encryption guarantees that even an adversary able to exploit flaws in the QKD implementation cannot read secret messages in the short or mid-term future. This hybrid scheme can be a viable interim solution for the medium-term future, when Challenges 2–4 and 6 are (largely) overcome (see Table 16.1).

References

1. National Security Agency (NSA). Quantum key distribution (QKD) and quantum cryptography (QC). https://www.nsa.gov/Cybersecurity/Quantum-Key-Distribution-QKD-and-Quantum-Cryptography-QC/. Retrieved on November 6 (2024)
2. National Cyber Security Center (NCSC). Quantum security technologies. https://www.ncsc.gov.uk/whitepaper/quantum-security-technologies. Retrieved on November 6 (2024)
3. French Cybersecurity Agency (ANSSI), Federal Office for Information Security (BSI), Netherlands National Communications Security Agency (NLNCSA), and Swedish National Communications Security Authority, Swedish Armed Forces. Position paper on quantum key distribution. https://www.bsi.bund.de/SharedDocs/Downloads/EN/BSI/Crypto/Quantum_Positionspapier.html. Retrieved on November 6 (2024)
4. R. Renner, R. Wolf, The debate over QKD: A rebuttal to the NSA's objections. arXiv:2307.15116 (2023)
5. V. Scarani, C. Kurtsiefer, The black paper of quantum cryptography: Real implementation problems. Theor. Comput. Sci. **560**, 27–32 (2014)
6. E. Diamanti, H.-K. Lo, B. Qi, Z. Yuan, Practical challenges in quantum key distribution. npj Quantum Inf. **2**, 16025 (2016)
7. Quantum Communications Hub. Community response to the NCSC 2020 quantum security technologies white paper. https://www.quantumcommshub.net/news/community-response-to-the-ncsc-2020-quantum-security-technologies-white-paper. Retrieved on November 6 (2024)
8. R. Alléaume, *Quantum Cryptography and Its Application Frontiers* (Sorbonne Université, Habilitation, 2021). https://perso.telecom-paristech.fr/alleaume/HDRMainv10final.pdf
9. R. Renner, S. Wolf, The exact price for unconditionally secure asymmetric cryptography, in *Advances in Cryptology—EUROCRYPT 2004* (Springer, Heidelberg, 2004), pp. 109–125
10. Y. Dodis, D. Wichs, Non-malleable extractors and symmetric key cryptography from weak secrets, in *Proceedings of the Forty-First Annual ACM Symposium on Theory of Computing* (ACM, New York, 2009)
11. C. Portmann, R. Renner, Security in Quantum Cryptography. Rev. Mod. Phys. **94**, 025008 (2022)
12. Federal Office for Information Security (BSI). Implementation attacks against QKD systems. https://www.bsi.bund.de/SharedDocs/Downloads/EN/BSI/Publications/Studies/QKD-Systems/QKD-Systems.html. Retrieved on November 6 (2024)
13. I.W. Primaatmaja, K.T. Goh, E.Y.-Z. Tan, J.T.-F. Khoo, S. Ghorai, C.C.-W. Lim, Security of device-independent quantum key distribution protocols: a review. Quantum **7**, 932 (2023)
14. V. Zapatero, T. van Leent, R. Arnon-Friedman, W.-Z. Liu, Q. Zhang, H. Weinfurter, M. Curty, Advances in device-independent quantum key distribution. npj Quantum Inf. **9**, 10 (2023)
15. E.B. Barker, Q.H. Dang, Recommendation for key management part 3: application-specific key management guidance. Technical report, National Institute of Standards and Technology (2015)
16. H.J. Briegel, W. Dür, J.I. Cirac, P. Zoller, Quantum repeaters: the role of imperfect local operations in quantum communication. Phys. Rev. Lett. **81**(26), 5932–5935 (1998)
17. N. Sangouard, C. Simon, H. de Riedmatten, N. Gisin, Quantum repeaters based on atomic ensembles and linear optics. Rev. Mod. Phys. **83**(1), 33–80 (2011)
18. K. Azuma, S.E. Economou, D. Elkouss, P. Hilaire, L. Jiang, H.-K. Lo, I. Tzitrin, Quantum repeaters: from quantum networks to the quantum internet. Rev. Mod. Phys. **95**, 045006 (2023)

19. X. Liu, J. Hu, Z.-F. Li, X. Li, P.-Y. Li, P.-J. Liang, Z.-Q. Zhou, C.-F. Li, G.-C. Guo, Heralded entanglement distribution between two absorptive quantum memories. Nature **594**(7861), 41–45 (2021)
20. D. Lago-Rivera, S. Grandi, J.V. Rakonjac, A. Seri, H. de Riedmatten, Telecom-heralded entanglement between multimode solid-state quantum memories. Nature **594**(7861), 37–40 (2021)
21. J. Rabbie, K. Chakraborty, G. Avis, S. Wehner, Designing quantum networks using preexisting infrastructure. npj Quantum Inf. **8**(1), 5 (2022)
22. V. Scarani, H. Bechmann-Pasquinucci, N.J. Cerf, M. Dušek, N. Lütkenhaus, M. Peev, The security of practical quantum key distribution. Rev. Mod. Phys. **81**, 1301–1350 (2009)
23. B. Dowling, T.B. Hansen, K.G. Paterson, Many a mickle makes a muckle: A framework for provably quantum-secure hybrid key exchange, in *Post-Quantum Cryptography* (Springer International Publishing, Berlin, 2020), pp. 483–502
24. N. Vyas, R. Alléaume, Everlasting secure key agreement with performance beyond QKD in a quantum computational hybrid security model. arXiv:2004.10173 (2020)

Renato Renner is a professor of theoretical physics at ETH Zurich, where he leads the research group for Quantum Information Theory. Prior to his appointment at ETH, he was a postdoctoral researcher at the Department of Applied Mathematics and Theoretical Physics (DAMTP) at the University of Cambridge, UK. During his doctoral studies in the Computer Science Department of ETH, he developed a security proof for quantum key distribution. His current research, apart from quantum cryptography, encompasses the foundations of quantum theory as well as the interplay between quantum physics and general relativity.

Ramona Wolf is a junior professor at the University of Siegen (Germany), where she leads the research group for Quantum Cryptography. Prior to her current role, she was a postdoctoral researcher at ETH Zurich in the group of Renato Renner, and she obtained her PhD in physics from Leibniz University Hanover (Germany) in 2020. Her research focuses on the security of quantum key distribution and its connection to the foundations of quantum theory, and she has written the first textbook on quantum key distribution.

Open Access This chapter is licensed under the terms of the Creative Commons Attribution 4.0 International License (http://creativecommons.org/licenses/by/4.0/), which permits use, sharing, adaptation, distribution and reproduction in any medium or format, as long as you give appropriate credit to the original author(s) and the source, provide a link to the Creative Commons license and indicate if changes were made.

The images or other third party material in this chapter are included in the chapter's Creative Commons license, unless indicated otherwise in a credit line to the material. If material is not included in the chapter's Creative Commons license and your intended use is not permitted by statutory regulation or exceeds the permitted use, you will need to obtain permission directly from the copyright holder.

Chapter 17
Quantum Technologies for Space Applications

Davide Venturelli and Filip Wudarski

Abstract Quantum technologies are becoming increasingly significant in space applications and defense. Quantum communication offers secure methods for data transmission, which have already been demonstrated in Earth-to-satellite links, paving the way for advanced communication systems and quantum networks. Quantum sensing is expected to play a vital role in GPS-denied navigation and precise Earth measurements on space stations and satellites. This chapter reviews the latest advancements in quantum communication and quantum sensing for space applications and explores their future developments and potential impact.

17.1 Introduction

Space science and quantum science represent the farthest frontiers of our understanding, each at opposite ends of the scale spectrum. The former investigates cosmic objects like planets, solar systems, and galaxies, while the latter focuses on understanding phenomena present in atomic and subatomic realms. Both scientific disciplines have technological derivatives which have driven societal progress that has influenced billions of people, and both promise to shape our future [1]. Therefore, it is not surprising that space technologies are impacting quantum technologies and vice versa.

For example, quantum communication satellites, like Quantum Experiments at Space Scale (QUESS) program with Micius satellite [2, 3], are combining space and quantum science to enable secure, long-distance communication. Similarly, quantum sensors [4] are being considered for applications in space exploration, offering unprecedented precision in measuring gravitational fields and increasing the hope of detecting dark matter [5]. Finally, the field of quantum computing is poised to revolutionize computational sciences, which inevitably will have strong

---

D. Venturelli (✉) · F. Wudarski
Universities Space Research Association (USRA), Research Institute for Advanced Computer Science (RIACS), Washington, DC, USA
e-mail: DVenturelli@usra.edu; FWudarski@usra.edu

© The Author(s) 2026
J. Jang-Jaccard et al. (eds.), *Quantum Technologies*,
https://doi.org/10.1007/978-3-031-90727-2_17

impact on space exploration, as computational techniques directly and indirectly support critical aspects of research, development, preparation, and control of each space mission. Therefore, space agencies like NASA [6, 7] or ESA [8–10] invest their resources in various quantum programs. Here, we focus on the current state-of-the-art in quantum technologies and explore how they are entering the realm of space exploration.

Today, the term "quantum technologies" mostly refers to the second wave of technological advancements[1] emerging from quantum mechanics, focused on the manipulation of quantum systems, ideally without loss of quantum resources like superposition or entanglement. This quantum control enables quantum information processing, which forms the foundation for quantum computing, communication, and sensing. The quantum resources provide capabilities to quantum technologies to surpass classical approaches in processing power, precision, and security. However, accurately manipulating fragile quantum states to achieve the desired outcomes is challenging from both theoretical and engineering perspectives. Experimental realization of fully fledged quantum devices requires a sophisticated hardware and software stack. Despite significant progress in developing hardware dedicated to quantum purposes, further advancements are still required to bring these technologies to high technology readiness levels (TRLs). Among the most pressing obstacles are noise and scalable systems engineering.

Despite the relatively early maturity of the second wave of quantum technologies (what in quantum computing community was dubbed noise intermediate scale quantum (NISQ) era), existing prototypes are already expected to allow researchers and users to develop innovations that will benefit the space ecosystem.

We will focus on quantum sensing and quantum communication providing a high-level overview of their functionality and applications that are relevant to civil space science and programs. For a deeper understanding of the theory and concepts related to these, we recommend standard textbooks such as [11, 12].

17.1.1 Quantum Sensing

Quantum sensing is often described as a method for measuring various physical quantities, whether quantum or classical, using quantum objects or states. Quantum coherence, and in particular quantum entanglement, serves as a resource for accurately determining values of physical quantities such as magnetic and electric fields, rotation, time/frequency, pressure, gravity, and more [4, 13, 14]. Quantum sensors are exceptionally sensitive, often detecting values that are orders of magnitude

---

[1] The first wave is associated with technologies such as lasers, transistors, or microwave ovens that rely on quantum effects, but do not actively manipulate on a low level. The UK Defence Science and Technology Laboratory (DSTL) classifies these technologies into "Quantum 1.0" and "Quantum 2.0," respectively.

smaller than those measurable by classical sensors. Fundamentally, the sensitivity of these sensors scales proportionally with the inverse of the transduction and relaxation times and is fundamentally bounded by the Heisenberg limit that is not only theoretically reachable but also more accurate than what one expects from the classical theory. Transduction refers to the changes in transition energy of quantum states in response to the external parameter of interest, while relaxation time is intrinsically linked to the interaction between the quantum system and its surrounding environment, i.e., decoherence noise.

Quantum sensors are based on controllable quantum states, which can be realized in various physical systems, including atomic spins, trapped ions with electronic or vibrational states, Rydberg atoms, nuclear spins, superconducting qubits, and even muonic spins. Quantum sensors can also use photons, phonons, atoms, or molecules for interferometry or optomechanics. These highly sensitive states can be utilized in space missions for precise gravitational mapping [14] or vehicle navigation, as well as in space-borne Earth observation and climate research. Recently, quantum sensing has been developed for radar and LIDAR-like applications [15], pushing the boundaries of classical sensitivity and accuracy. Moreover, atomic clocks are utilized for accurate time measurements that enable proper functionality of geopositioning systems like Global Positioning System, Global Navigation Satellite System, and Galileo and BeiDou systems.

Furthermore, quantum sensors have the potential to deepen our fundamental understanding of physics by providing data critical for developing and testing new theories. In the USA, this opportunity was well recognized in the Decadal Survey for the Biological and Physical Science (BPS) Division of NASA as well as investments by the Department of Energy as part of the National Quantum Initiative, with notable centers such as the Superconducting Quantum Materials and Systems Center at Fermilab and the Q-SEnSE NSF Institute leading the way with dedicated programs.

However, it is important to highlight some of the key challenges in advancing quantum sensing technology, particularly its integration into larger systems such as autonomous vehicles or satellite networks. This requires not only sophisticated control software but also sufficient stability of quantum states, which, in laboratory settings, often benefit from frequent recalibration to ensure optimal performance, but in space would pose additional obstacles to overcome.

PNT and Atom Interferometry Given the above, the prime space application of quantum sensing relates to position navigation and timing (PNT)—particularly in the areas of accelerometry and gyroscopy—and gravity measurement, including gravimetry and gravity gradiometry. The prime technology that has been explored for the above is atom interferometry. The International Space Station (ISS) currently houses a cutting-edge quantum matter research facility called the Cold Atom Laboratory (CAL). Initially launched in 2018, the CAL was upgraded in 2020 to support advanced research capabilities, including light-pulse atom interferometry (LPAI) and experiments with dual atom species. In the near future, the ISS will integrate a newly developed Bose-Einstein Condensate Cold Atom Laboratory (BECCAL), which promises to be a fully autonomous, cloud-accessible platform for conducting quantum matter experiments in microgravity conditions [16]. NASA is currently developing a quantum gravity gradiometer utilizing ultracold quantum matter for a low-earth orbit (LEO) mission. This project builds upon the GRACE mission, which previously used classical accelerometers to map Earth's gravity gradient. The primary objective is to precisely track and monitor mass distribution changes caused by various phenomena, including climate change, tidal movements, water aquifer fluctuations, and ice cap melting. Traditionally, deploying a specialized atom-interferometer sensor requires a lengthy development process spanning a decade or more. The scientific and technological advancement necessitates creating physics testbeds to mature relevant technologies and methodologies to a deployable standard.

Machine-Learning for Atom Interferometry Optical lattice-based sensing with cold atoms represents a promising yet still-emerging technology that promises to overcome some limitations of LPAI. Despite its relative immaturity, this approach already supports the world's most precise atomic clocks and is driving the development of compact, robust inertial and gravitational sensors. The technique involves preparing and confining atoms within an optical lattice created by intersecting counter-propagating laser beams. This method allows for remarkably precise control of the lattice potential, which directly translates to precise manipulation of the atom ensemble's momentum states. Unlike traditional atom interferometry, where atoms move freely between laser pulses, the shaken lattice interferometry (SLI) approach continuously traps atoms within the optical lattice during measurements [17]. The technological advantages of SLI are significant. The lattice fields generate trapping forces substantially stronger than gravitational forces, rendering the system highly resistant to vibrations and rotations. This approach enables sensors that can be over ten times more sensitive than traditional interferometry devices while maintaining a compact form factor [18]. Moreover, the system's ability to dynamically reconfigure measurement sequences allows for extraordinary flexibility—creating a field-programmable quantum sensor capable of measuring various signals, including acceleration, rotation, gravity, and gravity gradients. These characteristics make SLI particularly attractive for applications with strict size, weight, and power constraints, such as space-based deployments. Researchers can configure the sensor for specific performance requirements, such as large dynamic range, high precision, or real-time bias rejection. The technology's remarkable flexibility and extensibility position optical lattice-based quantum sensing as a potential cornerstone for emerging quantum sensing research and applications.

However, significant theory scientific challenges remain, particularly concerning many-body atomic interactions. While these interactions typically degrade interferometer performance, researchers have already demonstrated techniques to utilize such interactions for improving system performance, such as achieving momentum state squeezing in free-space interferometers.

Superconducting Sensors A novel promising approach to quantum sensing for space applications has been recently put forward: magnetic levitation. The magnetic suspension of diamagnetic and superconducting materials offers compelling advantages, notably in reducing experimental noise and creating innovative opportunities for integrating levitated objects with solid-state electronic systems. One particularly intriguing approach involves developing a quantum levitation platform featuring a superconducting sphere interfaced with a superconducting qubit [19]. This sophisticated experimental configuration enables extraordinarily precise positional measurements of the suspended sphere, with significant potential for detecting minute forces and interactions at the quantum scale. The broader implications of such research extend beyond immediate technological applications, potentially offering insights into fundamental physical phenomena, including potential investigations related to dark matter detection and gravitational wave measurement techniques.

Ultimately, the development of advanced inertial sensors would represent a breakthrough in navigation technology. The ambitious goal is to enable autonomous navigation for extended periods—specifically, maintaining position uncertainty within one meter over 100 days—without relying on external references like GPS. Current classical sensor technologies fall dramatically short of this target, underperforming by four to five orders of magnitude.

While space applications are very compelling, it should be noted that terrestrial deployment of technologies would open unprecedented opportunities for scientific and practical applications. Researchers could monitor volcanic activity with extraordinary detail, detect hidden underground structures like tunnels, and identify mineral deposits at depths unreachable by conventional ground-penetrating radar techniques. These capabilities would have profound implications for geological research, resource exploration, and environmental monitoring.

17.1.2 Quantum Communication for Space

Quantum communication is a promising field poised to revolutionize secure communication in response to emerging threats from quantum computing. Historically, at the heart of this advancement is quantum key distribution (QKD), which offers mathematically proven long-term security (assuming no new fundamental laws of physics), in ideal conditions. Traditional QKD was limited to a few hundred kilometers due to signal loss in fibers or terrestrial free-space. However, satellite-based QKD, using low-Earth orbit, extends this range to a global scale, far surpassing previous limitations [20, 21].

Beyond QKD, now the worldwide attention has been primarily on the establishment of "quantum networking" capabilities, rallying around the far-future concept of the "quantum internet" [22]. Deployment of quantum communication and quantum internet on scale can provide additional layer of data protection which is an increasingly important issue for the current digital society. Yet, challenges such as atmospheric turbulence, beam diffraction, and background noise remain. In particular, low data rates and the influence of the environment that causes decay of entanglement are still insufficient to encode secrets on a larger scale. Advanced techniques like high-precision pointing and tracking systems, large telescopes, and filtering mechanisms help mitigate these issues. Integrating terrestrial quantum networks with space-based quantum communication infrastructure is a key objective, aiming to create a global quantum web that connects quantum devices like computers, sensors, and simulators.

Before arbitrarily scalable connectivity, the first technical goal is to advance the maturity of the quantum networking components (e.g., repeaters, entanglement swappers, photon sources and detectors, clock synchronization, quantum memories), and the second is to demonstrate distributed quantum processing, which is also an enabling capability for scalable quantum computing.

Maturity Quantum communications rely on clock synchronization that enables correct interpretation of incoming signals. Therefore, quantum clock synchronization protocols are developed to introduce not only higher accuracy in time measurements necessary for accurate signal readings but also extra layer of security, as classical synchronization methods are susceptible to malicious attacks. The quantum procedure is based on using entangled pulses between atomic clocks, that through entanglement purification operation one can reduce errors [23].

The development of quantum communication follows several complementary paths. Satellite-based communication poses unique engineering challenges, some of which are not directly related to core quantum technologies. Meanwhile, the quantum components, including repeaters, detectors, fiber optics, and antennas, are being developed on the ground with potential for space deployment [24]. In parallel with engineering advancements, scientists and policymakers are working on standardization and certification protocols to help streamline progress [25].

Recent advancements in quantum communication signal a growing trend toward establishing global quantum networks, leveraging space-based infrastructure to overcome the limitations of terrestrial fiber-optic channels. By utilizing satellites, researchers are addressing the challenge of distance and signal degradation inherent in fiber-optic systems. This shift toward space-based solutions is further underscored by ongoing developments aimed at expanding coverage and enhancing reliability.

The European Commission roadmap [1] for advancing space-based quantum communication includes significant milestones, such as the SAGA mission, which aims to implement satellite-based quantum cryptography (PM-QKD) by 2028 and expand to entanglement-based communication (ENT-QKD) by 2035. Alongside technological advancements, standardization and certification efforts are crucial, involving collaboration among quantum physicists, cryptography experts, and engineers. Major standardization bodies, like ETSI, ISO, or NIST, are actively working on these aspects to ensure the security and reliability of quantum cryptographic systems.

In the USA, agencies such as the National Science Foundation have made significant investments, recently establishing a Center for Quantum Networks dedicated to architecting future quantum communication infrastructure. Within this context of expanding quantum capabilities, NASA's Space Communications and Navigation (SCaN) program has proposed innovative mission concepts for space-based quantum communication. These concepts envision satellites capable of transmitting and receiving quantum signals between ground stations and potentially between satellites themselves. SCaN anticipates that a low-earth orbit (LEO) platform like the International Space Station (ISS) could potentially serve as a critical infrastructure for distributing quantum entanglement between ground stations separated by distances up to 1,200 kilometers.

17.2 Conclusion

Quantum technology holds transformative potential for advancing space science and technology. Devices based on quantum mechanics can offer fundamentally higher precision, faster computation, and more secure communication. As a result, we are already witnessing a global trend of deploying quantum technology in space-related programs and their auxiliary fields. However, we are still in the early stages of the second wave of quantum technology, and widespread adoption remains a distant reality. Nevertheless, coordinated efforts among governments, space agencies, academia, and industry are in full swing to accelerate these advancements. These multi-institutional collaborations, supported and incentivized by governments, are especially crucial for space applications. Additionally, national security concerns play a significant role in shaping quantum initiatives worldwide. The pursuit of powerful quantum computers capable of breaking some of today's cryptographic codes is driving the development of secure quantum communication, which becomes even more robust when satellites are involved. Interestingly, the rise of quantum algorithms offering provable speedups is also pushing the envelope of classical algorithms, particularly in post-quantum cryptography. This led to the emergence of quantum-inspired algorithms, a new class that sometimes offers significant improvements over previous methods. Meanwhile, institutions such as NIST are releasing standards for classical protocols that can withstand attacks from potential *quantum hackers*.

Noteworthy benefits are expected from quantum sensors and measurements, in particular for space applications. Fundamentally, better accuracy offered by quantum control methods will impact space and aerospace navigation through sensitive electric, magnetic, and gravitational field mapping. Additionally, deploying quantum sensing devices on satellites for monitoring environmental and weather patterns will bring us more data with higher resolution, that in conjunction with AI-powered, algorithmic and QML approaches enable us to build better forecasting and nowcasting models.

References

1. R. Kaltenbaek, A. Acin, L. Bacsardi, P. Bianco, P. Bouyer, E. Diamanti, C. Marquardt, Y. Omar, V. Pruneri, E. Rasel, et al., Quantum technologies in space. Exp. Astron. **51**(3), 1677–1694 (2021)
2. C.-Y. Lu, Y. Cao, C.-Z. Peng, J.-W. Pan, Micius quantum experiments in space. Rev. Mod. Phys. **94**(3), 035001 (2022)
3. D. Castelvecchi, China's quantum satellite clears major hurdle on way to ultrasecure communications. Nature **15** (2017). https://www.nature.com/articles/nature.2017.22142
4. C.L. Degen, F. Reinhard, P. Cappellaro, Quantum sensing. Rev. Mod. Phys. **89**(3), 035002 (2017)
5. R. Ebadi, M.C. Marshall, D.F. Phillips, J. Cremer, T. Zhou, M. Titze, P. Kehayias, M. Saleh Ziabari, N. Delegan, S. Rajendran, et al., Directional detection of dark matter using solid-state quantum sensing. AVS Quantum Sci. **4**(4) (2022). https://arxiv.org/abs/2203.06037
6. E.G. Rieffel, S. Hadfield, T. Hogg, S. Mandrà, J. Marshall, G. Mossi, B. O'Gorman, E. Plamadeala, N.M. Tubman, D. Venturelli, et al., From ansätze to z-gates: A NASA view of quantum computing, in *Future Trends of HPC in a Disruptive Scenario* (IOS Press, New York, 2019), pp. 133–160
7. E.G ,Rieffel, A.A. Asanjan, M.S. Alam, N. Anand, D.E. Bernal Neira, S. Block, L.T. Brady, S. Cotton, Z.G. Izquierdo, S. Grabbe, et al., Assessing and advancing the potential of quantum computing: A NASA case study. Futur. Gener. Comput. Syst. **160**, 598–618 (2024)
8. Policy white papers on quantum technologies for space. https://qtspace.eu/policy-white-papers-on-quantum-technologies-for-space/, 2017–2019. Accessed on 2024-11-9
9. ESA Agenda 2025 (2021). Accessed on 2024-11-9
10. ESA Technology Strategy v1.2 (2021). Accessed on 2024-11-9
11. M.A. Nielsen, I.L. Chuang, *Quantum Computation and Quantum Information* (Cambridge University, Cambridge, 2010)
12. I.B. Djordjevic, *Quantum Communication, Quantum Networks, and Quantum Sensing* (Academic Press, New York, 2022)
13. S. Schmitt, T. Gefen, F.M. Stürner, T. Unden, G. Wolff, C. Müller, J. Scheuer, B. Naydenov, M. Markham, S. Pezzagna, et al., Submillihertz magnetic spectroscopy performed with a nanoscale quantum sensor. Science **356**(6340), 832–837 (2017)
14. B. Stray, A. Lamb, A. Kaushik, J. Vovrosh, A. Rodgers, J. Winch, F. Hayati, D. Boddice, A. Stabrawa, A. Niggebaum, et al., Quantum sensing for gravity cartography. Nature **602**(7898), 590–594 (2022)
15. R.G. Torromé, S. Barzanjeh, Advances in quantum radar and quantum LiDAR. Prog Quantum Electron **93**, 100497 (2023)
16. K. Frye, S. Abend, W. Bartosch, A. Bawamia, D. Becker, H. Blume, C. Braxmaier, S.-W. Chiow, M.A. Efremov, W. Ertmer, et al., The Bose-Einstein condensate and cold atom laboratory. EPJ Quantum Technol. **8**(1), 1 (2021)
17. C. LeDesma, K. Mehling, J. Shao, J.D. Wilson, P. Axelrad, M. Nicotra, D.Z. Anderson, M. Holland, Demonstration of a programmable optical lattice atom interferometer. Phys. Rev. Res. **6**(4), 043120 (2024)
18. M.M. Rybak, P. Axelrad, C. LeDesma, D.Z. Anderson, T. Ely, Application of shaken lattice interferometry based sensors to space navigation. Adv. Space Res. **71**(10), 4288–4301 (2023)
19. J. Hofer, R. Gross, G. Higgins, H. Huebl, O.F. Kieler, R. Kleiner, D. Koelle, P. Schmidt, J.A. Slater, M. Trupke, et al., High-Q magnetic levitation and control of superconducting microspheres at millikelvin temperatures. Phys. Rev. Lett. **131**(4), 043603 (2023)
20. S.-K. Liao, W.-Q. Cai, J. Handsteiner, B. Liu, J. Yin, L. Zhang, D. Rauch, M. Fink, J.-G. Ren, W.-Y. Liu, et al., Satellite-relayed intercontinental quantum network. Phys. Rev. Lett. **120**(3), 030501 (2018)

21. J. Yin, Y. Cao, Y.-H. Li, S.-K. Liao, L. Zhang, J.-G. Ren, W.-Q. Cai, W.-Y. Liu, B. Li, H. Dai, et al., Satellite-based entanglement distribution over 1200 kilometers. Science **356**(6343), 1140–1144 (2017)
22. S. Wehner, D. Elkouss, R. Hanson, Quantum internet: A vision for the road ahead. Science **362**(6412), eaam9288 (2018)
23. J.S. Sidhu, S.K. Joshi, M. Gündoğan, T. Brougham, D. Lowndes, L. Mazzarella, M. Krutzik, S. Mohapatra, D. Dequal, G. Vallone, et al., Advances in space quantum communications. IET Quantum Commun. **2**(4), 182–217 (2021)
24. J. Rödiger, Quantum key distribution, in *Trends in Data Protection and Encryption Technologies* (2023), pp. 41–45
25. M. Loeffler et al., Current standardisation landscape and existing gaps in the area of quantum key distribution. https://ec.europa.eu/info/funding-tenders/opportunities/portal/screen/opportunities/horizon-results-platform/29227 (2021). OPENQKD report, accessed on 2024-11-11

Davide Venturelli is the Co-founder and Business Advisor of SensoriumTL, a senior research scientist at NASA, and a fellow at USRA. His research projects include variational algorithms and physics-informed quantum neural networks (NSF ExpandQISE) as well as work on the Superconducting Quantum Materials and Systems Center at NASA. He has received multiple professional awards, including recognition as PI/Co-PI, and holds patents such as "Quantum Optimization for Multiple Input and Output Processing." He earned an MSc in theoretical and mathematical physics from the École Normale Supérieure de Lyon in 2007, followed by a PhD in 2011 from SISSA in Theory of Condensed Matter and Computer Simulations.

Filip Wudarski earned a PhD in theoretical and mathematical physics from Uniwersytet Mikołaja Kopernika w Toruniu in 2015. He has worked as a scientist at NASA Ames Research Center and later at USRA. His work includes the 2018 publication "Entanglement Witnesses from Mutually Unbiased Base."

Open Access This chapter is licensed under the terms of the Creative Commons Attribution 4.0 International License (http://creativecommons.org/licenses/by/4.0/), which permits use, sharing, adaptation, distribution and reproduction in any medium or format, as long as you give appropriate credit to the original author(s) and the source, provide a link to the Creative Commons license and indicate if changes were made.

The images or other third party material in this chapter are included in the chapter's Creative Commons license, unless indicated otherwise in a credit line to the material. If material is not included in the chapter's Creative Commons license and your intended use is not permitted by statutory regulation or exceeds the permitted use, you will need to obtain permission directly from the copyright holder.

Summary Part II

Part II of the book explored the evolving landscape of quantum communication technologies and their impact on secure information exchange. This part covered various aspects of quantum communication, including the threats posed by quantum computers to current encryption systems, quantum random number generators (QRNG), quantum key distribution (QKD), and post-quantum cryptography (PQC). It also examined enterprise readiness for the quantum era and perspectives on the ongoing QKD versus PQC debate.

Quantum random number generators (QRNGs) were identified as playing a crucial role in generating secure cryptographic keys by producing truly random numbers based on quantum phenomena—unlike classical methods, which rely on deterministic algorithms. The use of QRNGs was recognized for enhancing encryption strength and eliminating vulnerabilities associated with predictable random number generation. The discussion highlighted that commercially available QRNG devices were increasingly being integrated into cybersecurity frameworks. However, it was also noted that QRNGs faced limitations related to cost, complexity, and the requirement for specialized hardware, all of which hindered broader adoption. Future developments were expected to focus on improving accessibility and embedding QRNGs into everyday devices, thereby enabling scalable, quantum-safe security.

The ongoing debate between post-quantum cryptography (PQC) and quantum key distribution (QKD) centered on their respective strengths and limitations (see the detailed comparison in the following table). PQC was regarded as a practical solution that could be integrated with existing infrastructure, making it more scalable for widespread adoption. However, it was noted that PQC relies on assumptions regarding the computational hardness of certain mathematical problems—assumptions that could potentially be undermined by unexpected advances in quantum computing. In contrast, QKD was argued to offer unconditional security based on the laws of quantum mechanics but posed greater challenges in terms of scalability due to infrastructure requirements, high costs, and technical complexities. QKD also required specialized hardware and secure communication channels, which limited its practicality. Emerging trends suggested a complemen-

Table 1 Comparison between PQC and QKD

Aspect	PQC	QKD
Security	Computational: No 100% guarantee of reliability	Physics-based: No-cloning theorem of quantum mechanics ensures complete security
Implementation	Software-based solution on classical hardware	Hardware-based solution requiring specialized quantum devices
Communication media	Compatible with any digital media (e.g., wires, radio waves, optical, etc.)	Only compatible with optical media (e.g., fiber optics or free-space optical)
Cost	Low: Can be implemented on existing infrastructure	High: Requires new quantum hardware and infrastructure
Repeater compatibility	Compatible with current digital repeater technology	Requires new quantum repeaters, posing additional security risks
Mobile device compatibility	Fully compatible with existing mobile networks	Limited: Requires line-of-sight nodes (e.g., satellite, microwave links)
Digital signature compatibility	Variations of standards are being developed	None: Not compatible with existing digital signature standards

tary approach, in which hybrid systems combine QKD for high-security use cases with PQC for broader applications, offering a pragmatic pathway toward quantum-safe communication (Table 1).

The emergence of space-based quantum communication was presented as a promising avenue for overcoming the limitations of terrestrial QKD systems. It outlined how satellite-based QKD enables the establishment of global secure communication networks by bypassing the distance constraints inherent to fiber-optic systems. The successful demonstration of the Micius satellite by China highlighted the feasibility of this approach and initiated international collaborations aimed at developing space-based quantum communication infrastructure. Nevertheless, the discussion acknowledged key challenges, including high costs, technical complexity, and the need to ensure system robustness against environmental factors. Future trends were expected to focus on enhancing the scalability and resilience of these systems, integrating them with terrestrial networks, and exploring novel quantum technologies to support secure communication in space.

Part III
Quantum Technology Ecosystem Analysis

The rapid advancements in quantum technologies are reshaping global innovation landscapes, with nations and industries striving to harness their transformative potential. Part III explores this evolving ecosystem through a comprehensive analysis of global quantum strategies, investment trends, and sector-specific applications. It highlights key tools for tracking quantum technology developments, examines the convergence of various quantum fields, and presents case studies demonstrating quantum's impact across industries, including finance—a sector with notable parallels to defense. These insights provide valuable guidance for shaping quantum adoption strategies in cybersecurity and beyond.

Chapter 18
Global Quantum Strategies

Brendan Karch

Abstract Many countries have created national quantum strategies in order to centralize or coordinate quantum research, innovation, commercialization, and talent development in their countries. This chapter comparatively analyzes four national quantum strategies from Canada, Denmark, the Netherlands, and the UK. Each country embraces its own model for quantum strategy, with some favoring large, generative investments, while others pursue more decentralized or additive investments. The overall financial commitments may seem large in the aggregate but constitute a modest per annum spending. Countries that have yet to create their own national strategy can learn from the diverse models for building quantum ecosystems.

18.1 Introduction

Experts debate the precise timing for a commercial "breakthrough" in quantum technologies, yet there is widespread agreement that long-term investments are required, particularly for quantum computers with useful real-world advantages and applications. These investments are being made not just in research and development, but in the wider ecosystems that will support a new quantum economy. For this broad set of tasks, governments have been playing an increasing role through the deployment of national funding schemes, programs, and initiatives. To coordinate these efforts, over a dozen countries have gone further by developing national quantum *strategies*.

Quantum strategies are generally more involved than quantum programs or initiatives, in that they are multi-stakeholder, cross-sectoral, and consider wider social implications. They create both a vision for a quantum-enabled society and concrete plans or funding mechanisms for bringing sectors together to achieve

---

B. Karch (✉)
Swissnex, Boston, MA, USA
e-mail: brendan.karch@swissnex.org

© The Author(s) 2026
J. Jang-Jaccard et al. (eds.), *Quantum Technologies*,
https://doi.org/10.1007/978-3-031-90727-2_18

this vision. According to the OECD, national science, technology, and innovation strategies generally incorporate the following characteristics:

- They express the government's vision on how the scientific field can contribute to the country's economy and society.
- They create public investment priorities and how to create structures to enable them.
- They help rally private and/or public actors around a common goal and facilitate coordination to enable a common vision [1].

Switzerland, while recently launching a Swiss National Quantum Initiative (NQI), has yet to create or deploy a national quantum strategy. However, several of its peer countries have. The aim of this chapter is to describe in detail the quantum strategies of four countries—Canada, Denmark, the Netherlands, and the United Kingdom—and then analytically compare their strategies and provide preliminary recommendations for Switzerland or other countries that may be considering creating their own strategy. While the two global leaders in quantum technologies, the USA and China, are also important, it is more difficult to draw useful comparisons given their large size and very different models—especially in the case of China, where public information is lacking and national autonomy is a primary aim.

These four countries were selected because they have developed extensive quantum strategies, because they are considered among the leading nations in quantum technologies, because they prioritize international engagement, and because the size of their populations and quantum programs provide considerable diversity as a basis of comparison.

18.2 National Quantum Strategies

18.2.1 Canada

Canada's National Quantum Strategy (short: "Canadian Strategy"), created by the Canadian Ministry of Innovation, Science, and Industry, debuted in January 2023, although spending had begun in 2021. The Canadian Strategy consists of three interlocking missions: to make Canada "a world leader" in quantum technologies, to focus on privacy and cybersecurity, and to become early adopters through both government and industry. The three core pillars to achieve these missions are research, talent, and commercialization, with CAD 360 million (CHF 228 million) in targeted public funding planned over seven years starting in 2021 [2].[1]

---

[1] All currencies were converted to CHF using prevailing market rates at the time of authorship. Euros and USD were not converted.

Program implementation through funding streams comes from a wide array of preexisting organizations and initiatives. Major funders for research and development of quantum technologies include the Canada First Research Excellence Fund (CFREF) and Natural Sciences and Engineering Research Council (NSERC). Through NSERC, a new "Alliance Quantum" funding scheme is devoting around CAD 130 million (CHF 82 million) over seven years to allow for greater research and development collaborations—with CAD 100 million (CHF 63 million) targeted for domestic collaborations and CAD 30 million (CHF 19 million) for international collaborations. The first round of international grants in 2024 provided up to CAD 300,000 (CHF 190,000) per project over 1–3 years [2, 3].

The focus of the Canadian Strategy leans heavily toward the computing sector, with the goal to amplify Canada's strong position in quantum hardware and software. Focus areas include hybrid computing, quantum simulators, and use cases in fields such as digital security, banking, or advanced manufacturing. On the commercialization side, innovation challenge programs are issuing calls for advancements such as quantum computing as a service, smaller dilution fridges, or computing prototypes [2]. There is also support promised for the quantum sensing sector, which follows an analogous strategy of investing in research, backing prototypes, supporting common standards, and using the government as an early adopter for technologies [2].

Canada benefited from significant early private and research investment, which helped to create a pioneering and robust startup ecosystem in quantum technologies. The country ranks second globally in the number of quantum startups (after the USA), with 28 in total. D-Wave launched the first commercial quantum-based computer, a quantum annealer, in 2011. Overall, estimated private funding in the last two decades into Canadian quantum technologies has totaled CAD 1.3 billion (CHF 825 million), close to the CAD 1.4 billion (CHF 888 million) in public investment, according to McKinsey. In fact, total investment in quantum startups in Canada from 2001 to 2023 has exceeded all investments in EU startups in the same time frame [4]. Incubators have played a large role, especially the Creative Destruction Lab from the University of Toronto, which has helped launch more than 50 quantum-related companies. The government has pursued commercialization through large grants and investments directly in companies, as well as challenge programs and regional innovation clusters such as Quantum City in Calgary or DistriQ in Sherbrooke [2, 5]. The Canadian Strategy is thus able to build its funding for commercialization on the shoulders of a very robust quantum private industry.

Given these strengths, Canada is highly optimistic about the scale of quantum technologies in its long-term future economy. The Canadian National Research Council estimated that by 2045 the national quantum industry would be valued at CAD 139 billion (CHF 88 billion) and constitute 3% of the country's GDP [2, 5]. If the quantum economy achieves this scale, then significant investments in talent and workforce development are needed—an area of action for the Canadian Strategy. Much of the national initiative for talent development comes from individual university programs, such as a new Bachelor's in Quantum Science at Université de Sherbrooke or a new Master's at the University of Waterloo. The Canadian

Strategy is also providing CAD 40 million (CHF 25 million) to Mitacs for internship and professional development training in quantum [6]. The government is likewise involved in broader science outreach programs to increase diversity in quantum [2].

Quantum security is a major pillar of the Canadian Strategy. Canada hopes to identify vulnerable communications and assets, work with researchers on post-quantum cryptography solutions, and also potentially build a quantum secure network [7]. In these activities, the government sees itself as enabling research and development, being an early adopter of critical technologies, and also promoting international collaboration and innovation exchange [2].

On the international front, Canada's association into Horizon Europe in 2024 has opened up new international funding and collaboration possibilities, although the full impact is still unfolding and will take time to assess [8]. Bilateral agreements with UK and US funding agencies also cover scientific exchange more broadly. The "Alliance Quantum" grants will specifically target international collaboration in quantum with funding at CAD 30 million (CHF 19 million) over seven years.

18.2.2 Denmark

Denmark's National Strategy for Quantum Technology (short: "Danish Strategy") was published in two parts by the Ministry of Higher Education and Science in June and September 2023. On a four-year timeline through 2027, the government intends to commit DKK 1 billion (CHF 126 million) for quantum research and innovation, and an additional DKK 200 million (CHF 25 million) for commercialization, security, and international collaboration [9].

The Danish Strategy funding programs are mainly administered via Innovation Fund Denmark. The fund is expected to shift its focus over time toward demonstration and scale-up technologies as the ecosystem matures. In order to advise the direction of programs and allocation of funds, a National Forum for Quantum Technology has been established [10]. The strongest academic research clusters to support this ecosystem are located at the University of Copenhagen, Technical University of Denmark, and Aarhus University.

Danish government expenditure is supplemented by significant private-sector funding. Most notably, the Novo Nordisk Foundation has established a Quantum Computing Program at the University of Copenhagen, pledging DKK 1.5 billion (CHF 189 million) in 2022 for a 12-year program to build fault-tolerant quantum hardware and algorithms to solve life-science problems [10]. To leverage private-sector computing expertise, part of the Novo Nordisk funding has been used to establish an IBM Quantum Hub at the University of Copenhagen [9]. Moreover, KPMG established its Global Quantum Hub in Denmark, collaborating with leading universities [11]. More recently, in February 2024, Novo Nordisk Foundation also pledged DKK 150 million (CHF 18.9 million) to establish a Copenhagen Center for Biomedical Quantum Sensing [12].

In commercialization of quantum technologies, two concrete measures stand out in the Danish Strategy. Denmark pledges to establish a Quantum House Denmark with approximately DKK 16 million (CHF 2 million) yearly funding. This physical hub will provide lab and office space, business development guidance, and networks spanning universities, startups, funders, and corporations. Closely connected will be a national test center, funded through Novo Nordisk. The second concrete measure is a new Quantum Fund administered by Denmark's Export and Investment Fund—although exact funding will be dependent on private co-investment and leftover funds from other initiatives [9].

In contrast to some other countries, Denmark only has a very modest startup ecosystem in quantum technologies. Sparrow Quantum, producer of single-photon chips, and Kvantify, a hybrid software builder, are among the most notable Danish players. Two other Danish quantum companies were recently acquired by international players: QDevil by Quantum Machines and NKT Photonics by Hamamatsu.

As part of the EU, Denmark benefits significantly from EU funding instruments such as Horizon Europe and the EU Quantum Flagship. From 2014 to 2020, Denmark received around DKK 500 million (CHF 63 million) from the EU framework programs for quantum projects [10]. Denmark is establishing strong security guardrails in navigating the international environment, particularly with non-EU actors, and prioritizes collaboration with NATO and other strong allies [9]. In 2023, Denmark was selected as the site of a new NATO Center for Quantum Technologies, hosted at the Niels Bohr Institute in Copenhagen [13].

Denmark's key internationalization initiative will be a new International Quantum Hub funded with DKK 10 million (CHF 1.25 million) yearly through 2027. It is intended as the primary entry point for international quantum collaborators to reach Danish authorities and the quantum ecosystem. The hub will likewise represent a coherent tone and Danish viewpoint on international and security policy questions related to quantum technologies [9].

18.2.3 Netherlands

The Netherlands' National Agenda for Quantum Technology (short: "Dutch Strategy") was published in September 2019. Uniquely among the countries covered, the Dutch Strategy created a single prominent institution, Quantum Delta Netherlands (QDNL), to execute the Dutch quantum strategy. QDNL was proposed as a "world-leading center and hub for quantum technology" analogous to Silicon Valley [14]. QDNL describes itself as an ecosystem, developing its own initiatives while also consolidating the naming of preexisting quantum centers under the umbrella of "Delta hubs" [15].

QDNL is uniquely positioned as a distinct nonprofit agency that is mandated to execute the government's strategy. To this end, the Dutch government in 2020 invested an initial EUR 23 million, followed in 2021 by an additional EUR 615 million over seven years, in QDNL to coordinate the Dutch quantum ecosystem.

This model has created a uniquely powerful and centralized institution that is nonetheless able to operate distinctly from government ministries [16].

QDNL has developed three specific technology catalyst programs in quantum computing and simulation, quantum networking, and quantum sensing. Additionally, they have four main action lines devoted to building quantum research, talent, societal impact, and the wider ecosystem. Much of the presence of QDNL in the ecosystem comes through initiatives, events, and programs; however, they also have built a physical site directly through the House of Quantum in Delft. This center was designed to support research, startup space, and facilities and programs that inspire interaction and collaboration among quantum players [17]. Other House of Quantum locations are planned, with the goal of creating an interconnected "national campus" for quantum technology development [18]. The development of a Dutch quantum national strategy has benefitted from the geographic density of quantum expertise. The three main preexisting quantum research centers (QuTech in Delft, QuSoft in Amsterdam, and QT/e in Eindhoven) are within roughly two hours travel distance [14].

Public investment in quantum technologies, research, and infrastructures far exceeds private investment in the Netherlands. As of 2024, the Netherlands has pledged a total of around EUR 1 billion in public investments. This dwarfs the roughly EUR 40 million in private investments made in Dutch quantum technologies, with around a dozen quantum companies active in the Netherlands [4].

Dutch international activities in quantum have largely focused on EU cooperation. In addition to being a core participant in Horizon Europe and EU Quantum Flagship programs, QDNL has set up a trilateral research program with Germany and France. The Dutch contribution to the trilateral program of EUR 62 million will fund joint centers of excellence, as well as strategic research and development projects through a trilateral call [19].

18.2.4 United Kingdom

The UK published its National Quantum Strategy (short: "UK Strategy") in March 2023. They had already committed GBP 1 billion (CHF 1.1 billion) in public funding since 2014 through the National Quantum Technologies Programme, but starting in 2023 have pledged another GBP 2.5 billion (CHF 2.8 billion) in the following 10 years [20]. The UK Strategy programs from 2024 to 2034 will be split into two five-year phases. The first phase includes new research hubs and centers, outcome-focused innovation programs, industry-led innovation, accelerator programs, training and talent development, international collaboration, and infrastructure investments [20].

Like many other countries, the UK is motivated by international competition. "We are in a global race," the UK Strategy states. "The UK was an early mover, but other countries are accelerating their own efforts" [20]. The UK Strategy's mission outlines several core performance metrics to achieve by 2034: for example, to maintain its top three national position in quality and impact of quantum publications; to fund 1,000 new postgraduate students; and to develop five new bilateral funding arrangements. On the innovation front, they aim to attract 15% of total global private equity investment to the UK, have a 15% share of the global quantum technology market, and motivate 75% of UK companies to prepare for quantum computing. Most of these figures represent meaningful leaps over current figures [20].

The UK has been an early mover in quantum research and innovation. Since 2014, the UK has funded a network of four Quantum Research Hubs at universities and institutions, such as the Quantum Metrology Lab at the National Physical Laboratory and the National Quantum Computing Centre (NQQC), focused on building a scalable device. This preexisting Quantum Program touts the distributed network of research hubs across the country, which also includes the Fraunhofer Centre for Applied Photonics in Glasgow, Scotland. In 2024, the UK government announced five new hubs for quantum technology development with an additional investment of GBP 160 million (CHF 178 million) [21].

The UK's early strength in quantum innovation is evidenced by around 50 quantum startups that have emerged (with government assistance) since 2014— the most in Europe. These companies have attracted a combined GBP 425 million (CHF 474 million) in private investment [20]. At least 160 companies are active in the UK quantum sector, which ranks second globally in private equity investment after the USA [20, 22]. The UK Strategy aims to leverage its GBP 2.5 billion (CHF 2.8 billion) in public investment to attract an additional GBP 1 billion (CHF 1.11 billion) in private funding by 2033 [20]. The UK Strategy also hopes to attract further quantum businesses to the UK, such as with the return of PsiQuantum or the IBM collaboration on a National Centre for Digital Innovation [20, 23].

Aside from challenges general to quantum technology deployment, specific UK challenges include demand for quantum skilled labor, higher salaries, especially in the USA, and competition from larger countries and multinational corporations—all of which can erode the UK's strong early position in the "quantum race" [20]. To compete for talent, the UK has special workforce development provisions. They aim to double the number of PhDs in quantum or supporting technologies in the 2024–2034 period to over 1,000, with an initial 2-year investment of GBP 25 million (CHF 28 million). They also will expand a STEM outreach program in schools and push for enhanced visa pathways for foreign talent [20, 24].

The UK Strategy emphasizes the application of quantum technologies in a few key sectors to strengthen their overall economy and society, in particular sustainability, security/defense, life science, and data analytics/AI. The SparQ program run through the NQQC will explore these and other early applications. Defense, in particular, is seen as a useful early adopter and purchaser of quantum technologies, providing government support for emerging technologies [20]. More broadly, the NQQC, in addition to serving as a research and development hub, will also explore critical applications, standards, and regulations and act as a first purchaser for prototype platforms [20].

The UK has made notable advances in international partnerships. The government signed its first major joint statement for bilateral cooperation with the USA in 2021. The UK Strategy's goal is to develop this into a "comprehensive program of bilateral arrangements." Since 2021, additional quantum MoUs or partnerships have been announced with several countries, including Australia, Canada, Denmark, South Korea, and Germany [20].

18.3 Comparative Analysis

Given the different timescales, goals, and country population sizes, it is very difficult to make a strict quantitative comparison between the quantum strategies of Canada, Denmark, the Netherlands, and the UK. One can, however, roughly compare the pledged public investment on a per person, per annum (pp/pa) basis. On this metric, Canada's public quantum investment in its national strategy is modest, at less than CHF 1 pp/pa. The UK and Netherlands each have pledged slightly over CHF 4 pp/pa in their strategies, while Denmark has pledged around CHF 6.4 pp/pa. Thus, while the headline spending numbers for the various quantum strategies are designed to impress, the amount of taxpayer funds going toward supporting the emergence of this specialized technology is relatively modest.

Qualitative comparisons between the different countries' strategies reveal both fundamental differences in philosophy, but also similar strategies to shepherd quantum technologies to commercial viability. Canada and the UK are both notable for their very strong, early private sector investments in quantum research and innovation. The impressive array of quantum startups and established quantum companies in the two countries has been backed by an ecosystem of research translation, accelerators, supply chains, and investors, which combine to give Canada and the UK a strategic advantage. Their quantum strategies thus seek to build on these existing strengths. Denmark and the Netherlands, in contrast, are confronted with the task of building up a quantum commercial ecosystem from a less robust prior basis.

These different backgrounds inform the direction of investments and the level of centralization. Canada arguably has the "lightest touch" in terms of overall government coordination, as its effort can be seen mainly as a funding boost for regional hubs and bottom-up research and development clusters. On the opposite end of the spectrum is the Netherlands, which has created a new centralized organization, QDNL, that provides a single platform for all strategic quantum funding and activities. The UK sits in between these poles, investing heavily in regional clusters but also working to elevate the National Quantum Computing Centre into a robust institution for promoting its strategic priorities across sectors.

The level of government involvement can be seen in the relative balance of public vs. private investments. While all quantum strategies hope to create a robust commercial quantum sector, the UK and Canada aim to use their investments explicitly to attract sizable private sector funds. According to McKinsey, the UK has spent or pledged CHF 3.9 billion in public investment, compared to CHF 1.4 billion in private monies. In Canada, it is CHF 890 million public investment for CHF 820 million in private money [4]. In contrast, the level of prior private investment in quantum companies is comparatively small in the Netherlands and Denmark. In Denmark specifically, government investment is exceeded by a single huge corporate foundation—Novo Nordisk—which exerts major influence to steer quantum technologies toward use cases in biopharma and the life sciences. The question remains if the government or foundation investment can eventually yield a self-sustaining commercial industry, or if it instead leads to continued large-scale public subsidies. The German case may be the starkest example of this imbalance, with nearly CHF 5 billion in public investments spent or pledged, compared to around CHF 100 million in private investment [4].

Given these very large public investments, many countries feel that they are in a competitive landscape against other governments. The Dutch and UK strategies explicitly mention this; the Dutch Strategy argues that "urgent action [is] required" since "other countries are not standing still" [14]. Because of the government-driven nature of national quantum strategies, there is often significant weight placed on defense applications and government procurement of quantum technologies as an early boost for quantum commercialization. This was prominent in most quantum strategy documents.

The international strategies in the national quantum strategies are often among the least concrete sections. Overall, it is politically and bureaucratically challenging to direct significant funds to foreign research and development. Nonetheless, different strategies emerge. The UK, Canada, and the Netherlands have all engaged in bilateral (or trilateral) calls to build up specific relationships with other countries based on perceived mutual strengths and geographic proximity. This is especially valuable for countries outside EU programs. The Netherlands and Denmark also benefit from being core EU member states and are well integrated into the EU Quantum Flagship. Canada and the UK are also set to benefit from EU framework funding. Canada has also pledged significant funds for international research collaborations through "Alliance Quantum" grants. In a different vein, Denmark has pledged to establish an International Hub that serves as a single "open door" for international collaborators.

18.4 Recommendations

It is not feasible to make any specific policy recommendations for Switzerland or other countries without quantum strategies, based solely on this survey of several other countries' national quantum strategies. There is no single strategy for success, as each country has sought to identify and capitalize on its particular strengths.

In the Swiss case, the role of the Swiss National Quantum Initiative (NQI) will likely entail strengthening the core values and priorities of the Swiss quantum ecosystem, as identified by the Swiss Quantum Commission to include:

- Support for bottom-up, curiosity-driven research and innovation, rather than top-down directives
- Development of shared infrastructure and platforms
- Avoidance of direct subsidies, in favor of market processes and private competition
- Support education, workforce, and quantum literacy efforts
- International engagement
- Long-term, continued support necessary to reach quantum technology breakthroughs and commercial viability [25]

These priorities suggest that an overarching Swiss Quantum Strategy, if developed, may entail a "lighter touch" system of support for ongoing research and innovation, similar to the Canadian model, rather than a more centralized program as in the Dutch case. Nonetheless, given the perceived competition among national governments for resources and talent, and Switzerland's modest size, the country may also benefit from a more coordinated "public face"—especially for the public and international collaborators—that can help give visibility to Swiss excellence and build support for collaborations and public investments. As in Denmark and the Netherlands, the geographic density of Switzerland also lends itself to greater coordination of clusters, as opposed to dispersed regional hubs in countries like Canada. Other countries will need to respond to their specific conditions, such as the level of centrality in an organization and geographic density when designing their strategies.

In the Swiss case, reliance on bottom-up excellence in research, education, and innovation means that a national strategy will likely play a coordinating rather than a generative role in the development of a quantum ecosystem. Preexisting initiatives such as new master's programs in quantum engineering and bachelor's programs at multiple universities of applied sciences are already creating a growing workforce, and Switzerland can build on its strength as a world-leading talent factory. One main area where a Swiss Strategy might play a more "generative" role is in stimulating common infrastructure, perhaps even reaching an ambitious scale such as the UK's National Quantum Computing Centre.

The UK provides a similar model to Switzerland: it is a European country with a strong foundation of research that has previously been excluded from core EU funding schemes and thus has been pushed to collaborate on a more bilateral basis internationally. The UK strategy of developing several bilateral agreements has been mirrored in early Swiss efforts, such as the Joint Statement of Cooperation in Quantum Technologies with the United States. The Swiss government has also signed agreements to promote broader advanced technologies, sometimes including quantum, with several other countries. As Swiss research and innovation thrive on international collaboration, it is essential to create programs and platforms that invite the outside world to work with Switzerland on quantum. This might include new funding schemes, an international hub, or programs and initiatives using preexisting international platforms such as Swissnex.

18.5 Conclusion

As of early 2024, governments worldwide have announced a combined USD 42 billion in public investments in quantum technologies, which includes USD 10 billion in new funding announced in 2023 [4]. Many of these countries are explicitly steering this money to create a broader quantum ecosystems, backed by national strategies.

Time will tell if these public investments can sustain themselves, or whether government impatience or shifting priorities lead to a "quantum winter" in terms of public commitment. The Swiss ecosystem has sustained itself thus far largely on bottom-up energy, an excellent education and innovation pipeline, and long-standing infrastructures. This suggests that the current Swiss quantum ecosystem is more resilient, since it is less dependent on a single national program or initiative.

Nonetheless, given the competitive landscape as countries struggle to make large quantum breakthroughs, Switzerland will want to consider carefully whether a national quantum strategy can secure its future continued leading position and relevance in the emerging global quantum economy. The four peer countries studied here—all of whom are also strong international collaboration partners for Swiss quantum actors—provide lessons on how to structure such a potential strategy.

References

1. OECD National Strategies for STI. https://doi.org/10.1787/sti_in_outlook-2016-8-en (2016)
2. Canada's National Quantum Strategy. https://ised-isde.canada.ca/site/national-quantum-strategy/en/canadas-national-quantum-strategy (2022)
3. Alliance International Collaboration Quantum Grants. https://www.nserc-crsng.gc.ca/Innovate-Innover/aicq-cqai_eng.asp (2024)
4. McKinsey Digital Quantum Technology Monitor. https://www.mckinsey.com/capabilities/mckinsey-digital/our-insights/steady-progress-in-approaching-the-quantum-advantage (2024)
5. The Rise of Canada's Quantum Space. https://www.innovationnewsnetwork.com/rise-of-quantum-technology-in-canada/36126/ (2023)
6. National Quantum Strategy and Mitacs. https://www.mitacs.ca/our-events/national-quantum-strategy-and-mitacs/ (2024)
7. Defence Policy Update Focuses on Quantum Technology's Role in Making Canada Safe. https://theconversation.com/defence-policy-update-focuses-on-quantum-technologys-role-in-making-canada-safe-228079 (2024)
8. D. Matthews, Canada Officially Joins Horizon Europe, in *Science|Business* (2024)
9. National Strategy for Quantum Technology Part 2—Commercialisation, Security, and International Cooperation. https://www.eng.em.dk/Media/638315714019915522/National%20Strategy%20for%20Quantum%20Technology.pdf (2023)
10. Strategy for Quantum Technology Part 1—World-Class Reearch and Innovation. https://ufm.dk/en/publications/2023/strategy-for-quantum-technology-part-1-2013-world-class-research-and-innovation (2023)
11. Global Quantum Hub Opens in Denmark—KPMG Denmark. https://kpmg.com/dk/en/home/insights/2020/04/quantum-hub-at-kpmg-denmark.html (2023)

12. Researchers Aim to Advance Quantum Sensing to Transform Disease Diagnosis and Prevention. https://novonordiskfonden.dk/en/news/researchers-aim-to-advance-quantum-sensing-to-transform-disease-diagnosis-and-prevention/ (2024)
13. New Danish NATO Center for Quantum Technology. https://investindk.com/insights/new-danish-nato-center-for-quantum-technology (2024)
14. National Agenda on Quantum Technology. https://qutech.nl/2019/09/16/national-agenda-on-quantum-technology-the-netherlands-as-an-international-centre-for-quantum-technology/ (2019)
15. Quantum Delta NL. Delta Hubs. https://quantumdelta.nl/delta-hubs (2024)
16. How the US is Going Dutch on Quantum Research. https://www.nextgov.com/emerging-tech/2023/09/how-us-going-dutch-quantum-research/389956/ (2023)
17. Quantum Delta NL. Quantum Delta Programme Overview. https://quantumdelta.nl/programme-overview (2024)
18. About the House of Quantum. https://houseofquantum.com/about (2024)
19. Quantum Delta NL Awarded €60 million by National Growth Fund for Additional International Programme. https://quantumdelta.nl/news/quantum-delta-nl-awarded-eur60-million-by-the-national-growth-fund-for-an-additional-international-programme (2023)
20. UK National Quantum Strategy. https://www.gov.uk/government/publications/national-quantum-strategy (2023)
21. Five Hubs Launched to Ensure the UK Benefits from Quantum Future. https://www.ukri.org/news/five-hubs-launched-to-ensure-the-uk-benefits-from-quantum-future/ (2024)
22. K. Wheeler, *Technology Magazine* (2024). WhytheUKisWorldLeadingforQuantumCompanies
23. UK STFC Hartree Centre and IBM Begin Five-Year, $210 Million Partnership to Accelerate Discovery and Innovation with AI and Quantum Computing. https://newsroom.ibm.com/2021-06-03-UK-STFC-Hartree-Centre-and-IBM-Begin-Five-Year,-210-Million-Partnership-to-Accelerate-Discovery-and-Innovation-with-AI-and-Quantum-Computing (2024)
24. Quantum Ambassadors Programme. https://www.stem.org.uk/stem-ambassadors/quantum-ambassadors (2024)
25. Swiss Quantum Commission. Swiss Quantum Initiative—Strategy for 2025-2028: Recommendations for the allocation of public funding. https://quantum.scnat.ch/en/science_and_innovation (2023)

Brendan Karch is Chief of Staff and Head of Research at Swissnex in Boston and New York. Swissnex is a global network of science and technology consulates connecting Switzerland and the world in education, research, and innovation. Karch leads Swissnex's Project Quantum which works to connect the Swiss quantum ecosystem globally.

Open Access This chapter is licensed under the terms of the Creative Commons Attribution 4.0 International License (http://creativecommons.org/licenses/by/4.0/), which permits use, sharing, adaptation, distribution and reproduction in any medium or format, as long as you give appropriate credit to the original author(s) and the source, provide a link to the Creative Commons license and indicate if changes were made.

The images or other third party material in this chapter are included in the chapter's Creative Commons license, unless indicated otherwise in a credit line to the material. If material is not included in the chapter's Creative Commons license and your intended use is not permitted by statutory regulation or exceeds the permitted use, you will need to obtain permission directly from the copyright holder.

Chapter 19
Investment Trends in Quantum Computing

Loïc Maréchal

Abstract This chapter explores the ongoing substantial financial investments required for developing and commercializing quantum computing technology. Given the field's high uncertainty and long-term potential, investments are crucial for advancing breakthroughs in cryptography, materials science, and complex system simulations. The chapter examines the rise of quantum computing funding from the private equity and venture capital standpoints, highlighting key players like IBM and Google and emerging firms such as Rigetti and IonQ. It provides a detailed analysis of private funding trends, valuations, and geographic distribution, underscoring the sector's growth despite market volatility and regional concentration challenges. It also focuses on the discrepancies in funding allocation and performance among startups and the significant role of established companies like Microsoft, Google, and IBM in shaping the industry. Looking ahead, the chapter emphasizes the need for innovative financial models to assess investment returns, considering the nascent nature of quantum technology and the scarcity of financial data from private firms.

19.1 Introduction

Compared to most other emerging technologies, the massive infrastructure required for the development of quantum computing, along with its high uncertainty in efficiency and maturity horizon, requires heavy and long-term investments. These play a crucial role in determining the success of these initiatives. Quantum computing promises to revolutionize cryptography, materials science, and complex system simulations, driving competition among leading technology firms and research institutions. The increasing media coverage of the latest quantum computing achievements has also almost surely driven the most recent investments, reflecting

---

L. Maréchal (✉)
Institute of Entrepreneurship & Management, HES-SO Valais-Wallis, Sierre, Switzerland
e-mail: loic.marechal@hevs.ch

© The Author(s) 2026
J. Jang-Jaccard et al. (eds.), *Quantum Technologies*,
https://doi.org/10.1007/978-3-031-90727-2_19

the high stakes and potential rewards in this emerging field. For instance, IBM's significant budget for quantum research and Google's continued support of its quantum subsidiary, Google Quantum AI, are examples of the substantial funding fueling the quantum computing growth of quantum computing. Other notable companies include Rigetti Computing, IonQ, and D-Wave Systems, which have also attracted significant external funding from venture capital and private equity funds to advance their quantum technologies.[1,2] The share of financing in the sector has increased sharply over the last five years, mirroring the rising interest and expectations from the public and private sectors. Conversely, identifying a clear trend in the private funding of quantum early-stage firms remains challenging due to the nascent nature of the technology and its high entry barriers. Post-money valuations in the quantum computing sector have also sharply risen, highlighting growing investor confidence.[3] However, this increase is accompanied by significant time and cross-sectional volatility, likely due to uncertainties regarding the practical applications and timelines for quantum computing breakthroughs. This field's distribution of investment amounts shows significant outliers, underscoring the disparity between high-profile investments and the broader landscape. Furthermore, most investors and investees are based in the USA and China, indicating a regional concentration of resources and expertise. Despite the challenges, the substantial investments and increasing valuations suggest a robust growth trajectory. Continued investment is expected to drive further advancements, but stakeholders must remain aware of the associated risks and uncertainties inherent in pioneering such transformative technology. The following analyses tackle both public and private investments targeting private firms.

19.2 Outline of Investments

19.2.1 Investment Trends

Most of the following analyses use data from Crunchbase. Crunchbase is a database providing access to financial and managerial data on private companies. Its inception in 2007 was by TechCrunch, a US news service focusing on high-tech and startups. It is maintained by Crunchbase Inc. since 2015. This database is now adopted by academics (see, e.g., Besten [1]) and practitioners [1]. It is also used by international organizations such as the OECD (see, e.g., Dalle, Besten, and Menon; 2017) [2].

---

[1] **Venture capital**: capital investment in a project in which there is a substantial element of risk, typically startups.

[2] **Private equity**: capital investment in companies that are not publicly traded but typically larger than startups.

[3] **Post-money valuations**: a company's value after new capital injections from venture capitalists or angel investors are added to its balance sheet.

Crunchbase collects data by combining crowd-sourcing, machine learning, tracking top news publications, in-house processing, and relying on third-party providers. Crunchbase reports private and public investments that target private firms and updates its data daily.

The top panel of Fig. 19.1 reports the yearly evolution of funding rounds from venture capital or private equity targeted firms in quantum computing. The first spike in average and total funding in 2017 also marks the beginning of a regime change in these investments. Between 2016 and 2022, the average funding went from a mere USD 10 million to over USD 40 million. In the meantime, the number of funding rounds increased, along with investee companies, and the total funding increased tenfold, close to USD 1.4 billion in the year 2021. More strikingly, the total funding for 2024 is already close to USD 1.5 billion only for the first half of the year.

The bottom panel depicts the evolution of valuations following the funding rounds, post-money valuations (hereafter, PMVs), when available.[4] Before 2020, PMVs of quantum computing-related firms are virtually nonexistent. 2021 shows a first spike of available PMVs, following the massive funding rounds inflow (both in number and size). The interpretation regarding the first half of 2024 PMVs is the same as for funding rounds, with the notable exception that the median PMVs reached USD 100 million for the period, highlighting that not only valuations increase *per se* but also the analysts' willingness to report those of the sector.

Figure 19.2 depicts the distribution of the natural logarithm of funding amounts for all funding rounds targeting quantum computing firms.[5] The distribution mode and median are slightly above and below USD 3 million, respectively.

19.2.2 Geographic Location

Figure 19.3 reports the share of funding amount (left panel) and PMVs (right panel) for all countries that represent more than 4% of the total. Unsurprisingly, 48% of the total funding targets US quantum computing firms, and more than half of the recorded PMVs are accounted for in the USA. Canadian firms are second in terms of raised amount (12%); they only account for 6% of PMVs. In contrast, while Great Britain firms have raised only 10% of the total quantum computing funding, this translates into 32% of the PMVs. However, at this stage and for private firms, the data scope is too narrow to infer their relative performance. Finally, Chinese

---

[4] Unlike the public market, where the valuation is continuously observable through the market capitalization, valuations of private firms are scarce and often done after a significant funding round by dedicated analysts. This generates a selection bias toward large firms; however, this is the single metric publicly available regarding their financial performance.

[5] Since the funding round sizes distribution is heavily right-skewed, it is standard to use this transformation in financial analysis. For ease of interpretation, USD 1, 10, and 100 million correspond to logarithm values of 13.8, 16.1, and 18.4.

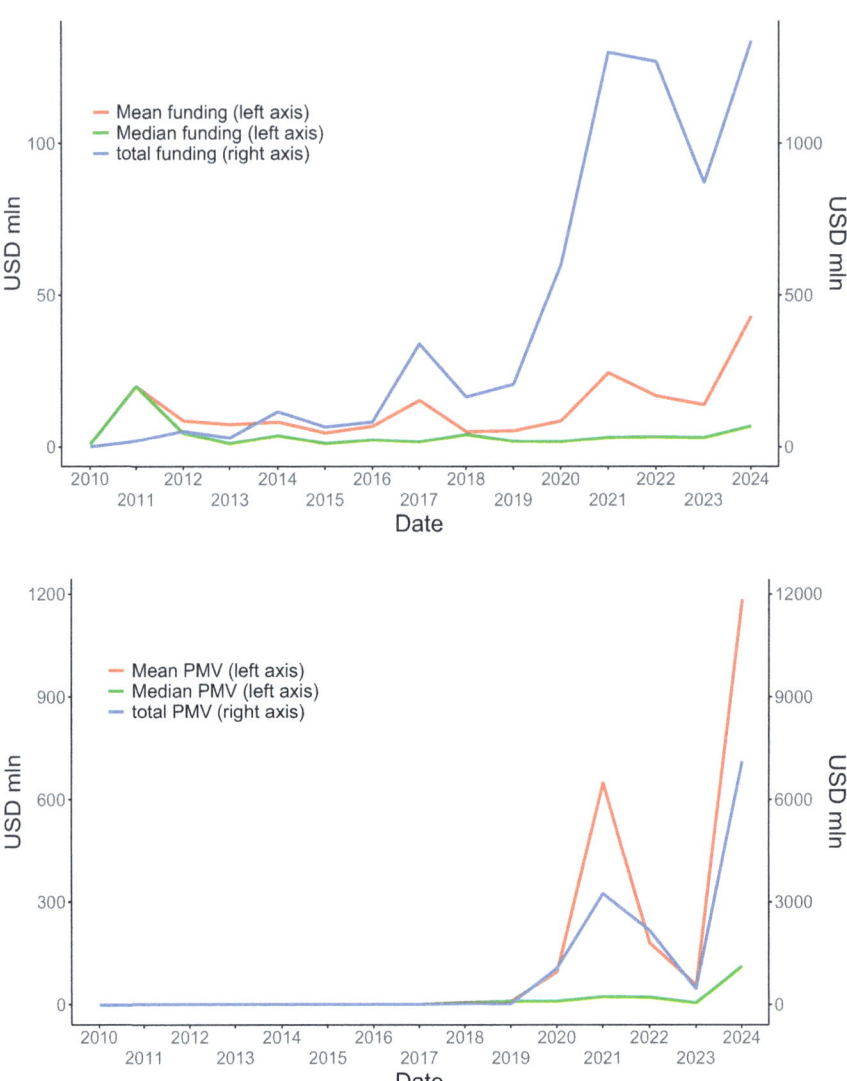

Funding amount and post-money valuations statistics of quantum computing-related firms

Fig. 19.1 The top panel depicts the yearly evolution of mean and median funding and total funding directed toward private quantum computing-related firms. The bottom panel depicts the yearly evolution of post-money valuations (when available) made on private and public quantum computing firms. Public firms' post-money valuations are considered once and correspond to the market capitalization available over their IPOs. Quantum computing firms are identified by selecting firms tagged with *Quantum Computing* in the Crunchbase sector classification. The data is from Crunchbase [3], and the period is Q1-2010–Q3-2024

19 Investment Trends in Quantum Computing

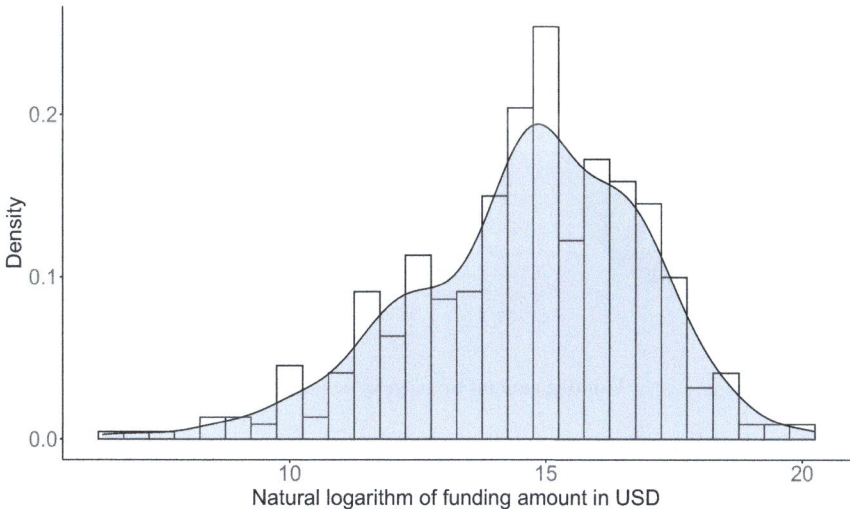

Natural logarithm funding distribution targeting quantum computing-related firms

Fig. 19.2 Distribution of natural logarithm funding amount in private firms tagged with *quantum computing*. The data is from Crunchbase [3], and the period is Q1-2010–Q3-2024

firms only account for 4% of the total funding and are not even reported in terms of PMVs. Three aspects may explain these counterintuitive results. First, Crunchbase has a representative bias toward the USA and, more generally, the Western world.[6] Second, China is more opaque and probably even more in such a strategic field. Third, it is likely that the popular view of the tremendous Chinese investments in quantum computing is mainly done through public investments and/or in national institutions.

19.3 Discretionary Evidence

19.3.1 Start-ups and Unicorns

Table 19.1 reports the total amount invested in the top 20 firms entirely dedicated to quantum computing. PsiQuantum vastly dominates the ranking in total funding, with nearly USD 1.3 billion raised since its inception. Yet, the latest valuation

---

[6] This bias is persistent across databases, and despite recent improvements, mitigating remains a challenge (see, e.g. Te et al. [4]).

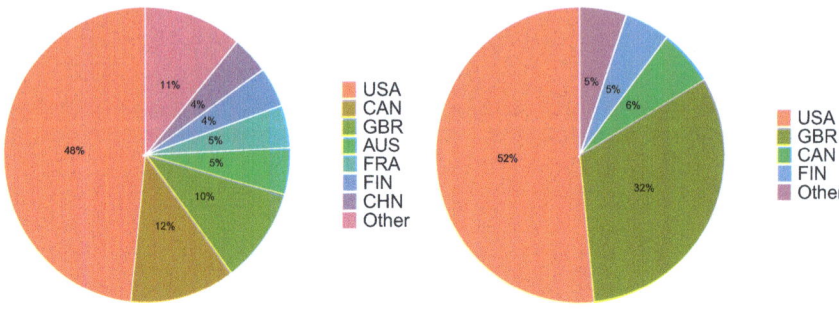

Funding amount by geographic location

Fig. 19.3 The left (right) panel reports the share of funding amount (post-money valuations) in private firms tagged with *quantum computing* by their most important locations. The data is from Crunchbase [3], and the period is Q1-2010–Q3-2024

available only implies a multiple[7] below 2.5. IonQ ranks second with USD 432 million for a 3.6 multiple. Interestingly, this low multiple is attained while the firm is now listed. Quantinuum, Exohood Labs, and Cambridge Quantum Computing have the highest multiple, with 16.31, 13.50, and 6.18, respectively. Some firms display large skewness in funding and considerable discrepancies in valuations and multiple. This might support the views of uncertainties attached to the sector as well as significant variations in each firm's specific quantum computing activities.

19.3.2 Public and Established Companies

It is hard to quantify the internal investments and R&D budget dedicated to quantum research and applications within established firms. However, the recent breakthroughs they have announced and their facilities support the view of a large amount. Moreover, most of these firms are already in the technology or IT sector and, thus, must be intrinsically innovative. Table 19.2 reports the list of the top listed companies in this field and their activities in the quantum computing sector. It highlights the significant dominance of tech giants like Microsoft, Nvidia, and Google, whose market caps far exceed those of other firms. Quantum computing research is being driven by diverse industries, including cloud computing (Microsoft, Google, Amazon), hardware (Intel, Nvidia), and specialized applications (Volkswagen, Toshiba). The table also underscores the role of companies with smaller market

---

[7] Multiple: In the context of venture capital, this term refers to the return multiple, indicating how much money an investor will make compared to their initial investment.

Table 19.1 This table reports financial performance metrics for quantum computing firms. "Total funding" (in USD million) is the total amount raised by the company over Q1-2010–Q3-2024 in their private stage. "Latest valuation" (in USD million) indicates either the post-money valuation if the company is still private (when available) or the current market capitalization (as of August 14, 2024) if the company had an IPO or a SPAC and is now listed. A listed firm is indicated with the superscript *. "Multiple" indicates the ratio between the two former values. Source: Crunchbase [3]

Company	Total funding (USD million)	Latest valuation (USD million)	Multiple
PsiQuantum	1,280.17	3,150	2.46
IonQ	432.00	1551*	3.59
Quantinuum	325.00	5,300	16.31
Rigetti Computing	298.45	164*	0.55
Xanadu	268.32	1,000	3.73
D-Wave Systems	267.99	208*	0.78
IQM Quantum Computers	249.12	900	3.61
Infleqtion	195.68	67	0.34
Origin Quantum	152.71	–	–
Oxford Quantum Circuits	146.46	–	–
PASQAL	142.08	–	–
Silicon Quantum Computing	133.40	–	–
Exohood Labs	112.00	1,512	13.50
Photonic	99.34	–	–
InVisage Technologies	98.00	–	–
Quantum Machines	93.00	–	–
Terra Quantum	90.00	53	0.59
Zapata Computing	82.06	16*	0.20
Quandela	73.08	–	–
Cambridge Quantum Computing	72.80	450	6.18

capitalizations, such as FormFactor, which focuses on niche areas like cryostat production. This diversity illustrates the broad applicability and interdisciplinary nature of quantum computing. The inclusion of market capitalization figures adds financial context to each company's engagement in the field, offering insights into the scale of their operations and influence in this rapidly evolving industry.

19.4 Future Work with Financial Methods

Given the novelty of the technology, the long-term horizon of the investments, and the secretive nature of the technology, either from private firms with no financial performance disclosure or from listed firms with budget tied to their overall R&D, it is hard to infer anything about the financial returns of this sector. In particular, the

Table 19.2 This table ranks the top listed firms active in the quantum computing sector by their market capitalization and describes their research activity. The market capitalization is recorded as of August 14, 2024. Source: Crunchbase [3]. **Top listed firms active in quantum computing**

Company	Research description	Market cap. (USD billion)
Microsoft	Azure cloud services and research—research in quantum computing	3,094
Nvidia	GPU and AI technology branches include quantum computing research	2,875
Google	Google Quantum AI—research in quantum computing	1,975
Amazon	Quantum computing services in AWS—research in quantum computing	1,783
Samsung	Electronics and semiconductor branches include quantum computing research	378
Alibaba	Quantum computing services are available through its cloud platform	189
IBM	Technology and research in quantum computing	177
Toshiba	Technology and research in quantum computing and cryptography	167
AT&T	Telecommunications branches include research in quantum networking	140
Honeywell	Quantum computing is part of its aerospace business	128
Siemens	Quantum computing research for industrial applications	114
Hitachi	Technology and research initiatives in quantum computing	107
Intel	Quantum computing hardware development and research	86
Volkswagen	Automotive research includes quantum computing for optimization purposes	44
Fujitsu	IT and computing branches include quantum computing research	31
Baidu	AI and technology research divisions include quantum computing research	29
Hewlett Packard	Technology and research initiatives in quantum computing	23
Tencent	Technology and research initiatives in quantum computing	22
FormFactor	Cryostat design and production for quantum computers	4

market lacks maturity for adjusted returns and systematic risk analyses. Instead, once enough successful exits, IPOs in particular, of these firms are observable, and one could use dedicated financial models to estimate these parameters. Such methods include [5, 6] to estimate the financial performance of such investments at the sector level [5, 6]. In particular, the latter research uses an ML algorithm to infer all valuations that are often missing in private equity datasets and are even more pronounced in the restricted quantum computing field based on correlated features. It also uses returns computed from investment rounds to exits, accounting for capital dilution, thereby estimating the financial performance with a maximum likelihood function that leverages information from all observable firms at once.

19.5 Recommendations

Emerging quantum computing technologies present significant opportunities for countries with a strong foundation in innovation, research, and a robust economic framework. To harness the full potential of this transformative technology, nations should consider adopting key investment strategies:

- Public-private collaboration: establish stronger partnerships between governmental agencies, academic institutions, and the private sector. Leading research institutions can collaborate with domestic firms and global players to drive innovation. Government funding for joint research initiatives and tax incentives for quantum startups can help cultivate a thriving quantum ecosystem.
- Targeted venture capital and private equity support: encourage venture capital and private equity firms to diversify their portfolios with investments in quantum computing startups. By providing early-stage financing, a nation can develop its existing quantum startup ecosystem and attract international talent, leveraging the country's reputation for stability and innovation.
- Developing its quantum research hubs: create dedicated research hubs focused on applied quantum technologies in sectors such as finance, healthcare, and cryptography. These hubs could attract foreign investment and position a nation as a leader in specialized applications of quantum computing, with a focus on real-world use cases.
- Focus on talent development: building a local talent pool skilled in quantum technologies is essential. A nation should invest in education programs preparing students and professionals for quantum computing careers, focusing on interdisciplinary physics, engineering, and finance skills.
- Strategic partnerships: as quantum computing requires massive infrastructure and resources, a nation should strategically partner or develop existing partnerships with global quantum leaders, such as the USA and the EU, to share research and technological advancements. This will allow firms to stay competitive and on the cutting edge of quantum developments.

By aligning policies, investment strategies, and educational initiatives, nations can secure a leading role in the global quantum computing industry. This strategic approach can drive innovation, attract economic benefits, and position them as key players in shaping the future of this groundbreaking technology.

19.6 Conclusion

Quantum computing is poised to transform industries such as cryptography, materials science, and complex system simulations, but its development requires sustained, large-scale investments due to the technology's high uncertainty and long-term horizon. This chapter analyzes the investment landscape in quantum computing, showing how financial backing from private equity, venture capital, and major tech firms has surged over the past decade. Key players like IBM, Google, Rigetti, and IonQ have driven innovation through internal research and external funding.

Investment trends show a sharp rise in funding since 2017, with significant growth in the number and size of financing rounds. Valuations of quantum startups have similarly increased, reflecting rising investor confidence. However, the volatility in post-money valuations and the concentration of investments in the USA and China highlight the sector's uncertainties and regional dynamics.

Although the market is still immature, with high variability in startup performance and a lack of reliable financial data from private firms, quantum computing investments appear to be on a robust growth trajectory. Financial support, especially from the public and private sectors, will drive future advancements. In the future, more sophisticated financial models will be necessary to assess the risk and returns associated with investments in this cutting-edge field.

References

1. M.L. Besten *den*, Crunchbase research: Monitoring entrepreneurship research in the age of big data. http://dx.doi.org/10.2139/ssrn.3724395 (2021)
2. J.-M. Dalle, M.L. Besten *den*, C Menon, Using Crunchbase for economic and managerial research. https://doi.org/10.1787/18151965 (2017)
3. Crunchbase, Inc., Historical company data, 2024. Crunchbase daily *.csv export, data retrieved on July 2024. https://data.crunchbase.com/docs/daily-csv-export
4. Y.-F. Te, M. Wieland, M. Frey, A. Pyatigorskaya, P. Schiffer, H. Grabner, Making it into a successful series a funding: An analysis of Crunchbase and Linkedin data. Journal of Finance and Data Science **9**, 100099 (2023)
5. J.H. Cochrane, The risk and return of venture capital. J. Financ. Econ. **75**, 3–52 (2005)
6. F. Burguet, L. Maréchal, A. Mermoud, The new risk and return of venture capital. J. Portfolio Manag. **50**(7), 116–147 (2024)

Dr. Loïc Maréchal is a researcher at the Institute of Entrepreneurship & Management (HES-SO Valais-Wallis) and the Cyber-Defence Campus (armasuisse). In this position, he uses financial methods to estimate the costs of cyberattacks and value cybersecurity firms to guide armasuisse's procurement decisions. He has taught finance at the Universities of Neuchâtel and Geneva, ESSEC Business School, and Les Roches. He has over ten years of experience in commodity markets, which includes working on trading desks and academic research, and five years of experience in the financial aspects of cybersecurity. His research includes publications such as "The New Risk and Return of Venture Capital," "TechRank," and "Cyber Risk and the Cross-Section of Stock Returns."

Open Access This chapter is licensed under the terms of the Creative Commons Attribution 4.0 International License (http://creativecommons.org/licenses/by/4.0/), which permits use, sharing, adaptation, distribution and reproduction in any medium or format, as long as you give appropriate credit to the original author(s) and the source, provide a link to the Creative Commons license and indicate if changes were made.

The images or other third party material in this chapter are included in the chapter's Creative Commons license, unless indicated otherwise in a credit line to the material. If material is not included in the chapter's Creative Commons license and your intended use is not permitted by statutory regulation or exceeds the permitted use, you will need to obtain permission directly from the copyright holder.

Chapter 20
Analysis of Quantum Trends in Open Software Repositories and Financial News

Thomas Berkane, Evgueni Rousselot, and Julian Jang-Jaccard

20.1 Introduction

Emerging data sources such as open software platforms like GitHub and financial newspapers can play a pivotal role in tracking trends in newly emerging technologies such as quantum. GitHub's strength lies in its vibrant developer community, where contributors share knowledge, exchange ideas, and collaborate on projects [1]. By monitoring these projects, individuals can stay informed about the latest advancements, challenges, and innovative solutions in technologies that impact fields like cybersecurity.

Complementing this, financial newspaper headlines provide a strategic perspective on quantum technology trends. Unlike technology news, financial news captures market sentiments, perceived value, and economic implications, often serving as early indicators of disruptive innovations. These insights reveal how quantum technologies are perceived by investors and industries, shedding light on their market expectations and relevance to critical sectors like defense. Together, GitHub and financial newspapers offer a comprehensive approach to understanding emerging technologies, bridging practical innovation with economic and strategic contexts.

T. Berkane · E. Rousselot · J. Jang-Jaccard (✉)
Cyber-Defence Campus, armasuisse, Lausanne, Switzerland
e-mail: thomas.berkane@ar.admin.ch; evgueni.rousselot@ar.admin.ch; julian.jang-jaccard@ar.admin.ch

© The Author(s) 2026
J. Jang-Jaccard et al. (eds.), *Quantum Technologies*,
https://doi.org/10.1007/978-3-031-90727-2_20

Table 20.1 Quantum topics

Areas	Topics
Quantum Computing	Qubits, Quantum Coherence Times, Quantum Gate, Quantum Circuit, Quantum Control Electronics, Quantum Error Correction, Quantum Processor Cooling, Quantum Computations, Quantum Algorithms, Quantum Simulators, Quantum Emulation, Quantum Optimization, Quantum Annealing
Quantum Communication	Quantum Entanglement, Quantum Key Distribution, Quantum Cryptography, Quantum Encryption

20.2 Analysis

In our study, we employed two complementary methods to monitor trends in quantum technologies: the GitHub REST API[1] and the financial information platform Refinitiv Eikon.[2] Guided by consultations with quantum experts, we identified 17 quantum topics from two primary branches of quantum technologies, selected for their substantial potential to significantly impact cyber defense capabilities, as outlined in Table 20.1.

To investigate open-source developments, we utilized the GitHub REST API to search for repositories pushed since January 1, 2023. The search criteria targeted repository names, descriptions, or README contents containing these identified quantum topics. This search process was executed twice, on November 16 and November 29, 2023, to capture any changes over time, such as the number of repositories and other characteristics. After the second run, we identified a total of 195 repositories relevant to quantum technologies, which were then used for further analysis. Concurrently, we used Refinitiv Eikon, a widely recognized news aggregation tool popular in the finance sector, to collect quantum-related news headlines spanning January 2017 to October 2023. Together, these approaches provided a dual perspective on the practical development and broader strategic landscape of quantum technologies.

20.3 Insights from GitHub

20.3.1 Based on Stars

In the context of GitHub, the "stars" for a repository represent the number of users who have marked the repository as interesting or noteworthy by clicking the "Star"

---

[1] https://docs.github.com/en/rest?apiVersion=2022-11-28.

[2] https://eikon.refinitiv.com/.

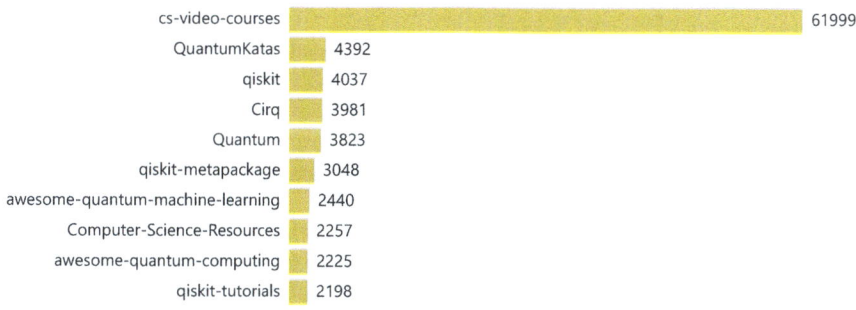

Fig. 20.1 Top 10 repositories by stars

button [2]. The sheer quantity of stars becomes an indicator of popularity, reflecting the level of interest and recognition a technology has garnered.

The results shown in Fig. 20.1 display the top 10 repositories based on the highest number of stars, offering the following insights.

- It is evident that a substantial segment of the developer community is presently immersed in acquiring knowledge about the concepts and theories associated with quantum technologies. This observation aligns with speculations from various reports [3–5] indicating that the majority of quantum technologies are still in an early stage of development. Six of the top 10 repositories (e.g., cv-video-courses, Quantum, awesome-quantum-machine-learning, computer-science-resources, awesome-quantum-computing) are dedicated to providing quantum learning materials.
- The developer community demonstrates a keen interest in quantum algorithm and simulation development, as evidenced by the popularity of quantum development kits such as QuantumKatas and qiskit, ranking second and third, respectively.
- There is a clear indication of growing interest in the advancement of low-level control for quantum circuit development—a crucial building block to unlock the full potential promised by quantum technologies. This interest is reflected in the popularity of Cirq at the fourth place among the GitHub repositories.

20.3.2 GitHub Trends

We conducted a time-series analysis of repositories exhibiting the highest growth rate in terms of number of stars (based on the relative growth rate).

Based on the results shown in Fig. 20.2, it is evident that an increasing number of quantum projects are emerging, each addressing different aspects of quantum technologies.

- As exemplified by a catalyst, the project with the highest growth rate, a growing number of projects are anticipated to focus on developing tools capable of

Fig. 20.2 Top 10 fastest growing repositories (based on the relative growth rate of stars)

compiling and executing both classical and quantum-based computing. This aligns with industry speculations [6], reinforcing the notion that future quantum computing implementations will integrate computing farms alongside classical computers, resulting in a hybrid system.
- Customized quantum developments are on the rise in various industries, notably in finance, as demonstrated by quantQ, which ranked second in growth rate.
- There is a substantial number of ongoing developer projects, like oqs-provider and sphincsplus, dedicated to quantum-safe cryptography (QSC). Solutions for QSC are anticipated to take effect sooner compared to other quantum technologies due to the well-understood vulnerability of current classical cryptography within the community [4, 6].
- Projects related to quantum simulation, as seen in SeQUeNCe and simulated-bifurcation-algorithm, are expected to continue growing, serving as crucial tools to assess the capabilities of quantum technologies.

20.4 Insights from Financial Newspaper

20.4.1 Topic Coverage

We conducted an analysis of trends and growth patterns, examining the frequency of coverage for quantum topics over time. This included identifying any notable spikes (or declines) and an overall assessment of the trajectory.

The results depicted in Fig. 20.3 illustrate the growth pattern of quantum topics mentioned in news headlines. From this graph, we derive the following insights.

- There is a significant upward growth rate in the quantum topics mentioned in news headlines—approximately averaging 250% growth every 2 years. This trend illustrates the robust and growing interest in quantum technologies within the financial market over the years.

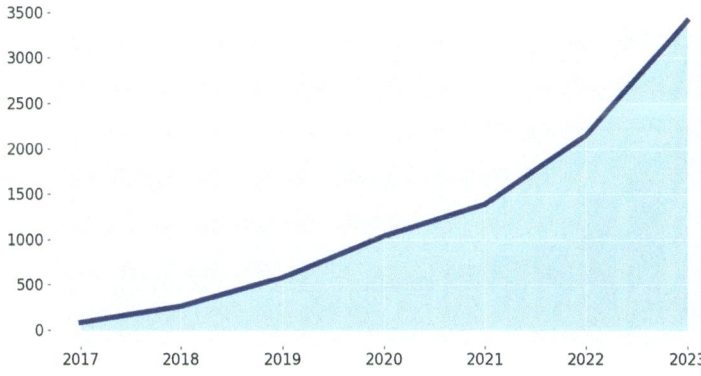

Fig. 20.3 Growth patterns over last 7 years (2017–2023)

- We observe a significant spike in interest each time a quantum breakthrough is achieved. For instance:
  - The surge in 2019 may be attributed to the moment when Google AI Quantum claimed Quantum Supremacy [7], demonstrating that quantum computers could solve certain problems exponentially faster than the best classical computers.
  - In 2020, researchers at Yale University [8] demonstrated a new error correction method crucial for preserving quantum states and ensuring the reliability of quantum computations. This method addresses the persistent challenges posed by noise and errors, which have been significant obstacles to the advancement of quantum [5].
  - The surge in mid-2022 may be due to the demonstration of an experimental realization of fault-tolerant quantum [9], proving that quantum scalability is possible, bringing the full potential of quantum computing one step closer.

20.4.2 Top Quantum Topics

As shown in Fig. 20.4, the top five most mentioned quantum topics are related to quantum communications (i.e., quantum_cryptography, quantum_communication, quantum_key_distribution, quantum_entanglement, quantum_internet). This indicates a heightened focus on securing and advancing communication technologies within the financial sector. The prominent mention of quantum cryptography and key distribution reflects a strategic interest in leveraging quantum technologies to support the security of financial transactions and communications, especially in response to the potential threat quantum computers pose to conventional cryptographic methods [4, 10]. This emphasis on quantum communication topics reflects

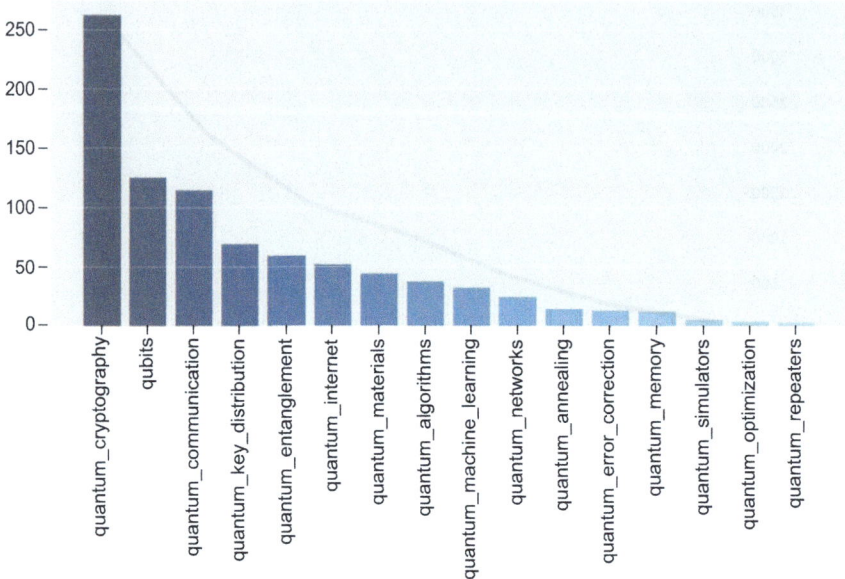

Fig. 20.4 Top most mentioned quantum topics

a recognition within the financial industry of the pivotal role quantum technologies can play in safeguarding communication networks and ensuring the integrity of sensitive financial data [6, 11].

20.4.3 Topic Correlations

We analyzed how quantum topics are related to each other by using cosine similarity, a method that measures how closely their content is connected in news headlines. To enhance the semantic understanding of each topic, we incorporated text descriptions of the relevant topics from Wikipedia.

Here are a few insights we derived from analyzing Fig. 20.5.

- With the highest correlation score of 0.76 between quantum_cryptography and quantum_key_distribution, it is evident that there is a strong interest in quantum cryptography as a means of protection from potential quantum attacks, where quantum key distribution (QKD) appears to be perceived as a practical implementation of this interest.
- The second and third highest correlations, at 0.72 and 0.62, respectively, between quantum_algorithms and quantum_machine_learning, in conjunction with quantum_computing, indicate a keen interest in quantum speedup. This interest enables financial markets to process vast amounts of data rapidly and

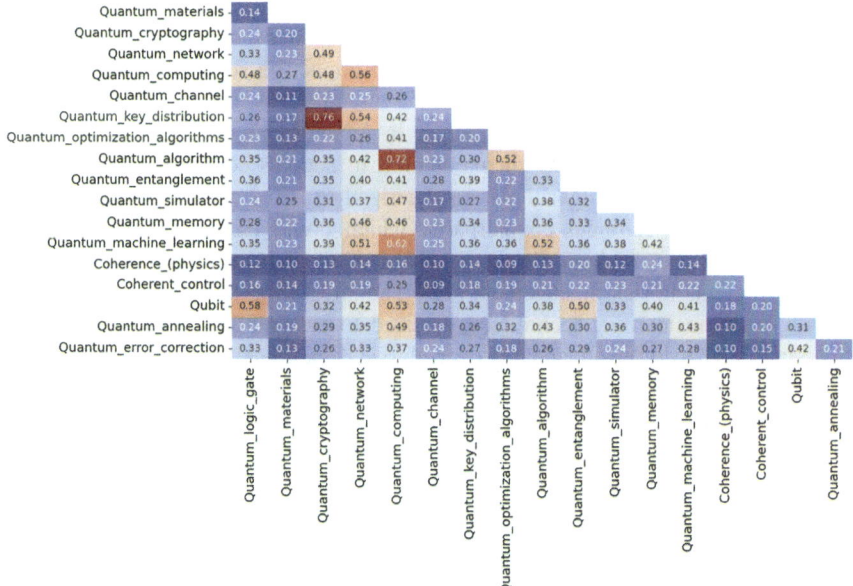

Fig. 20.5 Topic correlation using cosine similarity

accurately, optimizing investment decisions and facilitating risk analysis—a task traditionally considered one of the most challenging aspects of the finance sector [12].

20.4.4 News Headline Trends

Analyzing the trends in quantum finance within news headlines reveals several key insights.

- The concentration of the top five most mentioned quantum topics around quantum communications suggests that the financial sector recognizes the immediate value of quantum security in its efforts to strengthen protection against potential quantum threats.
- The increasing number of news headlines related to quantum entanglement and quantum internet suggests a growing interest in futuristic communication technologies. Quantum entanglement, where particles share states across any distance, is theorized to offer instantaneous correlation [6]. This feature has been proposed as a means to enhance secure communication, as any attempt to intercept or eavesdrop could disturb the entangled particles, potentially alerting users to security breaches. Similarly, the concept of a quantum internet, based on

entangled quantum bits (qubits) [6], aims to enable secure and efficient quantum information transmission on a larger scale. While these technologies hold promise, their practical implementation and impact on secure communications remain areas of ongoing exploration.
- There is a steady increase in interest in quantum algorithms and quantum machine learning, reflecting their potential to address complex computational challenges. Quantum algorithms are theorized to solve certain problems more efficiently than classical counterparts, which could enable faster and more accurate analyses of large datasets, optimization of investment strategies, and improvements in risk management [12]. The integration of quantum computing with machine learning techniques, referred to as quantum machine learning, is suggested to offer advantages over classical methods by uncovering hidden patterns and providing more precise predictions in financial data. The financial sector appears to be exploring these technologies as a means to potentially gain a competitive edge through faster and better-informed decision-making, although practical benefits remain under active investigation.

20.5 Recommendations

The observed trends in quantum technologies suggest several avenues for further exploration. In the realm of security, the growing emphasis on quantum-safe cryptography (QSC) highlights the need to address vulnerabilities in classical cryptographic systems. Projects such as oqs-provider and sphincsplus exemplify the push toward securing communications in anticipation of potential quantum threats. Similarly, advancements in quantum communication technologies, including quantum entanglement and quantum internet, could revolutionize secure communication networks. These technologies enhance data transmission security by detecting any interception attempts, making them particularly relevant for sectors handling sensitive information, such as defense, finance, and healthcare. Exploring and adopting these innovations should be a priority to reinforce security frameworks against future threats.

Quantum simulation tools, such as SeQUeNCe and simulated-bifurcation-algorithm, are also attracting interest for their potential to evaluate and advance quantum capabilities. These tools may play a pivotal role in testing and refining quantum systems, offering valuable insights into their practical applications in areas like defense modeling and optimization. Similarly, the rising focus on quantum algorithms and quantum machine learning presents opportunities to enhance analytical capabilities.

A critical area for development is hybrid computing systems, exemplified by projects like Catalyst. These systems integrate classical and quantum computing, reflecting an anticipated shift toward hybrid architectures. Such systems could offer flexible, scalable solutions by leveraging the strengths of both computing paradigms. Investing in hybrid computing could enable defense organizations to prepare for future computational demands, ensuring they remain agile and capable in an era of technological convergence.

While still in its early stages, strategic investments in quantum computing infrastructure could open opportunities for advanced modeling and simulations. These might include simulating complex cybersecurity scenarios to explore vulnerabilities or conducting war gaming and strategy simulations that could offer deeper insights into potential outcomes of military operations [6]. Although the field is still developing, exploring these possibilities may position the defense sector to benefit from future quantum breakthroughs.

20.6 Conclusion

In conclusion, this study demonstrates the value of leveraging diverse data sources, such as open software platforms and financial news, to monitor and analyze trends in quantum technologies. By examining GitHub repositories and financial headlines, the research highlights the growing interest and innovation in areas like quantum-safe cryptography, hybrid computing systems, and quantum communication technologies. While these advancements hold promise for potential impacts across sectors, including defense and finance, their practical applications remain in the early development stages.

References

1. E. Kalliamvakou, G. Gousios, K. Blincoe, L. Singer, D.M. German, D. Damian, The promises and perils of mining GitHub, in *Proceedings of the 11th Working Conference on Mining Software Repositories* (2014), pp. 92–101
2. H. Borges, M.T. Valente, What's in a GitHub star? understanding repository starring practices in a social coding platform. J. Syst. Softw. **146**, 112–129 (2018)
3. J. Gambetta, IBM's roadmap for scaling quantum technology, in *IBM Research (September 2020)* (2020)
4. D.F. Reding, J. Eaton, Science & technology trends 2020-2040. exploring the s&t edge, in *NATO Science & Technology Organization* (2020)
5. F. Vasconcelos, Quantum computing@ MIT: the past, present, and future of the second revolution in computing. arXiv preprint arXiv:2002.05559 (2020)
6. M. Krelina, Quantum technology for military applications. EPJ Quantum Technol. **8**(1), 24 (2021)
7. F. Arute, K. Arya, R. Babbush, D. Bacon, J.C. Bardin, R. Barends, R. Biswas, S. Boixo, F.G.S.L. Brandao, D.A. Buell, et al., Quantum supremacy using a programmable superconducting processor. Nature **574**(7779), 505–510 (2019)
8. P. Campagne-Ibarcq, A. Eickbusch, S. Touzard, E. Zalys-Geller, N.E. Frattini, V.V. Sivak, P. Reinhold, S. Puri, S. Shankar, R.J. Schoelkopf, et al., Quantum error correction of a qubit encoded in grid states of an oscillator. Nature **584**(7821), 368–372 (2020)

9. L. Postler, S. Heuβen, I. Pogorelov, M. Rispler, T. Feldker, M. Meth, C.D. Marciniak, R. Stricker, M. Ringbauer, R. Blatt, et al., Demonstration of fault-tolerant universal quantum gate operations. Nature **605**(7911), 675–680 (2022)
10. R. Orús, S. Mugel, E. Lizaso, Quantum computing for finance: Overview and prospects. Rev. Phys. **4**, 100028 (2019)
11. D.J. Egger, C. Gambella, J. Marecek, S. McFaddin, M. Mevissen, R. Raymond, A. Simonetto, S. Woerner, E. Yndurain, Quantum computing for finance: State-of-the-art and future prospects. IEEE Trans. Quantum Eng. **1**, 1–24 (2020).
12. Capgemini, The future for quantum technology in financial services. https://prod.ucwe.capgemini.com/wp-content/uploads/2023/07/D22206-2023-Quantum-Projects-ODS-Support-June-2023_The-Future-for-Quantum-Technologies-in-Financial-Services_POV_V7_07272023.pdf (2023)

Thomas Berkane was a research intern with the Technology Monitoring Team at the Cyber-Defence Campus. He is currently pursuing his engineering career at Harvard University.

Evgueni Rousselot was a research intern with the Technology Monitoring Team at the Cyber-Defence Campus. He is currently pursuing his studies at EPFL, Switzerland.

Dr. Julian Jang-Jaccard is the Science Lead for the Technology Monitoring Team at the Cyber-Defence Campus. Previously, she was an associate professor and Head of the Cybersecurity Laboratory at Massey University, New Zealand, and a pioneering member of the Cybersecurity Research team at CSIRO, Australia. At CSIRO, she developed practical cybersecurity solutions for leading Australian banks and telecommunications companies. She has published over 100 papers in prestigious venues, including IEEE and ACM, and received numerous multimillion-dollar research awards while collaborating with top ICT companies and universities worldwide. Dr. Jang-Jaccard holds MSc and PhD degrees from The University of Sydney, Australia, in 2002 and 2007, respectively.

Open Access This chapter is licensed under the terms of the Creative Commons Attribution 4.0 International License (http://creativecommons.org/licenses/by/4.0/), which permits use, sharing, adaptation, distribution and reproduction in any medium or format, as long as you give appropriate credit to the original author(s) and the source, provide a link to the Creative Commons license and indicate if changes were made.

The images or other third party material in this chapter are included in the chapter's Creative Commons license, unless indicated otherwise in a credit line to the material. If material is not included in the chapter's Creative Commons license and your intended use is not permitted by statutory regulation or exceeds the permitted use, you will need to obtain permission directly from the copyright holder.

Chapter 21
Bibliometric Analysis of Convergence of Quantum Technologies

Alexander Sternfeld, Andrei Kucharavy, and Dimitri Percia David

Abstract General-purpose methodologies for technological forecasting tend to rely on expert opinions on the state of a technological field. However, such analyses are generally considered incomplete in multidisciplinary fields where a single expert is typically incapable of having a complete overview of the area. To address this, such forecasts are usually augmented with unbiased and quantitative data mining approaches. This chapter aims to provide such an overview, focusing on the convergence potential in the quantum computing field. Here, recent advances in generative large language models (LLMs) development are leveraged to perform a bibliometric analysis of scientific literature on quantum computing. The analysis focuses on arXiv preprints, which are considered to be representative of the state-of-the-art in quantum computing research. Semantic triples are extracted from these preprints to represent the factual claims made in the papers. These triples are then analyzed to uncover emerging technological convergences. The results indicate an increasing convergence of core quantum computing technologies and computational complexity analysis through quantum circuits, likely indicating a rapid development of architectures dedicated to executing algorithms with a better quantum complexity. Additionally, a general indication of increased research maturity is observed, focusing on the utilization of existing technologies over the last two years.

21.1 Introduction

As governments and companies rely on accurate technological monitoring for their investment decisions, sound technological forecasts are essential (for an extensive literature review, see [1–4]). This need is particularly pronounced in the rapidly evolving field of cybersecurity, where disruptive technologies frequently emerge [5]. The short lifecycle of these technologies further complicates the application of

---

A. Sternfeld (✉) · A. Kucharavy · D. P. David
Institute of Entrepreneurship & Management, HES-SO Valais-Wallis, Sierre, Switzerland
e-mail: alexander.sternfeld@hevs.ch; andrei.kucharavy@hevs.ch; dimitri.perciadavid@hevs.ch

conventional forecasting methods to cybersecurity [6]. As a result, cybersecurity-specific technological forecasting heavily relies on algorithmic analysis, notably bibliometrics, to complement expert opinions [7, 8].

The recent advent of powerful and widely available LLMs has enabled more advanced and in-depth analyses of cybersecurity research compared to earlier quantitative methods [9, 10]. Specifically, natural language processing (NLP) techniques using term embeddings have facilitated the extraction of cybersecurity-specific terms for highly sensitive analyses of emerging technologies. These methods address limitations of previous approaches, such as the weak sensitivity of general-purpose tools like Google Trends, high rates of false positives and negatives in exact term matching due to linguistic ambiguity (e.g., Google N-gram), and delays in reflecting new technologies in ontology-based systems like OpenAlex [11].

Such an improved sensitivity is particularly interesting in the context of short-term forecasting of technological convergence potential. Synergetic convergence of existing technologies resulting in qualitatively new technology has gained attention as a powerful model of technological systems evolution [12]. Despite being a focus of bibliometrics-based technological forecasting, systematic analyses of convergence potential remained elusive, notably due to the linguistic ambiguity of terms referring to technologies, fluidity of technological definitions, and the fact that early indicators of convergence are rarely the central topic of documents revealing them [13].

Here, recent advances in LLMs are leveraged to extract claims about relationships between technologies from complete scientific articles. The focus is put on scientific articles' preprints, which reflect the earliest signals of technological situation change [5]. The extracted triples maintain the granularity of technology mentioned as close to the usage. At the same time, further processing through N-gram noun merging enables the investigation of more general trends, at the risk of related concepts merging, leading to an adjustable trade-off. To extract the trends indicative of potential technological convergence, the increase in co-occurrence of technologies mentioned and the evolution in the verbs articulating the technologies are investigated. Finally, technologies are clustered into related groups, to better understand whether an increased co-mention is due to an existing relationship refinement, or potentially disruptive technological convergence.

21.2 Methodology

21.2.1 Data Collection and Preprocessing

In this work, papers from the open-access archive *arXiv* are considered, for three main reasons. First, in fast-moving fields, recent breakthroughs are often published on preprint servers, given that peer review can take years before a final publication. Second, when submitting a work to arXiv, the authors must declare the domain of their article. Specifically, they can choose from a prespecified list of categories that are available on arXiv [14]. Therefore, when analyzing papers on arXiv, one can choose to study a subset of the available domains and extract terms that are specific to that domain of interest. Finally, arXiv preprints are in the public domain, avoiding copyright concerns, and encouraging article reuse, providing all raw PDF and LATEXfiles for download through a weekly updated Google Cloud Storage Buckets [15].

Here, arXiv papers from 12 categories related to quantum technologies are considered. Table 21.1 shows the categories, alongside their full names. Specifically, all papers between January 2020 and December 2023 are taken into account. The papers are filtered, to keep only those that have the term *quantum* in the abstract or title. This results in a final set of 48,930 papers for the triple extraction.

Before extracting the triples, several preprocessing steps are taken. First, the PDF files are converted to text, using the `PyMuPDF` library in Python [16]. Then, words that are split due to line breaks are merged, and bracketed citations are removed. Last, abbreviations are expanded using the Schwartz-Hearst algorithm [17]. Table 21.2 shows an example of a sentence before and after the preprocessing steps.

Table 21.1 The arXiv categories that are considered for this study, alongside their full names

Category	Full name
cs.CC	Computational Complexity
cs.CR	Cryptography and Security
cs.DC	Distributed, Parallel, and Cluster Computing
cs.DM	Discrete Mathematics
cs.DS	Data Structures and Algorithms
cs.ET	Emerging Technologies
cs.FL	Formal Languages and Automata Theory
cs.IT	Information Theory
quant-ph	Quantum Physics
physics.app-ph	Applied Physics
cond-mat.supr-cond	Superconductivity
cond-mat.quant-gas	Quantum Gases

Table 21.2 Illustration of the preprocessing steps. The parts in bold are altered during preprocessing

Uncleaned	Preprocessed
Large Language Models (LLMs) have **gotten** increasingly powerful, **LLMs** will automate various processes.	**LLMs** have **gotten** increasingly powerful, **LLMs** will automate various processes.

21.2.2 Triple Extraction

Semantic triples are the base building blocks for knowledge representation. Standardized by the W3C in 1999, they are most fundamental statements representing knowledge, as a subject–predicate–object relationship. Here, we will refer to subjects and objects as nouns, including compound nouns when multiple words are needed to convey the meaning—such as "quantum computing" as opposed to simply "computing"—and to predicates as verbs.

Previously, semantic triples saw limited success due to the human labor intensity of their extraction, lack of context awareness, and a divergence between the standardized knowledge representation and needs of concrete applications. In bibliometrics, until recently the sole major application was ontologies used for classification.

Our method leverages the LLMs to perform triple extraction that is aware of the context and is constrained to the vocabulary relevant to a specific technology monitoring task. Specifically, we use the `Meta-Llama-3-8B-Instruct` [18] generative instruction-tuned LLM, with a context length of 8,192 tokens, or about 24 pages. This model is open-weight, which improves the generalizability of the extraction method and allows for perfect replication. Although bigger models exist, their usage would lead to significant costs due to the needed computational resources.

For the extraction of the triples, few-shot learning is implemented, through a composite prompt to the base model. Specifically, the model is first given three sample texts with manually annotated triples. Then, the model is given a target text of 15 sentences, after which it will generate the corresponding triples.

Although using parameter-efficient fine-tuning of the model was tested to improve the performance, the preliminary results indicated a significant degradation in the quality of extracted triples [19]. Moreover, the advantage of only using few-shot prompting is that there is no need for training data or computational resources to fine-tune the model. Therefore, the extraction method can easily be adapted to new domains.

21.2.3 Qualitative Filtering

Before doing a downstream analysis, the triples are filtered based on their specificity. To illustrate, the term *lab* carries less information than the term *quantum*. First, the triples are filtered based on the frequency of the subject and object. All terms that are present in less than five triples in total are considered to be unusable, as the corpus does not contain sufficient information on them. The triples that contain either a subject or object from this group are thus removed.

Second, the triples are filtered to be specific to research, against the Gutenberg book corpus. The Gutenberg book corpus contains a large quantity of general books, and the aim is to keep only those words that are specific to scientific papers. By considering the frequency of words both in the arXiv corpus and in the Gutenberg corpus, those words that are specific to scientific papers are retained.

Last, a filter is applied to keep only the terms that are specific to the target domain. To illustrate, the terms *methodology* and *model* are used across multiple domains, whereas *quantum computing* is more domain-specific. This filtering is achieved by considering the cross-categorical entropy of extracted terms, according to arXiv categories.

21.3 Analysis

21.3.1 Triple Extraction

The triples are extracted from the 48,930 papers and are processed and filtered as described previously. This results in, on average, 51 triples per paper. These triples will be used to do both a quantitative and qualitative analysis for the technology forecasting related to quantum technologies.

To ensure our method aligns effectively with the conceptual framework of this book, we consulted our internal quantum experts and identified 20 quantum computing topics, each accompanied by a list of associated keywords. For example, the topic Quantum Key is associated with the keywords {quantum key distribution, key distribution quantum}. In this chapter, we focused on the 20 most common topics.

First, we match the compound nouns in triples to the 20 most common topics and analyze how the keyword prevalence evolves over time. Then, we investigated which compound nouns most often connect to each topic. In fact, a single topic such as "quantum computing" can match to both "quantum computation" and "quantum computer" compound nouns; those nouns are used in different contexts, one corresponding to the concept of technology, and the second to the concrete implementation. They are not used interchangeably and hence have to be treated separately, participating in semantic triples in different domains. Again, the change over time is taken into consideration. Last, a network of compound nouns based on the 20 topics is presented in Fig. 21.2. Here, one can see which techniques are most closely connected. Furthermore, a focus is put on those techniques that recently emerged and on those that have declined in popularity.

21.3.2 Trends

Figure 21.1 shows how the popularity of different quantum techniques has evolved over the past four years. In general, there has been an increase or no change in the number of triples extracted related to the top 20 quantum technologies. However, for

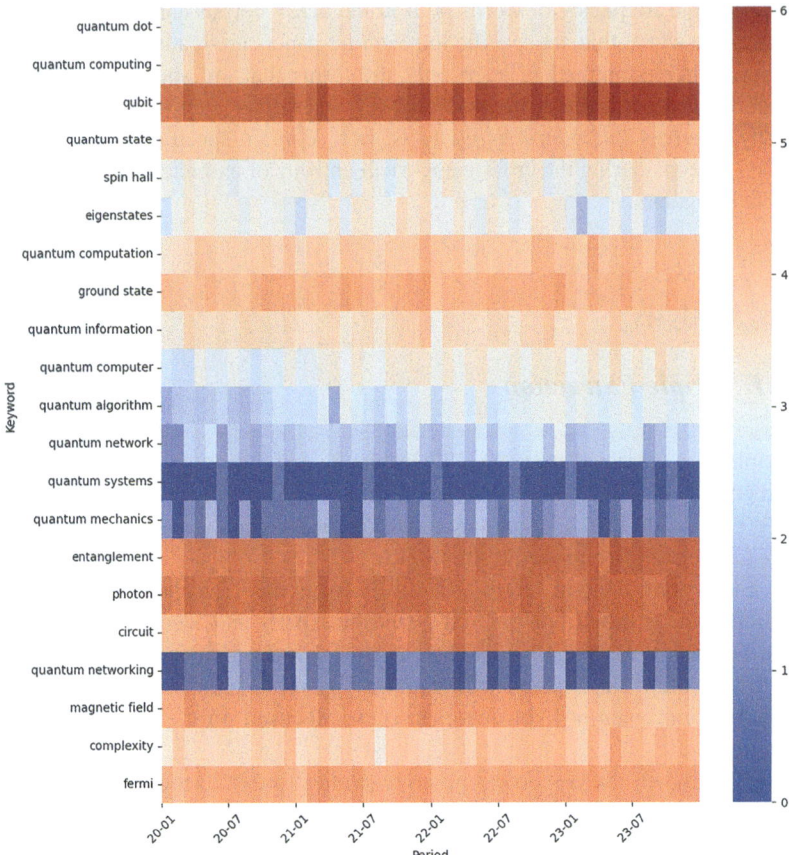

Fig. 21.1 Heatmap of the number of papers with triples related to the keyword, scaled by a natural logarithm. For ease of interpretation, the scaled values of 1, 3, and 6 correspond approximately to the absolute values of 3, 20, and 400

the topics related to *magnetic fields* there has been a decline in the number of triples extracted in 2023, suggesting a switching focus in research away from classical cold atom traps, such as Bloch et al. [20]. Furthermore, certain keywords are present much more frequently than others, specifically *qubit*, *entanglement*, and *photon*, which is expected for the core concepts in quantum computing.

Now, the relations between the different quantum concepts are taken into consideration. Figure 21.2 shows the key terms and their connections. As described in Sect. 21.3.1, a preliminary analysis by the editors provides us with lists of similar keywords. The visualized size of a term node and term name in Fig. 21.2 reflects the number of triples in which it is present, corresponding to its overall prevalence across the papers considered. Red relationships grew in presence in 2022 and 2023, whereas blue relationships became less present in 2022 and 2023.

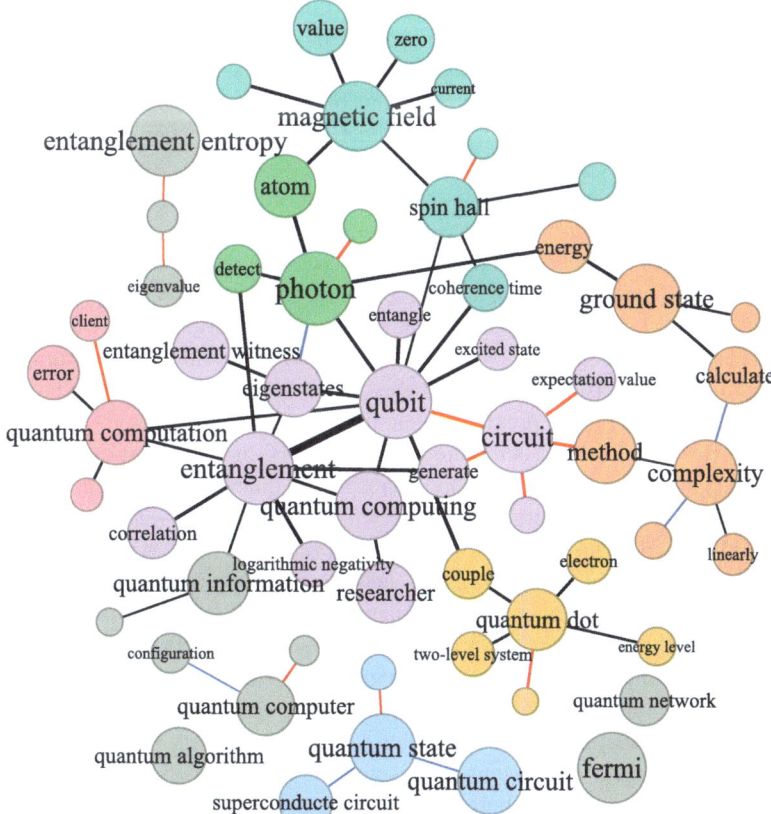

Fig. 21.2 Subjects and objects connected through triples. The size of each term reflects the number of triples extracted where the subject or object contains the key term or a term that is similar to the key term. If over 70% of the relations correspond to triples from papers in 2020 or 2021, the edge is colored blue, indicating waning relations. On the other hand, if over 70% of the relations correspond to triples from 2022 or 2023, the edge is colored red, corresponding to emerging relations. Black corresponds to the triples where the frequency of relations remained consistent between 2020 and 2023

To analyze the development of quantum technologies over time, the change in relationships is considered. The size of the edges is scaled based on the number of triples connecting the two nodes. Last, the network is clustered based on modularity, and each cluster is given a different color. Each cluster corresponds to technologies frequently co-mentioned together, often describing a single aspect of the field. For instance, the large pink cluster in the center of Fig. 21.2 covers the physical aspect of quantum computing, notably **qubit entanglement**.

The results indicate that in 2022 and 2023 certain concepts gained ground and became more popular. Most notably, there are many new relations around *circuit*, which likely refers to an increasing amount of research into quantum circuits. Interestingly, these new connections bridge the core quantum computation technologies with research on the computational complexity of quantum algorithms, suggesting a potential convergence point. Furthermore, a new connection can be seen between *client* and *quantum computation*. This could be a sign of a commercialization of quantum computing, where client-facing aspects of technology become increasingly important.

The findings also indicate certain relations that are becoming less popular. For example, the relations *(photon, eigenstates)* and *(quantum computer, configuration)*. It should be noted that there can be multiple causes of a relationship becoming less prominent over time. One cause can be an initial surge of research after a breakthrough, followed by slower development. Alternatively, certain research directions may have been surpassed by novel ideas, leading to the eventual disappearance of connections in the network. Overall, the decrease in technological co-mentions is less useful for convergence prediction than the co-mention increase.

Regarding the clustering structure of the network, it is interesting to observe a clear separation between the core concepts in quantum computation (*qubit, entanglement*—lavender), practical aspects (*error correction, quantum computation*—pink), theoretical aspects (*complexity, oracle, ground state*, and *density matrix renormalization group*—orange), and physics aspects (*quantum state, free fermion*—blue). One can also observe a diametral opposition between technologies implementing the actual quantum computation, with more classical atomic traps and photonic qubits on one side (*atom, photon, beamsplitter*—green), along with supporting technologies and supporting technologies (*magnetic field, vector potential*—teal), and quantum dot on the other side (*quantum dot, couple, electron*—yellow). Interestingly, there seems to be somewhat of a confusion in the extracted triples between the **quantum hall effect**, indeed a focal discussion point for ultracold atomic traps, and *spin hall effect*, postulated to exist in semiconductors without a need for a strong magnetic field, making it indeed a crucial technology for a *promising platform* for quantum computing.

From the point of view of technological convergence bridging different technologies, it seems that quantum circuits are emerging as a bridge between the core concept in quantum technology development and computational complexity operations. We hypothesize this is due to the increase in the research into architectures allowing algorithms with a better computational complexity for tasks of interest.

21.3.3 Maturity

As a last analysis, the predicates in the triples are analyzed. For this purpose, the red edges of the network in Fig. 21.2 are considered. These relationships have become more prominent between 2020 and 2023, which can be an indication of a growing technology. The triples corresponding to these edges are grouped and split into a group for 2020–2021 and a group for 2022–2023.

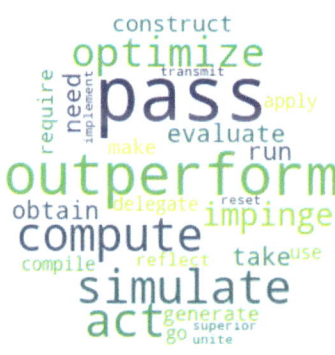 

(a) 2020-2021.   (b) 2022-2023.

Fig. 21.3 Wordclouds for the predicates corresponding to the red edges in Fig. 21.2, split up between the first 2 years and the last 2 years of the Jan 2020–Dec 2023 period

Figure 21.3 illustrates two-word clouds derived from the predicates of these groups. In the earlier triples, the most frequently occurring predicates are *outperform*, *pass*, and *optimize*, suggesting the introduction of novel techniques or the enhancement of existing ones. By contrast, the key predicates from 2022–2023 include *use*, *act*, *produce*, and *need*. These verbs reflect a shift toward the maturation of techniques, indicating their adoption and application in practice.

21.4 Conclusion

This work demonstrates a novel technology monitoring and convergence forecasting method that leverages LLMs to extract semantic entity triples from full-text scientific papers, applied to the field of quantum computing. The semantic triples extracted as a structured representation of scientific articles' claims are used to build a network that shows connections between different areas and evolves over time, along with the known relationships between concepts. This graph is used to search for indicators of technological convergence.

Thanks to this approach, three main insights are obtained. First, an overall growth in the volume of research related to quantum technologies is observed. Notable areas of increased focus include *entanglement*, *photons*, and *circuits*. The semantic network indicates a local conceptual linkage providing evidence of growing research into client-oriented quantum computation and suggesting a shift toward practical applications and the commercialization of quantum technologies.

Second, the results indicate a major technological convergence occurring over 2021–23, where quantum circuits are bridging core technologies in quantum computing with the theoretical complexity analysis, suggesting a rapidly developing research into quantum circuits implementing algorithms with improved quantum complexity.

Finally, there are signs of an overall transition in predicates of semantic triples involving technologies of interest toward the utilization of technologies rather than limitation and investigation-oriented ones between 2020 and 2023, suggesting a transition toward applied research in the quantum computing space.

Despite the limited scope of the data—focusing solely on scientific preprints—and the analysis, which examines only direct relationships between terms, the new method presented here proved effective. It identified several trends in quantum computing technology development, notably a potential instance of technological convergence driven by quantum circuits and algorithms that optimize quantum computational capabilities.

References

1. M. Coccia, Technometrics: origins, historical evolution and new directions. Technol. Forecast. Soc. Chang. **72**(8), 944–979 (2005)
2. C. Lee, A review of data analytics in technological forecasting. Technol. Forecast. Soc. Chang. **166**, 120646 (2021)
3. A. Haleem, B. Mannan, S. Luthra, S. Kumar, S. Khurana, Technology forecasting (TF) and technology assessment (TA) methodologies: a conceptual review. Benchmarking: Int. J. **26**(1), 48–72 (2019)
4. G. Calleja-Sanz, J. Olivella-Nadal, F. Solé-Parellada, Technology forecasting: recent trends and new methods, in *Research Methodology in Management and Industrial Engineering* (2020), pp. 45–69
5. D.P. David, L. Maréchal, W. Lacube, S. Gillard, M. Tsesmelis, T. Maillart, A. Mermoud, Measuring security development in information technologies: a scientometric framework using arxiv e-prints. Technol. Forecast. Soc. Chang. **188**, 122316 (2023)
6. T.U. Daim, D. Chiavetta, A.L. Porter, O. Saritas, *Anticipating Future Innovation Pathways Through Large Data Analysis* (Springer, Berlin, 2016)
7. F. Dotsika, A. Watkins, Identifying potentially disruptive trends by means of keyword network analysis. Technol. Forecast. Soc. Chang. **119**, 114–127 (2017)
8. P.H. Meland, S. Tokas, G. Erdogan, K. Bernsmed, A. Omerovic, A systematic mapping study on cyber security indicator data. Electronics **10**(9), 1092–1118 (2021)
9. A.R. Terryn, V. Hoste, P. Drouin, E. Lefever, Termeval 2020: shared task on automatic term extraction using the annotated corpora for term extraction research (acter) dataset, in *COMPUTERM* (2020)
10. K.K. Pal, K. Kashihara, U. Anantheswaran, K. Kuznia, S.V. Jagtap, C. Baral, Exploring the limits of transfer learning with unified model in the cybersecurity domain. ArXiv, abs/2302.10346 (2023)
11. M. Wursch, A. Kucharavy, D.P. David, A. Mermoud, LLMs perform poorly at concept extraction in cyber-security research literature. ArXiv, abs/2312.07110 (2023)
12. G. Dosi, Technological paradigms and technological trajectories: a suggested interpretation of the determinants and directions of technical change. Res. Policy **11**, 147–162 (1982)
13. T.U. Daim, G. Rueda, H. Martin, P. Gerdsri, Forecasting emerging technologies: use of bibliometrics and patent analysis. Technol. Forecast. Soc. Chang. **73**, 981–1012 (2006)
14. arXiv. arxiv category taxonomy. https://arxiv.org/category_taxonomy (2024). Accessed: 2024-02-29

15. arXiv.org submitters. arxiv dataset (2024)
16. Artifex. Pymupdf. https://pypi.org/project/PyMuPDF/ (2024). Accessed: 2024-02-29
17. A.S. Schwartz, M.A. Hearst, A simple algorithm for identifying abbreviation definitions in biomedical text, in *Pacific Symposium on Biocomputing. Pacific Symposium on Biocomputing* (2002), pp. 451–462
18. MetaAI. The llama 3 herd of models. ArXiv, abs/2407.21783 (2024)
19. A. Sternfeld, A. Kucharavy, D.P. David, A. Mermoud, J. Jang, LLM-resilient bibliometrics: factual consistency through entity triplet extraction, in *EEKE/AII@iConference* (2024)
20. I. Bloch, J. Dalibard, S. Nascimbene, Quantum simulations with ultracold quantum gases. Nat. Phys. **8**, 267–276 (2012)

Alexander Sternfeld is an associate researcher at the Reliable Information Lab, at the Institute of Entrepreneurship and Management (HES-SO Valais-Wallis). In this position, he is currently focusing on developing bibliometric methods for technology monitoring. He has obtained a bachelor's in economics and econometrics at Erasmus University Rotterdam. He then shifted his focus toward machine learning through a master's in data science at EPFL, Lausanne.

Prof. Dr. Andrei Kucharavy is an assistant professor at the Informatics Institute of HES-SO Valais-Wallis and the co-director of the HES-SO Gen Learning Center and the Reliable Information Lab. He holds a PhD from the University of Paris-Sorbonne (2017) and is an engineer of EPFL and Ecole Polytechnique (2013).

Dimitri Percia David is an associate professor of Data Science & Econometrics at HES-SO Valais-Wallis and co-head of the Reliable Information Lab, which focuses on applied machine learning, distributed computing, and digital trust. He co-founded the GenLearning Center, researching generative AI safety. He is a former CYD fellow and postdoc of the University of Geneva, and he chaired CRITIS 2021 and has a PhD in information systems from HEC Lausanne. Dimitri has over 8 years of experience in commodities trading and worked as a scientific collaborator at ETH Zurich.

Open Access This chapter is licensed under the terms of the Creative Commons Attribution 4.0 International License (http://creativecommons.org/licenses/by/4.0/), which permits use, sharing, adaptation, distribution and reproduction in any medium or format, as long as you give appropriate credit to the original author(s) and the source, provide a link to the Creative Commons license and indicate if changes were made.

The images or other third party material in this chapter are included in the chapter's Creative Commons license, unless indicated otherwise in a credit line to the material. If material is not included in the chapter's Creative Commons license and your intended use is not permitted by statutory regulation or exceeds the permitted use, you will need to obtain permission directly from the copyright holder.

Chapter 22
Quantum Ecosystem of Switzerland

Brendan Karch

Abstract Switzerland was an early pioneer in quantum research with the establishment of national research centers, resulting in the attraction of talent and investment for quantum technology startups since at least the early 2000s. Several university centers and research centers in Zurich, Basel, Lausanne, and Geneva, and beyond form the backbone of a robust quantum technologies ecosystem. Most quantum technology companies and startups active in Switzerland draw their IP from university labs. Furthermore, ecosystem builders in the commercial and governance space are emerging, especially in Basel and Geneva, to ensure widespread access to quantum computing and diverse applications for the technology. The maturity of the quantum ecosystem in Switzerland has relied largely on a bottom-up approach, but the newly formed Swiss Quantum Initiative is aiming to bring a level of coordination to the diverse ecosystem.

22.1 Introduction

Switzerland, despite being a small country with fewer than nine million inhabitants, maintains a robust ecosystem of quantum research, education, private-sector innovation, and governmental or international initiatives. As an early research pioneer in nanoscience and quantum physics, it maintains an integrated pipeline for bringing new ideas to market while also addressing the societal dimensions of new quantum technologies. In a competitive global ecosystem where other countries are investing heavily in quantum technologies, Switzerland can continue to innovate and prioritize international engagement.

B. Karch (✉)
Swissnex, Boston, MA, USA
e-mail: brendan.karch@swissnex.org

© The Author(s) 2026
J. Jang-Jaccard et al. (eds.), *Quantum Technologies*,
https://doi.org/10.1007/978-3-031-90727-2_22

22.2 Analysis

Curiosity-driven research at universities and research institutes constitutes the backbone of Swiss contributions to global efforts at achieving a second quantum revolution. Switzerland has been supporting basic scientific research into quantum technologies for decades. From 2001–2013, two National Centers for Competence in Research (NCCRs)—on nanoscale science and quantum photonics—coordinated large bodies of quantum-related research across Switzerland. From 2010 to 2022, NCCR QSIT (Quantum Science and Information Technology) played a leading role in organizing Swiss quantum researchers, while a newer research center, NCCR SPIN (ongoing since 2021), focused on the development of spin qubits. The cumulative investment in these NCCRs over two-plus decades will total about CHF 200 million, not including the research grants for individual research projects [1].

This investment in research has created a broad base of expertise across quantum technologies (e.g., computing, sensing, communications, algorithms, simulation, and theory). NCCRs have helped attract over 30 new professors to universities like the Swiss Federal Institutes of Technology in Zurich and Lausanne (ETH Zurich and EPFL), as well as the University of Basel, and the University of Geneva [2]. The investments are reflected in the importance of Swiss-affiliated quantum publications, which had the highest impact factor of any country in the world, relative to the global average, from 2016 to 2020 [3].

Four research universities are notable for their extensive contributions in the fields of quantum information science and theory: ETH Zurich, University of Basel, EPFL, and the University of Geneva. Launched in 2020, the Quantum Center at ETH Zurich encompasses 38 research groups from six departments. It interconnects quantum research and teaching across ETH departments and serves as a contact point for larger projects, including collaborations with industrial partners. The Center also helps to support ETH Zurich's interdisciplinary Master's Degree in Quantum Engineering. The Center for Quantum Science and Engineering (QSE Center) at EPFL serves as the school's research and teaching hub for all quantum efforts. The Center promotes research through collaborative grants, multidisciplinary education, and innovation. Its key focus areas are applied quantum algorithms and data science, along with quantum hardware materials and systems. The Center also helps to support EPFL's Master's Degree in Quantum Science and Engineering [2].

The Basel Quantum Center comprises 15 research groups at the University of Basel working on condensed matter, atomic, molecular, and optical systems, covering a broad range of applications in quantum computing, quantum sensing and metrology, quantum networking, and quantum simulation. The Quantum Center supports a PhD program and a cross-border postdoc cluster in collaboration with the University of Freiburg, Germany. A subset of the research groups are also involved in the affiliated Center for Quantum Computing and Quantum Coherence (QC2). The Geneva Quantum Centre at the University of Geneva brings together around 20 research groups building on a tradition of pioneering research in quantum sciences, most notably in quantum communications, quantum sensing, quantum materials, and the theoretical foundations of these domains. It targets broad education programs for the general public, schools, and the training of engineers and has launched new Bachelor's and Master's programs [2].

In addition to the four largest quantum research universities, the Paul Scherrer Institute (PSI) maintains a quantum computing hub in partnership with ETH Zurich in May 2021. It brings together the resources of ETH Zurich with PSI, the largest research institute for natural and engineering sciences in Switzerland. The Hub's central aim is to target the technical and scientific challenges on the way to realizing large-scale quantum computers based on both superconducting circuits and trapped ions. The Swiss Federal Laboratories for Materials Science and Technology (EMPA) features research into quantum nanomaterials. The University of Lugano (USI), meanwhile, features a group dedicated to cryptography and quantum information. The higher education landscape also includes Switzerland's Universities of Applied Sciences, where several institutions in regions such as Zurich, Lucerne, Fribourg, and northwest Switzerland are training students in quantum algorithms, engineering, or applications [2] (Fig. 22.1).

The private-sector innovation ecosystem in quantum technologies draws its strength from university research discoveries. Switzerland is the sixth leading country worldwide in number of quantum technology patents granted since the year 2000. Established large companies, most notably IBM, have been active in Switzerland in quantum research and technologies. From its research hub in Rüschlikon, IBM has worked on quantum research in many fields, with a focus recently on spin qubits and integration into the NCCR SPIN [4].

Pioneering Swiss startups such as ID Quantique and Zurich Instruments, spin-outs of the University of Geneva and ETH Zurich, respectively, have grown into important suppliers in the global quantum value chain. Zurich Instruments was founded in 2008 and has since developed into a leading global manufacturer of quantum computing control systems. ID Quantique is a global company with offices and engineering labs across the world founded in 2001. It has grown into a leading company for mature technologies in quantum key distribution (quantum-safe cryptography), random number generation, and photonic sensing. In 2007, Switzerland deployed the world's first commercial quantum cryptography system, developed by ID Quantique, which was used to secure elections in the State of Geneva [2, 5].

Many younger Swiss companies, many of them university spin-offs, are emerging with particular strengths in quantum microscopy and measurement, as well as enabling technologies such as photonics and precision nanomanufacturing. It is impossible to list all these companies; however, some notable examples include QZabre and Qnami, which work on ultrasensitive sensing technologies using manufactured diamonds with nanoscale nitrogen-vacancy centers. In the devices field, Basel Precision Instruments provides ultralow noise electronics, cryogenic microwave filters, and thermalizers. Miraex creates quantum interconnects between microwave and optical frequencies. Ligentec delivered low-loss photonic integrated circuits. And Enlightra (formerly MicroR Systems) focuses on low-noise microwave

Swiss Quantum Mapping

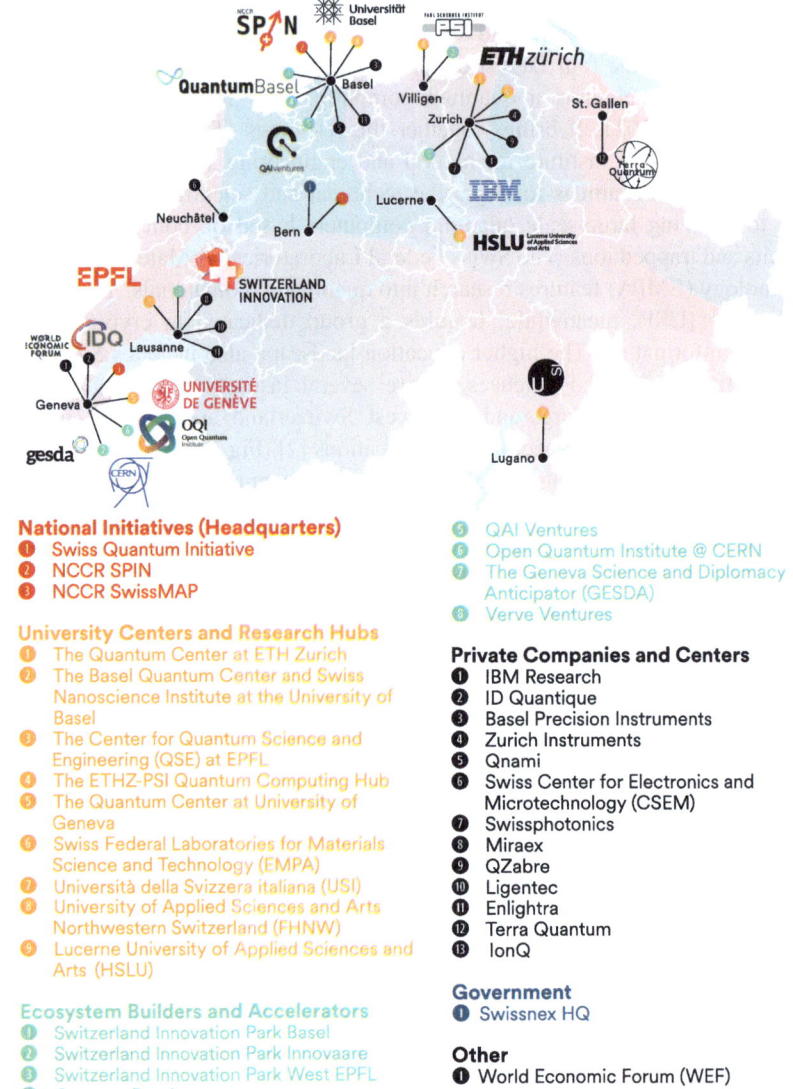

National Initiatives (Headquarters)
① Swiss Quantum Initiative
② NCCR SPIN
③ NCCR SwissMAP

University Centers and Research Hubs
① The Quantum Center at ETH Zurich
② The Basel Quantum Center and Swiss Nanoscience Institute at the University of Basel
③ The Center for Quantum Science and Engineering (QSE) at EPFL
④ The ETHZ-PSI Quantum Computing Hub
⑤ The Quantum Center at University of Geneva
⑥ Swiss Federal Laboratories for Materials Science and Technology (EMPA)
⑦ Università della Svizzera italiana (USI)
⑧ University of Applied Sciences and Arts Northwestern Switzerland (FHNW)
⑨ Lucerne University of Applied Sciences and Arts (HSLU)

Ecosystem Builders and Accelerators
① Switzerland Innovation Park Basel
② Switzerland Innovation Park Innovaare
③ Switzerland Innovation Park West EPFL
④ QuantumBasel

⑤ QAI Ventures
⑥ Open Quantum Institute @ CERN
⑦ The Geneva Science and Diplomacy Anticipator (GESDA)
⑧ Verve Ventures

Private Companies and Centers
① IBM Research
② ID Quantique
③ Basel Precision Instruments
④ Zurich Instruments
⑤ Qnami
⑥ Swiss Center for Electronics and Microtechnology (CSEM)
⑦ Swissphotonics
⑧ Miraex
⑨ QZabre
⑩ Ligentec
⑪ Enlightra
⑫ Terra Quantum
⑬ IonQ

Government
① Swissnex HQ

Other
① World Economic Forum (WEF)

Fig. 22.1 A mapping of selected Swiss institutions in quantum research and technology. This represents a partial overview and is not comprehensive. Original creation of Swissnex in Boston and New York

Table 22.1 Some key Swiss startups and companies active in quantum technologies [2]

Company	Region	Founded	Quantum specialization
ID Quantique	Geneva	2001	Cryptography, RNG, single photon detectors
Zurich Instruments	Zurich	2008	Qubit controllers, amplifiers, software
Ligentec	Lausanne	2016	Photonic integrated circuits
Qnami	Basel	2017	NV diamond sensing systems
Enlightra (formerly MicroR Systems)	Lausanne	2018	Multifrequency lasers
Basel Precision Instruments	Basel	2018	Ultralow noise electronics
QZabre	Zurich	2018	NV diamond scanning microscopes
Terra Quantum	St. Gallen	2019	Quantum services and algorithms
Miraex	Lausanne	2019	Quantum interconnects

generation, satellite up- and downlinks, as well as quantum laser sources. In the services field, Terra Quantum provides access to quantum algorithms, simulated quantum processing units, and quantum security solutions. These companies represent just a small cross-sample of the growing commercial quantum ecosystem in Switzerland [2] (Table 22.1).

Other important players at the private, national, and multinational levels are also working in Switzerland to build quantum ecosystems. The Swiss Center for Electronics and Microtechnology (CSEM), a public-private nonprofit innovation center, has developed key technologies in quantum sensing. The industry association Swissphotonics has significantly grown its portfolio and activities in the quantum space.

Most conspicuously, the new privately funded uptownBasel campus features the QuantumBasel Competence Center for Quantum & Artificial Intelligence, as well as the investment accelerator QAI Ventures, which have attracted top-level quantum companies and startups to the Basel area. The uptownBasel ecosystem of companies is making a significant investment of over CHF 500 million into the broader industry ecosystem, with only a portion of this amount specifically allocated to quantum technology development. They partnered with IBM to make uptownBasel a hub in the IBM quantum network. In addition, IonQ, a leading producer of trapped ion quantum computers based in the USA, announced in 2023 that they are establishing their quantum innovation center for the European, Middle East, and Africa (EMEA) region at QuantumBasel, which will include physical installation of two quantum systems [6].

At the international level the Open Quantum Institute (OQI), hosted at the European Organization for Nuclear Research (CERN) and incubated by the Geneva Science Diplomacy Anticipator (GESDA), is working to ensure that quantum technologies have broad benefits for the global scientific community and societies at large. Switzerland relies heavily on international collaborations to extend both its research and commercial impact. From 2016 to 2020, 89% of quantum publications from Switzerland featured international collaborators, among the highest rates in the world [3]. Finally, the Swiss State Secretariat for Education, Research, and Innovation (SERI) launched a new Swiss National Quantum Initiative (SQI) in 2023, tasked with defining frameworks for research calls, supporting infrastructure developments, promoting curricula, and strengthening international partnerships [7].

22.2.1 Maturity

The maturity of the quantum ecosystem in Switzerland varies by sector and technology. Thanks to long-term support for academic research in nanoscience and quantum physics, Switzerland maintains a strong research profile across most quantum subdisciplines. The fields of quantum sensing and communication are particularly strong. For example, CSEM has led international research on vapor cell-based atomic clocks, including the fabrication of microelectromechanical system (MEMS) cells and photonic-integrated chips for chip-scale atomic clocks. University spin-offs in nitrogen-vacancy diamond sensing technology such as Qnami and QZabre are also among global pioneers in the field. Additionally, pioneering quantum communications research from the University of Geneva results in ID Quantique, one of the oldest "pure quantum" companies in the world. The innovation sector in Switzerland has focused on producing technically advanced solutions that serve important scientific applications.

In terms of government involvement and multilateral engagement, the initiatives are relatively new. Switzerland's education and innovation sectors have long relied on bottom-up energy and associations. The SQI—led by a Commission and hosted at the Swiss Academy of Sciences—began operation in January 2023 with a mission to coordinate quantum activities at a national level. They are expecting to secure about CHF 80 million in funding from 2024 to 2028, which will enable a growing profile in supporting quantum research calls, infrastructure, and innovation. Internationally, the Swissnex network—an initiative of the Swiss State Secretariat for Education, Research, and Innovation (SERI)—has actively promoted increased visibility and connections for the Swiss quantum ecosystem since 2022 through its Project Quantum [8].

22.2.2 Swiss Trends in International Perspective

The steady pace of academic research and basic funding has resulted in a relatively stable and robust Swiss ecosystem, but there are concerns about remaining competitive in an increasingly hot global market for quantum science and technology. Significant recent headwinds in the Swiss quantum ecosystem included the 2021 exclusion from Horizon funding measures such as the European Union Quantum Flagship. Another, more abstract threat, comes from the potential for larger countries to focus on national programs over international collaborations, which remain essential for smaller countries like Switzerland. From 2016 to 2022, some 89% of Swiss quantum publications featured international partnerships [3].

Some Swiss actors express concern that, as other countries invest hundreds of millions to billions of dollars in public funding into quantum research and innovation (see chapter on Global Quantum Strategies), Switzerland's efforts may be too modest. At the same time, huge investments abroad may be raising expectations and hype for quick results in a field still working on fundamental discoveries. Switzerland is well positioned to persist through any hype cycles and remain a leading ecosystem. Its strengths reside in bottom-up collaboration, long-term commitment to research, strong international engagement, quality engineering, and a broad base of expertise across quantum subfields and enabling technologies.

22.3 Conclusion

The long-standing tradition of high-quality academic research in quantum technologies will likely continue to form the backbone of Swiss contributions to the second quantum revolution. At the same time, the Swiss quantum ecosystem has adapted in recent years to meet the growing commercial, government, and societal interest in applied quantum technologies. Since 2016, many new Swiss startups are actively deploying quantum technologies, with relative strengths in photonics and sensing.

The rise of private-sector actors has been accompanied by new ecosystem builders. The QuantumBasel initiative, for example, has grown into an internationally recognized brand. Swiss government's interest in coordinating the ecosystem can be seen with the creation of the Swiss Quantum Initiative, although the organization has operated with a light touch emphasizing the centrality of bottom-up energy rather than top-down mandates. Finally, initiatives such as the Open Quantum Institute at CERN, and Swissnex's Project Quantum, have emphasized the importance of a global cooperative approach, especially if quantum technologies are to be harnessed for socially beneficial purposes if and when they achieve decisive advantage.

References

1. M. Kern, The 'quantum' hype and public funding in Switzerland. https://e2-news.ch/en/news/the-quantum-hype-and-public-funding-in-switzerland (2023)
2. New Mapping of Swiss Quantum Ecosystem. https://swissnex.org/boston/news/new-mapping-of-swiss-quantum-ecosystem/ (2024)
3. I. Maye, Quantum publications: A bibliometric analysis. https://www.sbfi.admin.ch/sbfi/en/home/dienstleistungen/publikationen/publikationen-bestellen/quantum.html (2022)

4. IBM Research. Science of Quantum and Information Technology. https://www.zurich.ibm.com/st/ (2024)
5. IDQ Celebrates 10-Year Anniversary of the World's First Real-Life Quantum Cryptography Installation. https://www.idquantique.com/idq-celebrates-10-year-anniversary-of-the-worlds-first-real-life-quantum-cryptography-installation/ (2017)
6. US Quantum Company IonQ to Establish Presence in Basel. https://swissnex.org/boston/news/us-quantum-company-ionq-to-establish-presence-in-basel/ (2023)
7. Swiss Quantum Commission. https://quantum.scnat.ch/en/ (2024)
8. Swissnex Project Quantum. https://swissnex.org/quantum/ (2024)

Brendan Karch is Chief of Staff and Head of Research at Swissnex in Boston and New York. Swissnex is a global network of science and technology consulates connecting Switzerland and the world in education, research, and innovation. Karch leads Swissnex's Project Quantum, which works to connect the Swiss quantum ecosystem globally.

Open Access This chapter is licensed under the terms of the Creative Commons Attribution 4.0 International License (http://creativecommons.org/licenses/by/4.0/), which permits use, sharing, adaptation, distribution and reproduction in any medium or format, as long as you give appropriate credit to the original author(s) and the source, provide a link to the Creative Commons license and indicate if changes were made.

The images or other third party material in this chapter are included in the chapter's Creative Commons license, unless indicated otherwise in a credit line to the material. If material is not included in the chapter's Creative Commons license and your intended use is not permitted by statutory regulation or exceeds the permitted use, you will need to obtain permission directly from the copyright holder.

Summary Part III

Part III of the book provided an in-depth analysis of the global quantum technology ecosystem, focusing on strategies, investment trends, and sector-specific applications that drove quantum technology advancements. The analysis began with a look at the national quantum strategy in countries such as Canada, Denmark, the Netherlands, and the United Kingdom. These strategies ranged from centralized approaches that emphasize large-scale funding to decentralized models that promote innovation across sectors. Switzerland was presented as a case study, with recommendations for adopting a comprehensive national strategy that leveraged its strengths in academic research and industrial collaboration to enhance its quantum ecosystem.

A significant portion of the analysis focused on tracking investment trends and monitoring advancements in quantum technology. Increasing attention was given to hybrid quantum-classical systems, which sought to bridge the gap between theoretical research and real-world applications. The role of open-source platforms such as GitHub, along with newspaper headline analysis, was also explored, as these emerging data sources provided valuable insights into the progress and direction of quantum software and algorithm development. Additionally, bibliometric analyses of scientific publications highlighted a growing convergence of quantum technologies, indicating their increasing commercial viability.

Overall, this part emphasized the importance of strategic investments, global collaboration, and sector-specific applications in shaping the future of quantum technologies. By examining national strategies, investment patterns, and industry case studies, Part III offered a comprehensive overview of the evolving quantum landscape and its potential to drive innovation across various domains.

The manufacturer's authorised representative in the EU is Springer Nature Customer Service Centre GmbH, Europaplatz 3, 69115 Heidelberg, Germany. If you have any concerns regarding our products, please contact ProductSafety@springernature.com

Printed and bound by CPI Group (UK) Ltd, Croydon, CR0 4YY

23/03/2026

02076401-0014